1997 Consumer's Resource Handbook

United States Office of Consumer Affairs

Leslie L. Byrne
Special Assistance to the President and Director

Ella Green
Editor-in-Chief

Estelle L. Rondello
Managing Editor

Dinah Bembo
Associate Editor

Special thanks to the staff of the United States Office of Consumer Affairs

Sandy Aguilar
Stephanie Brown
Debra Huffman Church
Edna G. Cosby
Nellie Fegans

Barbara L. Hill
Fred Johnson
E. Waverly Land
Daisy Cherry Maggett
Michelle Muth

Howard Seltzer
Pamela L. Sidel
Juanita Yates

Appreciation to the National Association of Consumer Agency Administrators (NACCA) for assistance.

Single copies of the *Consumer's Resource Handbook* are available free by writing:
Handbook, U.S. Office of Consumer Affairs, 750 17th Street, NW, Washington, DC 20006–4607

This publication is printed on recycled paper.
October 1996

THE WHITE HOUSE

WASHINGTON

September 17, 1996

Dear Consumer:

Welcome to the *1997 Consumer's Resource Handbook*. It is most appropriate that this year's edition is dedicated to the memory of Secretary of Commerce Ronald Brown, a man who ardently supported consumer rights and who recognized the importance of this handbook in empowering American consumers with the knowledge and resources to make prudent, informed choices.

Today's increasingly competitive marketplace offers us a broad and diverse array of products and services. To select among them wisely, we must understand our rights as consumers and the standards of quality we should expect. The U.S. Office of Consumer Affairs, through publications such as this one, plays a vital role in educating the public on key consumer issues, protecting our rights, and enhancing our ability to make knowledgeable purchasing decisions.

I encourage you to use the valuable information in this handbook. By learning to choose and buy carefully and responsibly, you are helping to build a better and brighter future for all Americans.

Bill Clinton

Bill Clinton

Ronald H. Brown
Secretary of Commerce
1993–1996

It is appropriate and fitting that this edition of the Consumer's Resource Handbook is dedicated to the late Secretary of Commerce Ronald H. Brown. In many ways his life was dedicated to empowering people. From his career as a New York City welfare caseworker to his tenure as Secretary of Commerce, he inspired people to strive to do their very best. Whether he was leading a business trade mission to a foreign land or meeting with his employees in the office, he empowered us all through his example and leadership.

At the Commerce Department, he encouraged our employees to carry out the "Right to Service," established by President Clinton in their every day contacts with the public, our customers, to ensure that the Department delivers exceptional service. He continually supported the Department's consumer affairs efforts and last year held a special meeting with the winners of the Office of Consumer Affairs' National Consumer Week consumer awareness contest. He spent time online with STAT-USA customers answering questions on Customer Service Day to highlight the importance of serving our customers. He also understood the significance of consumers in the global marketplace.

Ron Brown was the first Secretary of Commerce to recognize the importance of the Consumer's Resource Handbook through the Department's financial support. The Handbook is an important educational tool for consumers as they seek to resolve their complaints or to acquire information from corporations and government offices.

On behalf of all the employees of the U.S. Department of Commerce, I thank you for dedicating this Handbook in the memory of the late Secretary of Commerce Ronald H. Brown.

Michael Kantor
Secretary of Commerce
October 1996

UNITED STATES
OFFICE OF CONSUMER AFFAIRS
Washington, D.C. 20201

October 1996

Dear Consumer:

It is with pride and sadness that we dedicate this edition of the Consumer's Resource Handbook to Ronald H. Brown, the late Secretary of Commerce. Secretary Brown had a long history of consumer advocacy and was a strong supporter of the U.S. Office of Consumer Affairs. While we are saddened by his sudden passing, we will always remember his devotion to country, his untiring efforts on behalf of consumers and his support of a free and fair marketplace. His legacy continues.

This ninth edition of the Consumer's Resource Handbook builds on the tradition of being a strong and effective tool for consumers. In April 1996, this Handbook received the prestigious "Mobius" award, presented by the Society of Consumer Affairs Professionals in Business (SOCAP). The award recognized the Handbook's value in helping consumers make informed decisions. This honor attests to the need and usefulness of the Handbook, which focuses on consumer issues that affect us all.

The information presented is based on the premise that consumers need to know their rights and how to make the right choices. Indeed, there are a number of laws which protect your rights before and after purchasing a product or service and many of those laws are referenced here. Today's marketplace, which is expanding rapidly through electronic shopping, has a wide variety of options for efficient, high quality goods and services to meet your needs and your pocketbook. But there, too, are numerous scams and frauds which take advantage of unsuspecting consumers.

This handbook offers information and advice to help you gain knowledge about your rights and about how to make the right choices—and, yes, how to protect yourself against unscrupulous dealers. Whether you are acquiring a product such as a car or making an investment in securities or seeking a service, you will find points to consider, questions to ask, and steps to take before and after you purchase an item or sign a contract.

I believe this Handbook will serve as a handy reference for you. It will help guide and protect you in the marketplace, so that whatever you buy, your choice will be a good one. We are proud to be at your service.

Sincerely,

Leslie L. Byrne
Special Assistant to the President and
Director

Contents

Contributors

The U.S. Office of Consumer Affairs wishes to express its gratitude to the contributors listed below who helped make possible the publication of the *1997 Consumer's Resource Handbook*.

Department of Agriculture
The Honorable Daniel R. Glickman
Secretary

Department of Defense
The Honorable William J. Perry
Secretary

Department of Energy
The Honorable Hazel R. O'Leary
Secretary

Department of Justice
The Honorable Janet Reno
Attorney General

Department of Veterans Affairs
The Honorable Jesse Brown
Secretary

Agency for International Development
The Honorable J. Brian Atwood
Administrator

Consumer Product Safety Commission
The Honorable Ann Brown
Chairman

Federal Communications Commission
The Honorable Reed E. Hundt
Chairman

Federal Deposit Insurance Corporation
The Honorable Ricki Helfer
Chairman

Federal Trade Commission
The Honorable Robert Pitofsky
Chairman

Securities and Exchange Commission
The Honorable Arthur Levitt, Jr
Chairman

Small Business Administration
The Honorable Philip Lader
Administrator

Chrysler Corporation
General Motors Corporation
Ford Motor Company
MasterCard International
Pacific Bell

What's in This Handbook

The information in this *Consumer's Resource Handbook* is presented in two parts: (1) tips on buying products and services and (2) contacts for information and assistance.

Part I of the *Handbook,* "Buying Smart," gives tips on getting the most for your money, handling your own complaint and writing a complaint letter. Part I also provides tips on a number of consumer issues such as choosing and using credit, protecting personal privacy and avoiding many types of frauds and scams.

Part II of the *Handbook,* "Consumer Assistance Directory," lists offices you can contact for help with problems or questions. This section provides individual names (where available), addresses, and telephone and fax numbers for contacts ranging from consumer organizations to corporations to government agencies at city, county, state and Federal levels. Some of these consumer assistance groups are highlighted below; for a complete list of agencies in Part II, see the "Contents."

Throughout the sections, a number of electronic addresses are listed for access through the worldwide web. The websites listed here omit http:// and begin with www (in the interest of space). Listed also are telephone numbers which provide access for hearing and speech impaired consumers; they are in **bold type.** A subject "Index" is at the end of the *Handbook* to help you locate information about specific topics.

National Consumer Organizations

There are a number of national organizations whose missions are defined as consumer assistance, protection and/or advocacy. Several of these organizations assist consumers directly; others are interested in hearing from consumers about problems and concerns; most, though not all, develop educational materials for consumers. Addresses, telephone numbers and descriptions of 30 of these organizations are listed in the "National Consumer Organizations" section of this *Handbook,* beginning on page 31.

Better Business Bureaus

There are 162 Better Business Bureaus (BBBs) and branches in the United States. These Bureaus are non-profit organizations supported primarily by local businesses. BBB's offer a variety of services, including general consumer information on products or services, business reliability reports, background information on local businesses and organizations, and records of a company's complaint-handling performance.

The Council of Better Business Bureaus, which is supported by national companies and the nation's BBBs, also offers consumer education programs, reports on charitable organizations, alternative dispute resolution services and assistance with complaints about the truthfulness and accuracy of national advertising, including children's advertising. A description of the Council is on page 32 and a list of BBBs operating in the United States begins on page 34.

Corporate Consumer Contacts

Many companies have consumer affairs or customer relations departments to answer questions or help resolve consumer complaints. The addresses and telephone numbers of more than 650 companies are listed in the "Corporate Consumer Contacts" section of this Handbook, beginning on page 39. If you write to the company, you may use the sample letter on page 8 as a guide.

Car Manufacturers

Most foreign and American car manufacturers have national or regional offices which handle consumer complaints not resolved by your local car dealer. The list of "Car Manufacturers" begins on page 64.

Trade Associations' and Other Dispute Resolution Programs

There are nearly 40,000 trade and professional associations in the United States representing a variety of interests (for example, banking, insurance, clothing manufacturing) and professions (for example, accountants, lawyers, doctors, therapists).

Some of these associations and their members have established programs to help consumers with complaints not resolved at the point of purchase.

Trade associations have various consumer functions, which are described in *National Trade & Professional Associations of the United States.* Check your local library for this book and related sources of help.

A list of "Trade Associations' and Other Dispute Resolution Programs" begins on page 68.

State, County and City Government Consumer Offices

State and local consumer protection offices can help you resolve consumer complaints and provide you with consumer education information. These agencies might mediate complaints, conduct investigations, prosecute offenders of consumer laws, license and regulate professions, promote strong consumer protection legislation, provide educational materials and advocate in the consumer interest. It is important to report complaints and suspected frauds and misrepresentations to these governmental agencies. Consumer complaints form the basis of most consumer protection law enforcement actions.

If you want to file a complaint, call your local consumer protection office to learn what you need to do. A list of "State, County and City Government Consumer Protection Offices" begins on page 71.

State Agencies and Commissions

In addition to state and local consumer offices, many states have special agencies and commissions to handle consumer questions and complaints about services for senior consumers and for disabled persons, as well as services provided by financial institutions and insurance companies. Other state agencies regulate securities, utilities and weights and measures. These state agencies are listed separately, beginning on page 85.

In addition, a variety of other helpful community services might be available in your area. For example, county and state Cooperative Extension Services offer information about health, safety, product comparisons, financial planning and nutritional needs. Information about these and other state and local services can be found at your library and in the telephone directory in the city/municipal, county or state government listings.

Military Commissary and Exchange Offices

Interested consumers will find a list of "Military Commissary and Exchange Offices" on page 105. The list includes the regional offices and headquarters for all the Armed Forces exchanges and commissaries.

Selected Federal Agencies

Many Federal Government agencies can help you with consumer questions and complaints. A number of these agencies have enforcement authority and/or complaint-handling responsibilities. The Federal agencies listed, beginning on page 107, respond to consumer complaints and inquiries.

Consumer Credit Counseling Services

Counseling services provide assistance to individuals having difficulty budgeting their money and/or meeting necessary monthly expenses. Many organizations, including credit unions, family service centers and religious organizations, offer some type of free or low-cost credit counseling.

The Consumer Credit Counseling Service (CCCS) is one non-profit organization that provides money management techniques, debt payment plans and educational programs. Counselors take into consideration the needs of the client as well as the needs of the creditor when working out a debt repayment plan. You can find the CCCS office nearest you by contacting the National Foundation for Consumer Credit, Inc., 8611 Second Avenue, Suite 100, Silver Spring, MD 20910–3372; Toll free: 800–388–CCCS.

Consumer Groups

Private and voluntary consumer organizations usually are created to advocate specific consumer interests. In some communities, they will help individual consumers with complaints. However, they have no enforcement authority. To find out if such a group is in your community, contact your state or local government consumer protection office. A list of the state and local offices begins on page 71.

Federal Information Center

The Federal Information Center (FIC), administered by the General Services Administration, can help you find information about the Federal Government's agencies, services, and programs. The FIC can also tell you which office to contact for help with problems.

You may call toll free from anywhere in the United States to 800–688–9889. Users of text telephones (TDD/TTY) may also call toll free by dialing 800–326–2996.

The FIC is open from 9 a.m. to 5 p.m. local time, except in Alaska (8 a.m. to 4 p.m.) and Hawaii (7 a.m. to 3 p.m.).

Consumer Information Catalog

The *Consumer Information Catalog* lists approximately 200 free or low-cost Federal booklets with helpful information for consumers. Topics include careers and education, cars, child care, the environment, Federal benefits, financial planning, food and nutrition, health, housing, small business and more. This free *Catalog* is published quarterly by the Consumer Information Center of the U.S. General Services Administration. Single copies of the *Catalog* only may be ordered by sending your name and address to Catalog, Consumer Information Center, Pueblo, CO 81009 or by calling 719–948–4000. Non-profit groups that can distribute 25 copies or more each quarter automatically can receive copies by writing for a bulk mail card.

You may visit the website at www.pueblo.gsa.gov or dial the bulletin board system on 202–208–7679.

Libraries

The local library can be a good source of help. Many of the publications mentioned in this *Handbook* can be found in public libraries. Some university and other private libraries also allow individuals to use their reference materials. Check your local telephone directory for the location of nearby libraries.

Media Programs

Local newspapers and radio and television stations often have "Action Line" or "Hot Line" services. These programs might be able to help consumers with their problems. Sometimes these programs, because of their influence in the community, are successful in helping to resolve consumer complaints. Some action lines select only the most severe problems or those that occur most frequently. They might not be able to handle every complaint.

To find these services, check with your local newspapers, radio and television stations, or local library.

Occupational and Professional Licensing Boards

Many state agencies license or register members of various professions, including doctors, plumbers, electricians, car repair shops, employment agencies, beauticians, and television and radio repair shops. In some states, local consumer agencies license or register some professions.

In addition to setting licensing standards, these boards also issue rules and regulations; prepare and give examinations; issue, deny or revoke licenses; bring disciplinary actions; and handle consumer complaints.

Many boards have referral services or consumer education materials to help you select a professional. If you contact a licensing agency about a complaint, the agency will contact the professional on your behalf and, if necessary, might conduct an investigation and take disciplinary action against the professional. This action can include probation or license suspension or revocation.

To find the local office of an occupational or professional licensing board, check your local telephone directory under the headings of "Licensing Boards" or "Professional Associations," or look for the name of the individual agency. If you need help locating the right office, contact your state or local consumer office.

Legal Help

Please note that some of the sources of help listed in the *Consumer's Resource Handbook* have a policy of declining complaints from consumers who have sought prior legal counsel.

Small Claims Court

Small claims courts were established to resolve disputes involving claims for small debts and accounts. While the maximum amounts that can be claimed or awarded differ from state to state, court procedures generally are simple, inexpensive, quick and informal. Court fees are minimal, and you often get your filing fee back if you win your case. Generally, you will not need a lawyer. In fact, in some states, lawyers are not permitted. If you live in a state that allows lawyers and the party you are suing brings one, do not be intimidated. The court is informal, and most judges make allowances for consumers who appear without lawyers.

Remember, even though the court is informal, the ruling must be followed, just like the ruling of any other court.

If the party bringing the suit wins the case, the party who lost often will follow the court's decision without additional legal action. Sometimes, however, losing parties will not obey the decision. In these cases, the winning party can go back to court and ask for the order to be "enforced." Depending on local laws, the court might, for example, order property to be taken by law enforcement officials and sold. The winning party will get the money from the sale, up to the amount owed. Alternatively, if the person who owes the money receives a salary, the court might order the employer to garnish or deduct money from each paycheck and give it to the winner of the lawsuit.

Check your local telephone book under the municipal, county or state government headings for small claims court offices. When you contact the court, ask the court clerk how to use the small claims court. Many state and local consumer agencies have consumer educational material to prepare you for small claims court (see page 71). To better understand the process, sit in on a small claims court session before taking your case to court.

Many small claims courts have created dispute resolution programs to help citizens resolve their disputes. These dispute resolution processes (e.g., mediation and conciliation) often simplify the process. For example, in mediation, both people involved in the small claims dispute meet, sometimes in the evenings or on weekends, and with the assistance of a neutral, third-party mediator, discuss the situation and create their own agreement.

The rate of success is high for dispute resolution through small claims court. Considering this, when you contact your small claims court, ask first about its mediation or conciliation process.

For additional information about dispute resolution, contact the American Bar Association, Section on Dispute Resolution, 740 15th Street, N.W., Washington, DC 20005, 202–662–1680.

Legal Aid

Legal Aid offices help individuals who cannot afford to hire private lawyers. There are more than 1,000 of these offices around the country staffed by lawyers, paralegals and law students. All offer free legal services to those who qualify. Funding is provided by a variety of sources, including Federal, state and local governments and private donations. Many law schools nationwide conduct clinics in which law students, as part of their training, assist practicing lawyers with these cases.

Legal Aid offices generally offer legal assistance with such problems as landlord-tenant relations, credit, utilities, family issues (e.g., divorce and adoption), foreclosure and home equity fraud, social security, welfare, unemployment and workers' compensation. Each Legal Aid office has its own board of directors which determines the priorities of the office and the kinds of cases handled. If the Legal Aid office in your area does not handle your type of case, it should be able to refer you to other local, state or national organizations that can provide advice or help. Check the telephone directory to find the address and telephone number of the Legal Aid office near you. If you would like a directory of Legal Aid offices around the country, contact the National Legal Aid and Defender Association, 1625 K Street, N.W., 8th Floor, Washington, DC 20006, 202–452–0620.

Legal Services Corporation

The Legal Services Corporation (LSC) was created by Congress in 1974. There are LSC offices in all 50 states, Puerto Rico, the Virgin Islands, Guam and Micronesia. To find the LSC office nearest you, check the telephone directory, call the Federal Information Center (FIC) toll free on 800–688–9889 or call the LSC Public Affairs Office at 202–336–8800. For a directory of all LSC programs, write or call:

Public Affairs
Legal Services Corporation
750 1st Street, N.E.
Washington, DC 20002
202–336–8800.

Finding a Lawyer

If you need help finding a lawyer, check with the Lawyer Referral Service of your state, city or county bar association listed in local telephone directories.

Complaints about a lawyer should be referred to your state, county or city bar association.

Part I.   Buying Smart

Protecting Yourself

Consumers are faced with a marketplace full of decisions. Ask the right questions before and after you buy and avoid consumer fraud and rip-offs.

Before You Buy

- Take advantage of sales but compare prices. Do not assume an item is a bargain just because it is advertised as one.

- Don't rush into a large purchase because the "price is only good today."

- Check to see if the company is licensed or registered at the local or state level.

- Contact your consumer protection office or Better Business Bureau (BBB) for any complaint recorded against the company. Request any consumer information they might have on the type of purchase.

- Be aware of such extra charges as delivery fees, installation charges, service costs, and postage and handling fees. Add them into the total cost.

- Ask about the seller's refund or exchange policy.

- Read the warranty. Note what is covered and what is not. Find out what you must do and what the manufacturer or seller must do if there is a problem.

- Don't sign a contract without reading it. Don't sign a contract if there are any blank spaces in it or if you don't understand it. In some states, it is possible to sign away your home to someone else.

- Before buying a product or service, contact your consumer protection office to see if there are automatic cancellation periods for the purchase you are making. In some states, there are cancellation periods for dating clubs, health clubs, and timeshare and campground memberships. Federal law gives you cancellation rights for certain door-to-door sales.

- Walk out or hang up on high-pressure sales tactics. Don't be forced or pressured into buying something.

- Don't do business over the telephone with companies you do not know.

- Be suspicious of P.O. Box addresses. They might be mail drops. If you have a complaint, you might have trouble locating the company.

- Do not respond to any prize or gift offer that requires you to pay even a small amount of money.

- Use unit pricing in supermarkets to compare what items cost. Unit pricing allows you to compare the price ounce-for-ounce, pound-for-pound, etc. Bigger packages are not always cheaper than smaller ones.

- Use coupons carefully. Do not assume they are the best deal until you've compared them to the prices of competitive products.

- Make sure all documents you sign are in a language you understand.

- Don't rely on a salesperson's promises. Get everything in writing.

After You Buy

- Read and follow product and service instructions.

- Be aware that how you use and take care of a product might affect your warranty rights.

- Keep all sales receipts, warranties, service contracts and instructions.

- If you have a problem, contact the company as soon as possible. Trying to fix the product yourself might cancel your right to service under the warranty.

- Keep a written record of your contact with the company.

- If you have a problem, check with your consumer protection office to find out about the warranty rights in your state.

- If you paid for your purchase with a credit card, you have important rights that might help you dispute charges. (See the Consumer Tips section, page 22.)

- Check your contract for any statement about your cancellation rights. Contact your consumer protection office to see if a cancellation period applies.

- If you take the product in for repair, be sure the technician understands and writes down the problem you have described.

Red Flags of Fraud

Consumer protection offices urge consumers to be aware of the red flags of fraud. Walk away from bogus offers. Toss out the mail or hang up when you hear:

- "Sign now or the price will increase;"

- "You have been specially selected . . . ;"

- "You have won . . . ;"

- "All we need is your credit card (or bank account) number—for identification only;"

- "All you pay for is postage, handling, taxes . . . ;"

- "Make money in your spare time—guaranteed income . . . ;"

- "We really need you to buy magazines (a water purifier, a vacation package, office products) from us because we can earn 15 extra credits . . . ;"

- "I just happen to have some leftover paving material from a job down the street . . . ;"

- "Be your own boss! Never work for anyone else again. Just send in $50 for your supplies and . . . ;"

- "A new car! A trip to Hawaii! $2,500 in cash! Yours, absolutely free! Take a look at our . . . ;"

- "Your special claim number entitles you to join our sweepstakes . . . ;" or

- "We just happen to be in your area and have toner for your copy machine at a reduced price."

Remember, the smart consumer always looks at the total price before deciding and checks out the company and product before buying.

Stay away from telemarketers who want to:

- send a courier service for your money;

- have you send money by wire;

- automatically withdraw money from your checking account;

- offer you a free prize but charge handling and shipping fees;

- ask for your credit card number, checking or savings account number, Social Security number or other personal information; and

- get payment in advance especially for employment referrals, credit repair, or providing a loan or credit card.

- Stay away from lotteries, pyramid schemes and multi-level sales schemes. They are all good ways to separate you from your money.

Complaining Effectively

Save all purchase-related paperwork in a file. Include copies of sales receipts, repair orders, warranties, canceled checks, contracts, and any letters to or from the company. When you have a problem:

- Contact the business that sold you the item or performed the service. Calmly and accurately describe the problem and what action you would like taken.

- Keep a record of your efforts to resolve the problem. When you write to the company, describe the problem, what you have done so far to try to resolve it and what solution you want. For example, do you want your money back, the product repaired or the product exchanged?

Allow time for the person you contacted to resolve your problem. Keep notes of the name of the person you spoke with, the date and what was done. Save copies of all letters to and from the company. Don't give up if you are not satisfied.

- Contact the company headquarters if you have not resolved your problem at the local level. Many companies have a toll-free 800 number. Look for it on package labeling, in a directory of 800 telephone numbers (available at your local library), by calling 800–555–1212 (toll free) or by referring to the many corporate consumer contacts, beginning on page 39. Address your letter to the consumer office or the company's president.

Writing a Complaint Letter

Whom To Contact

- Check the product label or warranty for the name and address of the manufacturer.

- If you need additional help locating company information, check the reference section of your local library for the following books: *Standard & Poor's Register of Corporations, Directors and Executives; Standard Directory of Advertisers; Trade Names Dictionary;* and *Dun & Bradstreet Directory.*

- If you have the brand but cannot find the name of the manufacturer, the *Thomas Register of American Manufacturers* lists the manufacturers of thousands of products. Check your local library.

- Each state has an agency (possibly the corporation commission or secretary of state's office) that provides addresses for companies incorporated in that state.

- Remember, do business with a company you will be able to find later. It might be difficult to find companies in other states or those listing post office boxes as addresses. Even if you have an address, it might be only a mail drop, so be sure you know where the company you are doing business with is located physically.

What To Say

- Include in the letter your name, address, home or work telephone numbers, and account number, if any.

- Make your letter brief and to the point. Include the date and place you made the purchase, who performed the service, such information about the product as the serial or model number or warranty terms, what went wrong, with whom you have tried to resolve the problem, and what you want done to correct the problem.

- Use the sample consumer complaint letter on the following page as a guide.

- Include copies, not originals, of all documents.

- Be reasonable, not angry or threatening, in your letter. Type your letter, if possible, or make sure your handwriting is neat and easy to read.

What To Do Next

- Keep a copy of your complaint letter as well as all letters to and from the company.

- You might want to send your complaint letter with a return receipt requested. This will cost more, but it will give you proof that the letter was received and will tell you who signed it.

- If you feel you have given the company enough time to resolve the problem, send a copy of your letter to, or file a consumer complaint with, your local or state consumer protection agency; such specific state agencies as banking, insurance and utilities; or local Better Business Bureau. Their addresses can be found starting on pages 71, 89 and 34, respectively. Include information about what you have done so far to try to resolve your complaint. If you think a law has been broken, contact your local or state consumer protection agency right away.

Sample Complaint Letter

(Your Address)
(Your City, State, ZIP Code)
(Date)

(Name of Contact Person, if available)
(Title, if available)
(Company Name)
(Consumer Complaint Division, if you have no contact person)
(Street Address)
(City, State, ZIP Code)

Dear (Contact Person):

Re: (account number, if applicable)

On (date), I (bought, leased, rented, or had repaired) a (name of the product with serial or model number or service performed) at (location, date and other important details of the transaction).

Unfortunately, your product (or service) has not performed well (or the service was inadequate) because (state the problem). I am disappointed because (explain the problem: for example, the product does not work properly, the service was not performed correctly, I was billed the wrong amount, something was not disclosed clearly or was misrepresented, etc.).

To resolve the problem, I would appreciate your (state the specific action you want—money back, charge card credit, repair, exchange, etc.) Enclosed are copies (do not send originals) of my records (include receipts, guarantees, warranties, canceled checks, contracts, model and serial numbers, and any other documents).

I look forward to your reply and a resolution to my problem, and will wait until (set a time limit) before seeking help from a consumer protection agency or the Better Business Bureau. Please contact me at the above address or by phone at (home and/or office numbers with area codes).

Sincerely,

(your name)

Enclosure(s)
cc: (reference to whom you are sending a copy of this letter, if anyone)

- describe purchase
- name of product, serial numbers
- include date and place of purchase

- state problem
- give history

- ask for specific action
- enclose copies of documents

- allow time for action
- state how you can be reached

Keep copies of your letter and all related documents

Consumer Tips

A number of suggestions are included here to help you become a smarter consumer. They cover a broad range of topics. If you are repairing, leasing, or buying a car; buying a home; investing in commodities or securities; or purchasing any number of products or services in the marketplace, the tips offer ways to make the best decisions and to be alert to fraud or scams. Covered also are the various marketing schemes, such as telemarketing, mail order, and door-to door sales.

Check with your local consumer protection office and Better Business Bureau for other consumer information on a variety of topics. Their addresses and phone numbers are listed on pages 71 and 34, respectively.

Car Repair, Purchase, Renting and Other Concerns

Car Repair

- Choose a reliable repair shop recommended to you by family or friends or an independent consumer rating organization. Check out the repair shop's complaint record with your state or local consumer protection office or Better Business Bureau.

- When you take the car to the shop, describe the symptoms. Don't diagnose the problem.

- Get more than one estimate. Get them in writing.

- Make it clear that work cannot begin until you have authorized it. Don't authorize work without a written estimate or, if the problem can't be diagnosed on the spot, insist that the shop contact you for your authorization once the trouble has been found.

- Don't sign a blank repair order. Make sure the repair order reflects what you want done before you sign it.

- Is the repair covered under warranty? Follow the warranty instructions.

- Ask the shop to keep the old parts for you.

- Get all warranties in writing.

- Some car manufacturers might be willing to repair certain problems without charge even though the warranty has expired. Contact the manufacturer's zone representative or the dealer's service department for assistance.

- Keep copies of all paperwork.

Some states, cities and counties have special laws that deal with auto repairs. For information on the laws in your state, contact your state or local consumer protection office.

Buying a Used Car

- Check newspaper ads and used car guides at a local library so you know what's a fair price for the car you want. Remember, prices are negotiable. You also can look up repair recalls for car models you might be considering.

- Call the Auto Safety Hotline at (800) 424–9393 to get recall information on a car. Authorized dealers of that make of vehicle must do recall work for free no matter how old the car is.

- Shop during daylight hours so that you can thoroughly inspect the car and take a test drive. Don't forget to check all the lights, air conditioner, heater and other parts of the electrical system.

- Do not agree to buy a car unless you've had it inspected by an independent mechanic of your choice.

- Ask questions about the previous ownership and mechanical history of the car. Contact the former owner to find out if the car was in an accident or had any other problems.

- Check with your local department of motor vehicles to find out what you need in order to register a car.

- Ask the previous owner or the manufacturer for a copy of the original manufacturer's warranty. It still might be in effect and transferable to you.

- Don't sign anything that you don't understand. Read all documents carefully. Negotiate the changes you want and get them written into the contract.

- For information on recalls and safety issues, see page 10 under new car sales.

Buying from a Private Individual

Generally, private sellers have less responsibility than dealers for defects or other problems.

- Check with your state's motor vehicle department on what you will need to register a vehicle.

- Make sure the seller isn't a dealer posing as an individual. That might mean the dealer is trying to evade the law and might be an indicator of problems with the car. Look at the title and registration. Make sure the seller is the registered owner of the vehicle.

- Ask the seller lots of detailed questions about the car.

- Have the car inspected by your mechanic before you agree to buy it.

Buying from a Dealer

Check the complaint records of car dealers with your state or local consumer protection agency or Better Business Bureau.

- Read the "Buyers Guide" sticker required to be displayed in the window of the car. It gives information on warranties, if any are offered, and provides other information.

- In most states, used cars may be sold "as is." If the "as is" box is checked off on the "Buyers Guide," you have no warranty.

- If the "warranty" box is checked off on the "Buyers Guide," ask for a copy of the warranty and review it before you agree to buy the car.

- Have the car inspected by your mechanic before you agree to buy it.

- Some states have laws giving extra protection to used car buyers. Contact your state or local consumer protection office to find out what rights you might have.

To order a free publication on buying a used car, contact the Federal Trade Commission, Public Reference Section, 6th and Pennsylvania Avenue, N.W., Room 130, Washington, DC 20580, 202–326–2222.

Buying a New Car

- Evaluate your needs and financial situation. Read consumer magazines and test drive several models before you make a final choice.

- Find out the dealer's invoice price for the car and options. This is what the manufacturer charged the dealer for the car. You can order this information for a small fee from consumer publications you can find at your local library.

- Find out if the manufacturer is offering rebates that will lower the cost.

- Get price quotes from several dealers. Find out if the amounts quoted are the prices before or after the rebates are deducted.

- Keep your trade-in negotiations separate from the main deal.

- Compare financing from different sources, for example, banks, credit unions and other dealers, before you sign the contract.

- Read and understand every document you are asked to sign. Do not sign anything until you have made a final decision to buy.

- Think twice about adding expensive extras you probably don't need to your purchase, for example, credit insurance, service contracts or rustproofing.

- Inspect and test drive the vehicle you plan to buy, but do not take possession of the car until the whole deal, including financing, is finalized.

- Don't buy on impulse or because the salesperson is pressuring you to make a decision.

- The National Highway Traffic Safety Administration's Auto Safety Hotline at 800–424–9393 (toll free) distributes recall and safety information on used and new cars, trucks, motorcycles, motor homes, child seats and other motor vehicle equipment; vehicle crash test information; tire quality grading reports; child seat registration forms; and other safety literature. You should report all vehicle and child seat defect information to the Hotline (see page 29).

- The Center for Auto Safety (see page 31) monitors auto defects. To see if there is a pattern of repeated complaints on a certain vehicle model, write the Center for Auto Safety, 2001 S Street, N.W., Suite 410, Washington, D.C. 20009 and include the vehicle make, model and year and a self-addressed stamped envelope.

Credit and Sublease Brokers

A new and rapidly growing area of consumer fraud involves con artists who prey on people who have bad credit and who are having problems getting loans to buy cars. There are two main schemes:

- The "credit broker" promises to get a loan for you in exchange for a high fee. In many cases, the "broker" takes the fee and disappears, or simply refers you to high-interest loan companies.

- The "sublease" broker charges a fee to arrange for you to "sublease" or "take over" someone else's car lease or loan. Such deals usually violate the original loan or lease agreement. Your car can be repossessed even if you've made all of your payments. You also might have trouble insuring your car.

To protect yourself:

- check with your state or local consumer protection agency to find out if the broker is required to be licensed;

- do not do business with a company that does not appear to be complying with state law;

- do not pay for services in advance.

To order a free publication on how to buy a new or used car, contact the Federal Trade Commission, Public Reference Section, 6th and Pennsylvania Avenue, N.W., Room 130, Washington, DC 20580, 202–326–2222.

Car Leasing

- Shop around for the best leasing deal. Read lease promotions carefully. The attractive low monthly payment might be available only if you make a large down payment (capitalized cost reduction) or a balloon payment at the end of the lease.

- Beware of open-end leases. They require the consumer to pay the difference if the vehicle is worth less at the end of the lease than was estimated originally.

- The Consumer Leasing Act requires leasing companies to give you important information in writing before you sign a contract. Read the documents given to you by the leasing company and make sure you understand them before you sign anything. In particular, look for:

—up-front costs, for example, security deposits, down payments, advanced payments and taxes;

—the terms of the payment plan;

—termination costs, for example, excess mileage penalties, excessive wear and tear charges, and disposition charges; and

—penalties for early termination or default.

When you have paid off a car loan, you own the car. When you have paid off the lease, you own nothing.

To order a free publication on car leasing, contact the Federal Trade Commission, Public Reference Section, 6th and Pennsylvania Avenue, N.W., Room 130, Washington, DC 20580, 202–326–2222.

Lemon Laws

Almost every state has a new car "lemon law" that allows the owner a refund or replacement when a new vehicle has a substantial problem that is not fixed within a reasonable number of attempts. Many specify a refund or replacement when a substantial problem is not fixed in four repair attempts or the car has been out of service for 30 days within the first 12,000 miles/12 months. If you believe that your car is a lemon:

- contact your state or local consumer protection office for information on the laws in your state and the steps you must take to resolve the situation;

- give the dealer a list of symptoms every time you bring it in for repairs; keep copies for your records;

- get copies of the repair orders showing the reported problems, the repairs performed and the dates that the car was in the shop; and

- contact the manufacturer, as well as the dealer, to report the problem. Some state laws require that you do so to give the manufacturer a chance to fix the problem. Your owner's manual will list an address for the manufacturer.

If the problem isn't resolved, you might have the option of participating in an arbitration program offered by the manufacturer or your state. Contact your state or local consumer protection office for information.

Lemon Law Summary is available upon request by sending a self-addressed, stamped (55 cents) envelope to the Center for Auto Safety, 2001 S Street, N.W., Suite 410, Washington, DC 20009.

Vehicle Repossessions

When you borrow money to buy a car, you should know that:

- The lender can repossess if you miss a payment or for any default (a violation of the contract).

- The lender can repossess without advance notice.

- After repossession, the lender might be able to accelerate, meaning the lender can require the borrower to pay off the entire balance of the loan in order for the borrower to get the vehicle back.

- The lender can sell the vehicle at auction.

- The lender might be able to sue the borrower for the deficiency if it sells the car for less than the borrower owes. This is true even in voluntary repossessions.

- The lender cannot commit a "breach of the peace," for example, breaking into a home or physically threatening someone, in the course of a repossession.

If you know you're going to be late with a payment, talk to the lender to try to work things out. If the lender agrees to a delay or to modify the contract, be sure you get the agreement in writing.

Some states have laws which give consumers additional rights. Contact your state or local consumer protection office for more information.

To order a free publication on vehicle repossessions, contact the Federal Trade Commission, Public Reference Section, 6th and Pennsylvania Avenue, N.W., Room 130, Washington, DC 20580, 202–326–2222.

Renting a Car

Federal law does not cover short-term car and truck rentals. However, there are state laws that do. You should contact your state or local consumer protection office for more information on laws in your area.

- Shop around for the best rates.

- Compare all fees, in addition to the daily/weekly rate, before renting.

- Most car rental contracts make the consumer liable for all damage to the vehicle, no matter who caused it. Before buying a rental company's collision or loss damage waiver, check with your own car insurance company and your credit card company to see if they cover car rentals and to what extent. It pays to do your homework because these policies can add $3 to $15 per day to your rental charges! Rental companies also might sell loss of use and liability insurance. Check with your insurance agent in advance, so you do not duplicate coverage you already have.

- If you pay by credit card, some rental companies will place a hold or freeze on your account during the rental period. Others might start to charge your account before the rental period is over. Find out the company's policy in advance.

- Carefully inspect the vehicle and its tires before renting and write down all the dents and scratches you see.

- Check refueling policies. You can refill at a local gas station, you can let the car rental company refuel the car at its price, which is usually higher, or you can pay in advance for a refill which will cost you needlessly if there is any unused gas upon returning the vehicle.

- Contact your state or local consumer protection agency for information on state law or to report problems with your car rental.

- To order a free publication on car rental, contact the Federal Trade Commission, Public Reference Section, 6th and Pennsylvania Avenue, N.W., Room 130, Washington, DC 20580, 202–326–2222.

Mail Orders

Federal mail order rules require companies that take consumers' orders by mail to:

- Ship the merchandise within 30 days of receiving a completed order or within a different timeframe if it is stated in their ads;

- Notify consumers if shipment can't be made on time and give them the choice of waiting longer or receiving refunds; and

- Cancel their orders and return their money (or give them credits on their charge accounts) if the revised shipping date can't be met, unless the consumers agree to another delay.

There also might be laws regarding mail order in your state. Contact your state or local consumer protection agency.

- Keep a record of the name, address and phone number of the company, goods you ordered, date of your order, amount you paid and method of payment.

- Keep a record of any delivery period that was promised.

- If you are told that the shipment will be delayed, write the date of that notice in your records and the new shipping date if you've agreed to wait longer.

- When you cancel an order that wasn't shipped on time, you have the right to get a refund within seven days or within one billing cycle for charged sales.

- When you use your credit card for mail order purchases and you don't receive the goods or services, or they were defective or misrepresented, use the credit card protection rights described in the section on Credit Cards, page 20.

- To limit some of the mail you do not want, you can sign up with the free Mail Preference Service operated by the Direct Marketing Association, a private trade group. It will instruct its mail marketing members to take you off their lists. To join, write to the Mail Preference Service, P.O. Box 9008, Farmingdale, New York 11735–9008.

To report violations of the Federal mail order rule, contact the Federal Trade Commission. For information on your state laws, contact your state or local consumer protection agency. To report a problem with mail order, contact the U.S. Postal Inspection Service or the Postal Crime Hotline at 800–654–8896.

Mail Fraud

- Read the offer carefully. Get the advice of another person whose opinion you trust.

- Deal only with companies or charities whose reputation and integrity are known.

- Never give your credit card number or personal, financial or employment information unless you know with whom you are dealing.

- Never send money for any "free" merchandise or services.

- Be careful of making impulse purchases.

- Keep a record of the order, notes of the conversation and copies of the advertisement, canceled check, receipt, letters and envelopes.

- Take the time to shop locally to compare mail order products, services and prices with those in local stores.

- Check out the company with the U.S. Postal Inspection Service, your state or local consumer protection agency, or the Better Business Bureau. Mail fraud is a Federal crime.

- Using your credit card or a money order might give you some recourse if you have a problem, despite your carefulness.

Be suspicious of "free gifts" that require a "tax payment" or "registration fee;" sweepstakes requiring an entry fee or purchase; employment or work-at-home opportunities requiring a fee; offers requiring your credit card number or bank account number; loans that require you to pay a fee in advance; mailings that look like they are from official government agencies when they are not; and prize notices requiring you to call a 900 number.

Telemarketing

While many legitimate businesses use the telephone to make their sales, it's easy for fraudulent companies to abuse the phone. Beware of the con artists who promise anything and deliver nothing, or at least not what customers thought they were getting.

Tips for Smart Telephone Shopping

- Always keep a record of the name, address and phone number of the company, goods you ordered, date of your purchase, amount you paid (including shipping and handling) and method of payment.

- Keep a record of any delivery period that was promised.

- If you are told that the shipment will be delayed, write the date of that notice in your records and the new shipping date, if you've agreed to wait longer.

- Don't give your credit card number, checking account number or other personal information to a telemarketer unless you are familiar with the company or organization, and the information is necessary in order to make your purchase.

Telephone Order Rights

Some states have telemarketing laws that require written contracts, automatic cancellation periods or registration of telemarketing companies. Contact your state or local consumer protection agency.

Federal telephone order rules require companies that take consumers' orders by phone, computer or fax to:

- Ship the merchandise within 30 days of receiving a completed order or within a different timeframe if it is stated in their ads;

- Notify consumers if shipment can't be made on time and give them the choice of waiting longer or receiving refunds; and

- Cancel their orders and return their money (or give them credits on their charge accounts) if the revised shipping date can't be met, unless the consumers agree to another delay.

Use Caution and Common Sense

- Don't be pressured into acting immediately or without the full information you need.

- Shop around and compare costs and services.

- Report all fraudulent activity to your consumer agency. Check out the company with your consumer protection agency or the Better Business Bureau.

- If the solicitation came by mail, call the Postal Crime Hotline at 800–654–8896 (toll free) for more advice on not becoming a victim.

- Call the National Fraud Information Center, administered by the National Consumers League, at 800–876–7060 (toll free) for information about telemarketing fraud.

Blocking Telemarketing Calls

You have the right under Federal law:

- to tell a company not to call you by phone or not to contact you in writing; the company must keep a list of these consumers and not contact them; keep a record for your file;

- not to get calls before 8 a.m. or after 9 p.m.;

- not to receive unsolicited ads by fax; and

- to be disconnected from a pre-recorded machine-delivered message within five seconds of hanging up.

Some states do not allow telemarketers to call people who do not want to receive calls. Contact your state or local consumer protection agency to check your state's rights.

To reduce telephone calls you do not want, you can sign up with the free Telephone Preference Service operated by the Direct Marketing Association, a private trade group. To join, write to the Telephone Preference Service, P.O. Box 9014, Farmingdale, NY 11735–9014.

To report violations of the telephone order rule, contact the Federal Trade Commission. If you made the telephone transaction in response to a postcard or other mailing, contact the U.S. Postal Inspection Service or the Postal Crime Hotline at 800–654–8896 (toll free). For information on the laws in your state, contact your state or local consumer protection agency.

Calls That Cost: 900 Numbers and Other Pay-Per-Call Services

Unlike 800/888 numbers which are free, you pay a fee when you call a 900-type number. The company or organization you're calling sets the price, not the telephone company. Most states do not regulate the cost of these calls. Charges can vary from less than a dollar to more than $50. Federal law requires that:

- consumers be told the cost of calling the number and given a description of the product and service. This must appear, in advertisements and for calls costing more than $2 dollars, in the introductory message or preamble at the beginning of the call;

- the cost of calling must be disclosed by flat rate, by the minute with any minimum or maximum charge that can be determined, or by range of rates for calls with different options; all other fees charged for services and the cost of any other service to which a caller might be transferred must be disclosed;

- consumers be given time to hang up after the introductory message without being charged; there must be a signal or tone to let them know when the preamble ends;

- no charges can be made for calling 800/888 numbers unless the consumer agrees in advance to be charged (see the next topic on "What You Need To Know About 800/888 Numbers");

- any pay-per-call services offering sweepstakes, prizes or awards must disclose the odds of winning or the factors for determining the odds;

- ads directed to children under age 12 are not allowed unless they are for legitimate educational services;

- ads directed primarily to people under the age of 18 must state that parents' consent is needed to call the number; and

- ads for information about Federal programs offered by private companies must state clearly that they are not endorsed, approved or authorized by government agencies.

Protect yourself from fraud by avoiding:

- ads that don't describe clearly the goods or services or the cost of the calls;

- offers of "free" gifts or prizes just for calling;

- promises of jobs, loans, credit cards for people with poor credit, "credit repair" or other services aimed at consumers who are in financial hardship;

- contests to win money in which little or no skill is required;

- services targeted to children under 12 which don't appear to serve any legitimate educational purpose; and

- offers of cheap travel or any other deals that seem to be "too good to be true."

Hang up if you're being switched from an 800/888 number to a 900 number without your prior consent.

What You Need To Know About 800/888 Numbers

Generally, you cannot be charged for 800/888 numbers. New rules prohibit charging callers to toll-free numbers for conveyance of information without explicit authorization through either a written agreement or payment by direct remittance; prepaid account; or debit, credit or calling card. The rules specify particular information that must be:

- included in presubscription agreements;

- disclosed orally to callers who wish to pay for an 800/888 information service by direct remittance; prepaid account; or debit, credit or calling card, and

- displayed on a telephone bill when charges are assessed for informational services provided for a toll-free number.

Further, all presubscription arrangements must be done in writing or through direct remittance; prepaid account; or debit, credit, charge or calling debt card. Charges for resubscribed information services must be displayed separately from charges for local and long distance service.

Your Rights and Recourse

- If you question 900-type number charges which appear on your phone bill, you can dispute the bill. Your local and long distance telephone service cannot be disconnected for disputed pay-per-call charges.

- In most cases, the charge for a pay-per-call service is collected by the local telephone company on behalf of the service provider. Follow the instructions on your bill immediately to dispute the charges. Keep a record of whom you talked to and the date, as well as copies of any letters you send. Pay the undisputed portion of your phone bill.

- Even if the telephone company removes the charges, the debt might be turned over to a collection agency by the service provider. Send the collection agency a letter explaining why you dispute the debt. (See the section on Credit Access and Use, page 19.)

- To avoid problems with 900-type numbers, you can request "blocking" from your local phone company. Blocking prevents 900 numbers from being dialed from your phone.

- If you suspect a violation of pay-per-call rules, contact your state or local consumer protection agency and the Federal Trade Commission. If the ad for the number came by mail, write to the U.S. Postal Inspection Service or call the Postal Crime Hotline at 800–654–8896 (toll free). If you are not satisfied with the way the phone company handled your complaint, contact the Federal Communications Commission. (See page 107 for information on how to contact Federal agencies.)

Door-to-Door Sales

- Ask to see the salesperson's personal identification and license or registration if that is required where you live. Make note of his/her name, the name and address of the company, and whether the salesperson carries proper identification.

- Ask for sales literature and then call local stores that might sell the same merchandise to compare prices. Some door-to-door products might be overpriced.

- Don't be pressured into buying something. Watch for the warning signs: an offer of a "free gift" if you buy a product, an offer that is only good for that day, or you're told that a neighbor just made a purchase.

- If you feel threatened or intimidated, ask the person to leave. Don't leave the person unattended in any room of your home. If you are suspicious, report the incident to the police immediately.

Cancellation Rights

- The "Door-to-Door Sales Rule" (or "Cooling Off Rule") gives you the right to cancel certain purchases costing $25 or more. Notify the company in writing by midnight of the third business day following the sale. Saturdays are considered business days, but Sundays and holidays are not.

- The seller must tell you about your cancellation rights and give you two dated copies of a cancellation form showing the seller's name and address and explaining your right to cancel.

- These Federal cancellation rights apply to purchases made in locations outside the seller's normal place of business; for example, at a house party, a temporarily rented room or in your home.

- States might have additional cancellation laws that protect consumers. Check with your state or local consumer protection agency for your rights.

- To cancel a contract, sign and date one copy of the cancellation form. Mail it within the 3-day limit, making sure it's post-marked before midnight of the third business day. Sending it by certified mail will show proof that it was mailed.

- If you were not given the cancellation form at the time of sale, your right to cancel continues until 3 days after the seller finally gives it to you. You can write your own letter cancelling the sale and send it return receipt requested.

- Once you cancel, you have a right to a refund within 10 days. The seller must let you know when the product will be picked up and must return any paperwork and trade-ins within that time.

- Within 20 days, the seller must pick up the item or reimburse you for any shipping expenses if you send it back yourself. If you do not return it, you still are responsible under the contract.

- Extend your rights! If you paid by credit card, canceled the contract within 3 days, have not yet paid the credit card bill and still have a problem getting a refund, dispute the charges with your credit card company under the Fair Credit Billing Act. (See the section on Credit Access and Use, page 19.)

Home Improvement

- Plan ahead. Know what you want or need to have done before contacting a contractor.

- Get detailed estimates from reputable contractors. Contact your local or state consumer agency and Better Business Bureau for information on contractors' licensing or registration requirements, complaint records and for brochures containing advice.

- Contact your local building inspection department to check for permit and inspection requirements.

- Call your insurance company to find out if you are covered for any injury or damage that might occur and be sure your contractor has the required insurance for his/her workers and subcontractors.

- Insist on a complete written contract. Know exactly what work will be done, the quality of materials that will be used, timetables, the names of any subcontractors, the total price of the job and the schedule of payments.

- You have cancellation rights (usually 3 business days) in many home improvement contracts. Before you sign a contract, check with your local consumer agency to find out if you have cancellation rights and how they apply.

- Understand your payment options. You can get your own loan or the contractor might arrange financing. Be sure you have a reasonable payment schedule at a fair interest rate.

- Some state laws specify payment schedules, for example, only allowing a certain percentage of the total cost to be made as a down payment. Contact your state or local consumer agency to find out what the law is in your area.

- Lien rights, which might give the contractor or subcontractors the ability to "attach" your home for unpaid bills, vary from state to state. Ask your local consumer agency to explain the situation where you live.

- You need to be especially cautious if the contractor:

—comes door-to-door or seeks you out;

—just happens to have material left over from a recent job;

—tells you your job will be a "demonstration;"

— offers you discounts for finding him/her other customers;

—quotes a price that's too cheap;

—pressures you for an immediate decision;

—has workers or suppliers who tell you they have trouble getting paid;

—can be reached only by leaving messages with an answering service; or

—drives an unmarked van or has out-of-state plates on his/her vehicle.

Home Financing

- Check the real estate or business sections in the newspaper for information on current interest rates. Call several lenders for rates and terms based on the type of mortgage you want.

- When buying a newly constructed home, compare the interest rate and terms offered through the builder's sales office with those offered by other lending institutions.

- When interest rates go down, you might save money by refinancing, but you probably should not refinance unless the new interest rate will be at least two percentage points below the rate you're paying currently.

- For an adjustable rate mortgage, or "ARM," find out the "cap" or the maximum interest rate that can be charged during the life of the loan. Ask how often the rate might change and what determines the rate change.

- Get a complete list of "closing" or "settlement" costs and find out which costs will be refunded if your loan is not approved.

- Be wary of financing that is based on "negative amortization." While the payments might be lower than in other types of loan agreements, they're not enough to cover the monthly interest charges. The portion of interest that is left unpaid is added to the principal, which means that each month, the borrower pays interest on a higher amount than before. With negative amortization, the debt actually keeps increasing rather than decreasing. You could end up owing a lot of money at the end of the loan or losing your home.

Home Equity Credit Lines

- Although a home equity credit line might allow you to take tax deductions you could not take with other types of loans, your home will be at risk if you cannot make the monthly payments.

- Some questions to ask when comparing home equity loan offers:

—How large a credit line can be extended?

—How long is the term of the loan?

—What is the minimum monthly payment? Is there a maximum?

—What is the annual percentage rate?

—If the interest rate "floats," or is adjustable, how much can it increase at one time? Is there a maximum rate?

—Are there any annual fees or transaction fees?

Reverse Mortgages

- If you own your home, a reverse mortgage loan will pay you in monthly advances or through a line of credit. It lets you convert your equity into cash which you can use for any purpose, while retaining your ownership in your home. Before you sign, be sure you understand all the terms and conditions.

- Interest rates on this type of loan might be higher and are charged on a compound basis. Application fees, points and closing costs also might be higher than other types of loans. Interest rates are not deductible on your income taxes until you repay the loan in full. There will be less equity for you and your heirs in the future.

For more information or to file a complaint, contact:

Department of Housing and Urban Development
Office of Single Family Housing
451 Seventh Street, S.W.,
Room 9272
Washington, DC 20410
202–708–2700

State and Local Consumer Protection Offices (See list beginning on page 71.)

Selecting a Financial Institution

Select a financial institution carefully by comparing the terms and prices of all of the services you need.

- Shop around. Do not do business with the first institution that seems willing to do business with you.

- Check the front door to see if the institution displays a government logo indicating that it is insured federally. Generally, if the institution is insured federally, an individual is covered for up to $100,000 in deposits if the institution fails.

If a financial institution is federally insured, you will see one of the following official signs posted at the entrance of the institution

For banks:

For savings associations:

For credit unions:

Truth in Savings Act

- Requires financial institutions to disclose the "Annual Percentage Yield," or "APY," on savings accounts. The APY tells you how much money you would earn if you kept $100 in the account for one year.

- Requires that the institution credit your entire deposit instead of crediting a portion of your deposit or using a "low balance per month" method. This increases your earnings.

- Requires that institutions have available a list of their fees for bounced checks, stop payment orders, certified checks, wire transfers or similar items. Ask for the list.

- Prohibits institutions from advertising "free" checking if there are hidden charges or requirements, for example, having to maintain a minimum balance to qualify.

Checking Accounts

- Before you open a checking account, find out what the fees will be for writing checks, for bounced checks, for the checks themselves and for other services. Ask if the institution will send you the canceled checks with your monthly statement. If not, find out the cost for copies of canceled checks. You might need them for proof of payment in some situations.

- Find out if the financial institution will waive checking fees if you have direct deposit of your paycheck. Some banking institutions will lower or even drop fees if your pay is deposited directly by your employer. Additional advantages of direct deposit are security, convenience and quicker access to your money.

Loans

- When shopping for a mortgage, check the real estate section of your local newspaper to find out the current interest rates. Check the rates for 30-year mortgages, 15 year mortgages and adjustable rate mortgages. Ask the lending institution to explain the differences.

- Most home improvement loans are secured by a mortgage on your home. It's better not to finance expensive credit life insurance or to consolidate other debts into this loan. Your home will be at risk for every extra dollar you borrow. If you don't make your payments, you could lose your home.

- For car loans, compare the rates offered by the car dealer with those of local lending institutions. Don't add expensive extras like credit life insurance to the total amount of the loan. You do not have to purchase credit insurance in order to get a loan.

Information and Assistance

Agencies responsible for carrying out consumer protection laws that cover financial services also provide information and assistance to consumers. For more information or to file a complaint, contact:

Federal Deposit Insurance Corporation (FDIC)
Office of Consumer Affairs
550 17th Street, N.W.
Washington, DC 20429
202–898–3536
Toll free: 800–934–3342
(Regulates state chartered banks that are not members of the Federal Reserve System.)

Board of Governors of the
Federal Reserve System
Division of Consumer and
Community Affairs
20th and C Streets, N.W.
Mail Stop 800
Washington, DC 20551
202–452–3693
TDD: 202–452–3544
(Regulates state chartered
banks and trust companies that
are members of the Federal
Reserve System.)

Comptroller of the Currency
Customer Assistance Unit
250 E Street, S.W.
Mail Stop 3–9
Washington, DC 20219
800–613–6743
(Regulates banks with national
in the name or N.A. after the
name.)

National Credit Union
Administration
Office of Public and
Congressional Affairs
1775 Duke Street
Alexandria, VA 22314–3428
703–518–6300
(Regulates federally chartered
credit unions.)

Office of Thrift Supervision
Division of Consumer and Civil
Rights
Office of Community
Investment
1700 G Street, N.W.
Washington, DC 20552
202–906–5900
Toll free: 800–842–6929
(Regulates Federal savings
and loans and Federal savings
banks.)

State Banking Authorities
(See Consumer Assistance
Directory, page 89.)

State and Local Consumer
Protection Offices
(See Consumer Assistance
Directory, page 71.)

Using a Debit Card

Many consumers are familiar with automated teller machine (ATM) cards issued by banks and credit unions. These cards can be used to access cash, make deposits, transfer funds and verify balances in checking and saving accounts. Now, consumers are learning that certain types of ATM cards, commonly called debit cards, can be used to purchase goods and services as well.

- Debit card purchases are deducted directly from your personal checking account, unlike credit cards which allow you to draw funds from a line of credit for which you are billed monthly.

- Purchases you make with a debit card are handled in one of two ways: either you punch in your personal identification number (PIN), just as you would with an ATM, or you sign for the purchase, similar to a credit card transaction.

- Consumer protection measures limit cardholder liability. You're never responsible for charges on cards you haven't accepted. If you report a lost or stolen debit card within 2 days of discovering its loss or theft, Federal regulations limit your liability to $50. State laws may provide additional protections. If you report the loss after more than 2 days after discovering the loss or theft of your card, liability is limited to $50 plus any amount resulting from your failure to notify the issuer sooner, up to $500. If you fail to report your unauthorized charges within 60 days of having been sent your monthly statement, your liability for unauthorized charges is $50 plus any amount that resulted from your delay in reporting.

- If your card is lost or stolen, you must work directly with the financial institution that issued the card. It is very important that you, the cardholder, report a lost or stolen card or suspected unauthorized use of a card immediately to your financial institution.

- Returns or disputes for goods and services you purchased with a debit card are treated the same as cash or checks. You should resolve the matter directly with the merchant, whose policies on refunds and returns usually govern these transactions.

- As with credit cards, some financial institutions charge fees for the use of a debit card. These fees are found in the disclosure statement that financial institutions send their customers.

Credit Access and Use

Equal Rights

The Equal Credit Opportunity Act guarantees you equal rights in dealing with anyone who regularly offers credit, including banks, finance companies, stores, credit card companies and credit unions. A creditor is someone to whom you owe money. When you apply for credit, a creditor may not:

- ask about or consider your sex, race, national origin or religion;

- ask about your marital status or your spouse, unless you are applying for a joint account or relying on your spouse's income or you live in a community property state (Arizona, California, Idaho, Louisiana, Nevada, New Mexico, Texas and Washington);

- ask about your plans to have or raise children;

- refuse to consider reliable public assistance income or regularly received alimony or child support; and

- discount or refuse to consider income because of your sex or marital status or because it is from part-time work or retirement benefits.

You have the right to:

- have credit in your birth name, your first name and your spouse's last name, or your first name and a combined last name;

- have a co-signer other than your spouse if one is necessary;

- keep your own accounts after you change your name or marital status or retire, unless the creditor has evidence you are unable or unwilling to pay;

- know why a credit application is rejected; the creditor must give you the specific reasons or tell you of your right to find out the reasons if you ask within 60 days; and

- have accounts shared with your spouse reported in both your names.

You also have a right to know how much it will cost to borrow money. The Truth in Lending Act requires a lender to inform you of the cost to borrow so that you have the opportunity to compare the cost and terms of credit offered by various lenders.

Credit Cards

Choosing a Credit Card

Credit card issuers offer a wide variety of terms. Consider and compare all the terms, including the following, before you select a card:

- Annual Percentage Rate (APR)—the cost of credit as a yearly rate.

- Free or Grace Period—allows you to avoid any finance charge by paying your balance in full before the due date. If there is no free period, you will pay a finance charge from the date of the transaction, even if you pay your entire balance when you receive your bill.

- Fees and Charges—most issuers charge an annual fee; some also might charge a fee for a cash advance or if you fail to make a payment on time or go over your credit limit.

Shop around for the terms that are best for you. Before giving money to a company that promises to help you get a credit card:

- Find out who the card issuer is and get the credit card terms in writing, including all the fees and whether a deposit is required;

- Try to apply to a card issuer directly, rather than giving money to a third party; if you don't get the credit card, you might not be able to get your money back;

- Beware of "credit cards" that only allow you to buy from certain overpriced, restricted goods catalogs; and

- Beware of companies that promise "instant credit" or guarantee you a credit card "even if you have bad credit or no credit history;" no one can guarantee you credit in advance; and

- Be cautious of offers for "secured" credit cards. These cards usually require you to set aside money in a separate bank account in an amount equal to the line of credit on the card to guarantee that you will pay the credit card debt. Some of these offers advertise that secured cards can be used to "repair" a bad credit record, but you should know that no matter how well you handle this account, your payment history on your past debts still will be taken into consideration when you apply to other lenders for credit or for employment or housing.

For a small fee, you can purchase a list of the most competitive interest rates and credit cards in the country and find out how to qualify for the lowest rate possible by contacting:

Bankcard Holders of America
524 Branch Drive
Salem, VA 24153
540–389–5445
Website: www.epn.com/bha

Using a Credit Card

Know your credit card protections. When you have used your card for a purchase and you don't receive the goods or services as promised, you might be able to withhold payment for the goods or services. Card issuers must investigate billing disputes. (See the section on Credit Billing and Disputes, page 22.)

If your card is lost or stolen, you are not liable for any charges if you report the loss before the card is used. If the card is used before you report it missing, the most you will owe is $50.

Protect your credit record. Pay bills promptly to keep finance charges low and to protect your credit rating. Keep track of your charges and don't exceed your credit limit. Report any change of address prior to moving, so that you receive bills promptly.

If you cannot pay off your full credit card balance each month, a lower interest rate will save you money. If you do pay off your balance in full each month, choose a card with no annual fee.

Preventing Credit Card Fraud

- Sign cards when they arrive, so no one can forge your signature on the cards and use them.

- Keep a record of your card numbers and expiration dates and the phone number of the card issuer in a safe place. If your card is stolen or missing, notify the card company immediately.

- Don't give your credit card number over the phone to unfamiliar companies or to people who say they need it to "verify" your identity in order to give you a prize.

- Destroy carbons and incorrect charge slips.

- Draw a line through blank spaces on charge slips. Do not sign a blank charge slip.

- Keep copies of all sales slips. Open credit card bills promptly and compare the sales slips with the charges on your bill.

- Report billing errors and unauthorized charges to your credit card company right away.

Credit Reporting

The Fair Credit Reporting Act controls how your credit history is kept, used and shared among lenders.

The three biggest credit reporting agencies, TRW, Equifax and Trans Union, have millions of credit files on consumers nationwide. Their toll-free numbers are:

- TRW—800–392–1122;

- Equifax—800–685–1111; and

- Trans Union—800–916–8800.

You can find other credit bureaus in your area by looking in the yellow pages under Credit Bureaus or Credit Reporting.

If you apply for credit, insurance, a job or to rent an apartment, your credit record might be examined. You can make sure yours is accurate.

- Get a copy once a year or before major purchases. Your report is generally free if you've been denied credit in the past 60 days. Otherwise, the credit bureau can impose a reasonable charge.

- Read the report carefully. The credit bureau must provide trained personnel to explain information in the report.

- Dispute any incorrect information in your credit record. Write to the credit bureau and be specific about what is wrong with your report. Send copies of any documents that support your dispute.

In response to your complaint, the credit bureau:

- must investigate your dispute and respond to you, usually within 30–35 days; information that is inaccurate or cannot be verified must be corrected or taken off your report; and

- cannot be required to remove accurate, verifiable information that is less than 7 years old (10 years for bankruptcies).

If you are dissatisfied with the results of the re-investigation, you can have the credit bureau include a 100-word consumer statement giving your version of the disputed information. You also can contact the source of the disputed information and try to resolve the matter.

If there is an error on a report from one credit bureau, the same mistake might be on others as well. You might want to contact the three major bureaus, as well as any local bureau listed in the yellow pages of your telephone book.

Credit bureaus sometimes sell your name to banks or others who want to send you offers for credit cards or other forms of credit. If you don't want your name included on such lists, write or call the three major credit bureaus and tell them not to release your name.

Credit Repair

You might see or hear ads from companies that promise to "clean up" or "erase" your bad credit and give you a fresh start. They charge high fees, usually hundreds of dollars, but do not deliver on their promises.

If you are thinking of paying someone to "repair" your credit, remember this:

- Negative credit information can be reported for 7 years (10 years for a bankruptcy).

- No one can require a credit bureau to remove accurate negative information before that period is up.

- There are no "loopholes" or laws that credit repair companies can use to get correct information off your credit report.

- No credit repair company can do anything you can't do for yourself. (See the section on Credit Reporting, page 21.)

- A "money-back guarantee" does you no good if the company has gone out of business or refuses to make good on its refund promise.

- The only way to "repair" bad credit is by good credit practices over a period of time.

Some credit repair companies promise not just to clean up your existing credit record but also to help you establish a whole new credit identity. Remember, it is illegal to make false statements on a credit application or to misrepresent your Social Security number. If you use such methods, you could face fines or even prison. Beware of any company or method that:

- encourages you to omit or lie about bad credit experience when you apply for new credit;

- tells you to use a new name or address or a new number, for example, an Employer Identification Number (EIN), in place of your Social Security number in applying for credit; or

- says it is legal to establish a new credit identity.

You can rebuild your good credit by handling credit responsibly. You might want to contact a Consumer Credit Counseling Service (CCCS) office. This is a non-profit organization that will provide help at little or no cost to you. For a CCCS office in your area, call 800–388–CCCS (toll free).

Credit Billing and Disputes

The Fair Credit Billing Act applies to credit card and charge accounts and to overdraft checking. It can be used for:

- billing errors;

- unauthorized use of your account;

- goods or services charged to your account but not received or not provided as promised; and

- charges for which you request an explanation or written proof of purchase.

Protect Your Rights

- Write to the creditor or card issuer within 60 days after the first bill containing the disputed charge is mailed to you. (Even if more than 60 days have passed since you were billed for the item, you still might be able to dispute the charge if you only recently found out about the problem.)

- Send your letter to the address provided on the bill; do not send the letter with your payment.

- In your letter, give your name and account number, the date and amount of the charge disputed, and a complete explanation of why you are disputing the charge. Be specific.

- To be sure your letter is received, and so you will have a record, you might wish to send it by certified mail, with a return receipt requested.

If you follow these requirements, the creditor or card issuer must acknowledge your letter in writing within 30 days after it is received and conduct an investigation within 90 days.

While the bill is being disputed and investigated, you need not pay the amount in dispute. The creditor or card issuer may not take action to collect the disputed amount, including reporting the amount as delinquent, and may not close or restrict your account.

If there was an error or you do not owe the amount, the creditor or card issuer must credit your account and remove any finance charges or late fees relating to the amount not owed. For any amount still owed, you have the right to an explanation and copies of documents proving you owe the money.

If the bill is correct, you must be told in writing what you owe and why. You will owe the amount disputed plus any finance charges. You may ask for copies of relevant documents.

Debt Collection

The Fair Debt Collection Practices Act applies to those who collect debts owed to creditors for personal, family and household debts, including car loans, mortgages, charge accounts and money owed for medical bills. A debt collector is someone hired to collect money owed by you. A debt collector may not:

- contact you at unreasonable times or places, for example, before 8 a.m. or after 9 p.m., unless you agree, or at work if you tell the debt collector your employer disapproves;

- contact you after you write a letter to the collection agency telling them to stop, except to notify you if the debt collector or creditor intends to take some specific action;

- contact your friends, relatives, employer or others, except to find out where you live and work, or tell such people that you owe money;

- harass you by, for example, threats of harm to you or your reputation, use of profane language or repeated telephone calls;

- make any false statement, including that you will be arrested; and

- threaten to have money deducted from your paycheck or to sue you, unless the collection agency or creditor actually intends to do so and it is legal to do so.

If you are contacted by a debt collector, you have a right to a written notice, sent within 5 days after you are first contacted, telling you:

- the amount owed;

- the name of the creditor; and

- what action to take if you believe you don't owe the money.

If you believe you do not owe the money or don't owe the amount claimed, contact the creditor in writing and send a copy to the debt collection agency with a letter telling them not to contact you.

If you do owe the money or part of it, contact the creditor to arrange for payment.

For more information:

Contact the Federal Trade Commission, Public Reference Section, 6th and Pennsylvania Avenue, N.W., Room 130, Washington, DC 20580, 202–326–2222.

To file a complaint:

Contact your state or local consumer protection agency, your state attorney general or your Better Business Bureau.

Investment Fraud

Commodities

Do your detective work before you invest: Call toll free 800–676–4632.

There are often similarities in sales pitches used to promote fraudulent commodity investments, and knowing these can help you protect yourself from being the next victim. Prospective investors are approached through a variety of methods, such as:

- print, TV and radio (advertising and infomercials);

- advertising on the Internet and commercial online services, including "chat rooms," where a potential customer may be approached online about a possible commodity investment vehicle;

- cold calls (unsolicited telephone calls), often from "boiler room" operations, using lead lists and lists of victims of prior investment scams; and

- social contacts, often using the common affinity of ethnic and religious affiliations.

Deceptive or fraudulent sales pitches often use misrepresentations and material omissions of fact to promote fantastic profits with little risk, and these sales pitches involve persistent, high-pressure contacts allowing little or virtually no time for reflection or investigation by the investor.

Proceed with caution when a salesperson:

- Tells you to borrow money, for instance, on a credit card, take out a mortgage on your home, or cash in your IRA to invest in commodities;

- Tells you to invest immediately, and then sends an overnight courier service to pick up your check and give you forms to sign;

- Says that you will double or triple your money quickly, profit is guaranteed (you can't lose your money), or that trading commodity futures and/or options on futures is risk-free;

- Downplays the risk disclosure documents and statement, which are required by Federal law, as insignificant or just a formality that you need not take seriously, or words to that effect; and

- Tells you to write false information on your account form, for example, to overstate your income.

After you invest, be aware of the following warning signs of trouble:

- Account statements that appear to be home-made or printed on home computers (they should be printed on letterhead stationery, without typographical errors); and

- Delays in receiving your money when you order the broker to close a trade and send you your balance.

Use the toll-free Consumer Protection Hotline before considering a commodity investment. Exchange-traded futures contracts and options on futures can be offered and sold to the public lawfully only through commodity brokers that are registered with the U.S. Commodity Futures Trading Commission (CFTC), the Federal regulatory agency for the futures and options markets.

To verify information about a register firm or individual, the National Futures Association (NFA), a CFTC-designated self-regulatory organization, maintains a toll-free Hotline at 800–676–4NFA (4632) to check/verify the registration status and disciplinary history (including customer complaints) concerning registered futures/options firms and registered salespersons (from outside the United States, reach the Hotline on 312–781–1410).

Check out free consumer protection information on CFTC's website (www.cftc.gov), including how a customer can file a complaint to institute reparations proceedings against commodity professionals registered with the CFTC and how a customer can e–mail information about a suspect firm or broker to CFTC's Division of Enforcement.

For additional information, contact CFTC's Office of Public Affairs at 202–418–5080; for information on how to file a customer complaint, call the Office of Proceedings on 202–418–5506. See page 107 for CFTC's mailing address.

Securities

- Before making a securities investment in stocks, bonds or mutual funds, you should get written financial information such as a prospectus or annual report.

- Be wary of promises of quick profits, offers to share "inside" information and pressure to invest before you have an opportunity to investigate.

- Never invest in a product that you don't fully understand. ASK QUESTIONS. The U.S. Securities and Exchange Commission (SEC) has a publication that lists questions you should ask (see listing at the end of this section).

- Words like "guarantee," "high return," "limited offer," or "as safe as a C.D." may be a red flag. No financial investment is risk-free and a high rate of return means greater risk.

- Select a broker or investment adviser who understands your financial objectives. Interview two or three to compare experience, education and professional background.

- Call the National Association of Securities Dealers, Inc. (NASD) on 800–289–9999 toll-free to find out about the disciplinary history of the broker.

- Call your state securities regulator to see if the investment and the salesperson are registered in your state. Often your state securities regulator can give you more information about the disciplinary history of brokers and investment advisors. (A list of state securities administrators begins on page 93.) You may also get a state contact by calling the North American Security Administrators Association (NASAA) at 202–737–0900 or see the state listing on the SEC website (see address below).

- Understand how the broker or investment adviser is paid. What fees will you pay to purchase, sell or maintain the account?

- If you have a problem with your broker or your account, talk with the firm's manager. If you can't resolve the problem with the firm, contact the U.S. Securities and Exchange Commission (see page 113) or your state securities regulator.

- For free publications, including "Ask Questions: Questions You Should Ask About Your Investment," "Invest Wisely: Advice from Your Securities Industry Regulators" and "Invest Wisely: An Introduction to Mutual Funds," call toll-free 800–SEC–0330. You may visit our website at www.sec.gov

How To Reduce Unwanted Solicitations and Guard Your Privacy

- Pay for local purchases with cash rather than by check or credit card.

- Ask manufacturers, catalogue or magazine subscription companies, charities and others with whom you do business not to sell your name to others for marketing purposes.

- Don't release your Social Security number except to an employer, government agency, lender or credit bureau that requires it to identify you.

- Don't give anyone your credit card or checking account numbers unless you're making purchases with them, and don't put credit card numbers on your checks.

- When filling out warranty or other information cards, don't include optional or unnecessary personal information.

- Federal law gives you the right to ask telemarketers to take your name off of their lists and not to call you again. Keep records of their names, addresses and the dates of your requests. File a complaint with the Federal Communications Commission (see page 111) if they don't remove your name from their marketing lists once you have made your request.

- Personal information is easily obtained by companies promoting sweepstakes, contests and prize offers. These three types of promotions are in the top ten consumer complaints nationwide. Be careful to check out the companies before deciding to do business with them or releasing personal or financial information. Contact your state or local consumer agency (see page 71) or Better Business Bureau (see page 34).

Review Files That Contain Information About You

The Medical Information Bureau (MIB) is a data bank used by insurance companies. You might want to obtain a copy of your file and make sure the information it contains is correct. Write to the Medical Information Bureau, P.O. Box 105, Essex Station, Boston, MA 02112.

Credit bureaus keep records about your credit history. You should review periodically your credit reports for accuracy. (See the section on "Credit Reporting" on page 21.)

To limit mail or telephone calls you do not want, you can sign up at no cost for a service that tells some of the telephone or mail marketing companies not to contact you. (See the sections on Telemarketing and Mail Orders, pages 13 and 12, respectively, for more information.)

Many states have their own privacy laws concerning telemarketing; employment; the use of Social Security, credit card or checking account numbers; medical records; mailing lists; credit reports; debt collection; computerized communications; insurance records and public data banks. Check with your state or local consumer agency about specific privacy rights or a referral to the appropriate agency.

Advance Fee Scams

Be wary of ads promising guaranteed jobs, guaranteed loans, credit repair, debt consolidation or similar claims. Many of these offers are only a way to get you to send money in advance in exchange for little or no service.

- Be cautious when responding to advertisements which use 900 telephone numbers. You can be charged substantial and differing amounts for calls to 900 numbers.

- Be careful with your personal information, including Social Security, credit card and bank account numbers, among others. Fraudulent businesses could use this information to make an unauthorized charge to your credit card or to withdraw money from your bank account.

- Before you make any payment, ask the business to send you a contract and other information stating the terms of the service and whether you can cancel the service and get a refund.

- Ask how long the firm has been in business and if it is licensed properly. Request that the company send you copies of its business or other licenses. Review all contracts carefully.

- Contact your state or local consumer protection agency and the Better Business Bureau to find out a company's complaint record.

- Some states have enacted laws banning or regulating these types of businesses. To find out the law in your state or to report a fraud, contact your state or local consumer protection agency.

- For information on the dangers of these types of scams, call the non-profit National Fraud Hotline at 800–876–7060 (toll free).

Special Contracts

Health Clubs

When you are considering whether to join a health club, be cautious of:

- joining clubs that have not opened—they might never open;

- low-cost "bait" ads—many "switch" you to expensive long-term contracts;

- promises that you can cancel anytime and stop paying— check the written contract for the terms of membership and any other promises;

- the fine print—many low-cost ads and contracts severely restrict hours of use and services;

- signing long-term contracts— consumer protection agencies report that many consumers quit using the club within a few months;

- automatic monthly billing to your charge card or debit from a checking account—these are easier to start than to stop; and

- unbelievably low one-time fees with no monthly dues.

Before you sign, be sure to:

- Check with your doctor before you begin an exercise program;

- Visit the club at the hours you will be using it;

- Check to see that promised equipment/services are actually available;

- Talk with current members regarding their satisfaction with the club;

- Check out several clubs before you sign a contract;

- Consider your commitment to a long-term program—good intentions seem to fade as the reality of the hard work sets in;

- Read the contract carefully before you sign. Is interest charged for a payment plan? Are all promises in writing?

- Check with your local or state consumer agency or Better Business Bureau for any laws in your state, cancellation rights or complaints against the company.

Dating Clubs/Matchmakers

When you choose to deal with a dating service, be sure to check:

- from how far away the referrals might come;

- the economic/professional status of dates;

- that dates are club members;

- your ability to review the video/profile/picture, etc., of a proposed date before your phone number is given or a meeting is arranged;

- that the information in your file is clear, e.g., wishes, interests, requirements, "won't accepts;"

- the length of the contract and the number of dates or introductions promised;

- the cost of any additional fee to extend/renew/continue the membership;

- any extra costs associated with club functions (parties, picnics, trips);

- what the club promises to do for the basic fee—there might be little relationship between the cost and performance of the club; beware of very high priced companies;

- that all "guarantees" are in writing;

- for figures on its percentage of success and the average length of time needed to locate an acceptable spouse if the club promises to find you a spouse; and

- the cancellation policy; check with your state or local consumer agency for your legal rights; contact your consumer agency or the Better Business Bureau to file a complaint.

Timeshares/Campgrounds

- Prizes and awards might be used in promoting timeshares and campgrounds. They sometimes are overvalued or misrepresented. Free awards might "bait" you into driving a long distance to the property, only to attend a long high-pressure sales pitch to obtain your prize.

- Be realistic. Make your decision based on how much you will use it and if it provides the recreational and vacation purposes you want. Don't decide to purchase based on an investment possibility. It might be difficult or almost impossible to resell.

- Ask about such additional costs as finance charges, annual fees and maintenance fees. Maintenance fees can go up yearly.

- Compare your total annual cost with that of hotels or your normal vacation expenses.

- Ask about availability during your vacation periods. Ask what other timeshares or campgrounds you may use with your membership.

- Talk with individuals who already purchased from the company about the services, availability, upkeep and reciprocal rights to use other facilities.

- Get everything in writing and make sure verbal promises are in the written contract. Have an attorney review any contracts/documents and make sure there are no blanks on papers you sign.

- Do you have cancellation rights? State laws vary. Check with your local or state consumer agency.

- Check with your consumer agency or the Better Business Bureau for any complaints against the company, seller, developer and management company.

To order a free publication on timeshares and health clubs, contact the Federal Trade Commission, Public Reference Section, 6th & Pennsylvania Avenue, N.W., Room 130, Washington, DC 20580, 202–326–2222.

Travel Scams

- Don't be taken by solicitations by postcard, letter or phone claiming you've won a free trip or can get discounts on hotels and airfares. These offers usually don't disclose the hidden fees involved, for example, deposits, surcharges, excessive handling fees or taxes.

- Some travel scams require you to purchase a product to get a trip that's "free" or "two-for-one." You'll end up paying for the "free" trip or more for the product than the trip is worth, and the two-for-one deal might be more expensive than if you had arranged a trip yourself by watching for airfare deals.

- Be wary of travel offers which ask you to redeem vouchers or certificates from out-of-state companies. Their offers are usually valid only for a limited time and on a space-available basis. The hotels are often budget rooms and very uncomfortable. The company charges you for the trip in advance, but will the company still be in business when you're ready to take the trip?

- Check the reputation of any travel service you use, especially travel clubs offering discounts on their services in exchange for an annual fee. Contact your state or local consumer protection agency or the Better Business Bureau.

- Request copies of a travel club's or agent's brochures and contracts before purchasing your ticket. Don't rely on oral promises. Find out about cancellation policies and never sign contracts that have blank or incomplete spaces.

- Never give out your credit card number to a club or company with which you're unfamiliar or which requires you to call 900 numbers for information.

- Don't feel pressured by requests for an immediate decision or a statement that the offer is only good "if you act now." Don't deal with companies that request payment in advance or that don't have escrow accounts where your deposit is held.

- Research cut-rate offers, especially when dealing with travel consolidators who might not be able to provide your tickets until close to your departure date.

- You can protect yourself by using a credit card to purchase travel services. If you don't get what you paid for, contact the credit card issuer and you might be able to get the charges reversed. Be aware that you have 60 days to dispute a charge. See page 22 for further information on billings and disputes.

Rent-To-Own

Although buying in a rent-to-own transaction sounds like a simple solution when you are short of cash, rent-to-own can be expensive. The rental charge can be three or four times what it would cost if you paid cash or financed the purchase at the highest interest rate typically charged in installment sales.

Before signing a rent-to-own contract, ask yourself the following questions:

- Is the item something I absolutely have to have right now?

- Can I delay the purchase until I have saved enough money to pay cash or at least make a down payment on an installment plan?

- Does a retail store offer a layaway plan for the item?

- Have I considered all my credit options, including applying for retail credit from the merchant or borrowing money from a credit union, bank or small loan company?

- Would a used item purchased from a garage sale, classified ad or secondhand store serve the purpose?

If you decide that rent-to-own is the best choice for you, here are some questions you should ask before you sign on the dotted line.

- What is the total cost of the item? The total cost can be determined by multiplying the amount of each payment by the number of payments required to purchase the item. Make sure to add in any additional charges, for example, finance, handling or balloon payments at the end of the contract.

- Am I getting a new or used item?

- Can I purchase the item before the end of the rental term? If so, how is the price calculated?

- Will I get credit for all of my payments if I decide to purchase the item?

- Is there a charge for repairs during the rental period? Will I get a replacement while the rented item is not in my possession?

- What happens if I am late on a payment? Will the item be repossessed? Will I pay a penalty if I return the item before the end of the contract period?

Comparison shop among various rent-to-own merchants. Contact your local or state consumer protection agency or Better Business Bureau to find out if there are any complaints on record against the business. Check for any specific state laws. Read the contract carefully and make sure you understand all the terms and get all promises in writing.

Remember, know what you are paying. Compare the cash price plus finance charges in an installment plan with the total cost of a rent-to-own transaction.

Long-term rent-to-own contracts cost so much more than installment plans that you could rent an item, make a number of payments, return the item, buy it on an installment plan and still come out ahead.

Product Safety and Recalls

Knowing how to use products correctly, reading instructions and being alert to hazards will help to ensure a safe environment around you. You also should pay attention to product recalls in the news and consumer magazines. Several Federal government agencies provide recall information on a variety of products, including toys, cars, child safety seats, food, and health and beauty aids.

- Read about major appliances, tools and other items before you buy. There are several consumer magazines at the library which give detailed information on the prices, features and safety of various products.

- Learn to use power tools and electrical appliances safely. If you don't know what a ground fault circuit interrupter (GFCI) is, find out. Read the instructions carefully before using the equipment.

- Don't use things for purposes the manufacturer never intended. Tools aren't kids' toys.

- Poolside safety demands non-climbable fencing, CPR training, a poolside phone, a GFCI and constant adult supervision to help ensure the protection of children. Some building codes require some of these safety features.

- Make sure toys are age appropriate. Your 10-year-old's baseball bat can be a lethal weapon in the hands of your 3-year-old slugger.

- Children should always wear bicycle helmets. Some states now require them. When shopping for helmets, look for the ANSI and/or SNELL sticker to ensure the safest helmet.

- Small parts can present choking hazards to children who put things in their mouths. Beware of balloons, balls, marbles and older children's toys.

- Baby items demand special attention. Cribs, baby walkers and baby gates have changed dramatically as the result of new safety requirements. Don't buy used baby items that can't comply with current standards.

- Garage and tag sales are places where small appliances, power tools, baby furniture and toys with safety defects, lead paints or other hazards get passed along to new owners. Make sure these types of items meet current safety requirements.

- If you spot a product defect, design flaw, allergic reaction or hidden hazard, contact the U.S. Consumer Product Safety Commission or your state or local consumer protection agency.

- Read product labels. Some products can turn into deadly poisons when mixed with other products, stored improperly or used in poorly vented areas.

- Keep all medicines, cleaning products, wood finishes, toxic art supplies and paints out of the sight and reach of young children. Keep leftover products in their original containers. Have the poison control emergency number near your phone. Get rid of old and dated products.

- Look for tamper-resistant packaging on foods and medicine.

- Watch out for dinnerware decorated with lead paint or glaze and lead crystal decanters. If there's no way to ensure the items are lead-free, don't buy them.

- Contact the Auto Safety Hotline at 800–424–9393 (toll free) to report safety problems, and to obtain recall and safety information on new and used cars, trucks, motorcycles, motor homes, child seats and other motor vehicle equipment.

For consumer education material or to file a complaint, contact:

(consumer products, other than cars, food or drugs)
U.S. Consumer Product Safety Commission (CPSC)
Washington, DC 20207
<u>Product Safety Hotline</u>:
Toll free: 800–638–CPSC;
800–638–2772
TDD toll free: 800–638–8270
Fax-on-Demand: 301–504–0051
(dial from handset of fax machine)
Website: www.cpsc.gov
E-mail: info@cpsc.gov

(For more information about CPSC's Product Safety Hotline and Fax-on-Demand services, see page 107.)

(vehicles, child safety seats and other motor vehicle equipment)
National Highway Traffic Safety Administration (NHTSA)
Washington, DC 20590
<u>Auto Safety Hotline and Fax-on-Demand</u>:

202–366–0123
Toll free outside DC:
800–424–9393
TDD: 202–366–7899

TDD toll free outside DC: 800–424–9153
Website: www.nhtsa.dot.gov

(food, drugs, medical devices, such radiological products as microwave ovens, televisions and sunlamps)
U.S. Food and Drug Administration
Recall and Emergency Coordinator
Refer to the white pages of your local telephone book for your regional FDA office.

Recalls
Item 595Z
Pueblo, CO 81009
(Write to this address to receive a free publication prepared by the U.S. Office of Consumer Affairs that explains which Federal agencies issue consumer product recalls, the kinds of products each of them covers, how to report product safety problems, and how to find out about warnings or recalls that have been announced.)

State and Local Consumer Protection Office (See page 71.)

Nutrition Labeling

The new food label format offers more complete, useful and accurate nutrition information than has been available in the past. Shoppers are now able to compare the nutritional value of every packaged food on the grocery shelf.

Nutrition Labeling Panel—Content

The revamped nutrition panel on each food product is called "Nutrition Facts" and lists the following mandatory dietary components:

- total calories;
- calories from fat;
- total fat;
- saturated fat;
- cholesterol;
- sodium;
- total carbohydrates;
- dietary fiber;
- sugars;
- protein;
- vitamins A and C;
- calcium; and
- iron.

Voluntary dietary components that can be listed on the label include calories from saturated fat, polyunsaturated fat, mono-unsaturated fat, potassium, soluble fiber, insoluble fiber, sugar alcohol, other carbohydrates, and essential vitamins and minerals.

Nutrition Labeling—Format

All nutrients must be stated as a percentage of their "Daily Value" (the daily nutrient intake level recommended by public health authorities) to show how much of a day's ideal total of a particular nutrient a consumer is getting. For example, if a serving of soup contains half the amount of sodium that is recommended for consumers daily, the food label shows the "Daily Value" of sodium in that soup as 50%. These percentages are based on a daily intake of 2,000 calories.

Serving Sizes

Serving sizes have been standardized and reflect more closely the amount of food usually eaten at one time. The serving size for similar products from different manufacturers are comparable.

Nutrient Content Descriptors

Food manufacturers are required to use standardized definitions when making claims concerning the nutrient contents of foods, for example, "light," "low-fat," "free," "reduced calories" and "high fiber."

Health Claims

Product claims about the relationship between a nutrient or food and the risk of a disease are limited to specific types of claims in seven areas. For example, if a product makes a health claim related to the link between calcium and osteoporosis, the product must contain at least 200 milligrams of calcium and must be a form of calcium that can be absorbed easily by the body.

The claims must be stated so that the consumer can understand the relationship between the nutrient and the disease.

For more information, contact:

Food and Drug Administration
Consumer Affairs and Information
Department of Health and Human Services
5600 Fishers Lane
Room 16–75 (HFE–88)
Rockville, MD 20857
301–443–3170 or
Toll free: 800–532–4440

Department of Agriculture
Center for Nutrition Policy and Promotion
1120 20th Street, N.W.
Room 200
Washington, DC 20036
202–418–2312
Website:
www.usda.gov/fcs/cnpp.html

Introducing '%Daily Value'
The Key to Healthy Eating

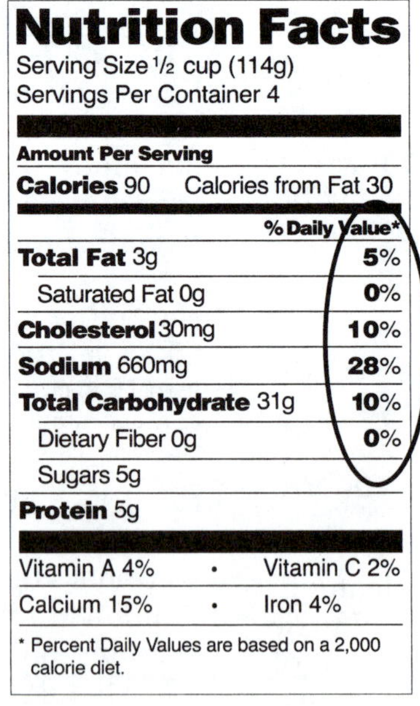

There's a new nutrition tool called "%Daily Value" that allows you to easily determine whether a food contributes a lot or a little of a particular nutrient. A high percentage means the food contains a lot of a nutrient. A low percentage means it contains a little. You don't have to worry about doing calculations.

Let's say you're trying to eat less fat. You come across two different brands of frozen mixed vegetables in sauce. One of the packages lists 5% as the %Daily Value for total fat. The other package gives 15%. Which should you choose? The one with 5% because 5 is a significantly lower number than 15.

Source: Food and Drug Administration, 1994

Part II. Consumer Assistance Directory

National Consumer Organizations

These organizations define their missions as consumer assistance, protection and/or advocacy. The descriptions below are based on information they provided. The services they provide vary. Those that assist individuals with marketplace problems are specified. Otherwise, these organizations do not assist consumers with individual complaints, although many are interested in hearing from consumers about problems, issues and trends in connection with their advocacy and consumer education activities. Most, though not all, develop and distribute consumer education and information materials; several are professional associations primarily or exclusively concerned with improving consumer protection or customer service; and many are engaged in advocacy of consumer interests before government, the courts and the news media. Where informational or educational materials are offered, there might be a charge; contact the organization to find out.

Alliance Against Fraud in Telemarketing (AAFT)

1701 K Street, N.W.
Suite 1200
Washington, DC 20006
202–835–3323
Fax: 202–835–3323

The alliance, coordinated by the National Consumers League, is an international coalition of public interest groups, trade associations, labor unions, businesses, law enforcement agencies, consumer reporters and consumer protection agencies. AAFT members promote cooperative educational efforts to alert potential victims to the threat of telemarketing fraud and steps consumers can take to protect themselves.

American Association of Retired Persons (AARP)

Consumer Affairs Section
601 E Street, N.W.
Washington, DC 20049
202–434–6030
Fax: 202–434–6466

AARP's Consumer Affairs Section advocates on behalf of mid-life and older consumers, develops and distributes consumer information, and educates the private sector about the specific needs of older consumers. Programs and materials on housing, insurance, funeral practices, eligibility for public benefits, financial security, transportation and consumer protection issues are developed, with special focus on the needs and problems of older consumers.

American Council on Consumer Interests (ACCI)

240 Stanley Hall
University of Missouri
Columbia, MO 65211
573–882–3817
Fax: 573–884–6571
E-mail: acci@showme.
missouri.edu
Contact: Anita B. Metzen,
Executive Director

Serving the professional needs of consumer educators, researchers and policymakers, ACCI publications and educational programs foster the production, synthesis and dissemination of information in the consumer interest.

American Council on Science and Health (ACSH)

1995 Broadway, 2nd Floor
New York, NY 10023–5860
212–362–7044
Fax: 212–362–4919

A non-profit public education group, ACSH's goal is to provide up-to-date, sound information on the relationship between health and chemicals, foods, lifestyles and the environment. Booklets and special reports on a variety of topics are available, as is a quarterly magazine, *Priorities*.

Bankcard Holders of America (BHA)

524 Branch Drive
Salem, VA 24153
540–389–5445
Fax: 540–389–3020

A non-profit organization, BHA assists consumers in saving money on credit, getting out of debt and resolving credit problems. It offers lists of low-rate and secured credit cards, more than 20 guides and brochures on credit topics, including a cost/benefit guide to rebate/frequent flier programs, as well as a newsletter.

Call for Action

5272 River Road
Suite 300
Bethesda, MD 20816
301–657–8260 (network information)
Fax: 301–657–2914
TDD: 301–657–9462

Call for Action assists consumers with marketplace problems. An international non-profit hotline, Call for Action is affiliated with radio and television stations and helps consumers and small businesses through mediation of marketplace disputes. A list of the affiliated radio and television stations is available by contacting the hotline.

Center for Auto Safety (CAS)

2001 S Street, N.W., Suite 410
Washington, DC 20009
202–328–7700

CAS assists consumers with auto-related problems. CAS advocates on behalf of consumers in auto safety and quality, fuel efficiency, emissions and related issues. For advice on specific problems, CAS requests that consumers write; include a brief statement of the problem or question; year, make and model of the vehicle; and a stamped self-addressed envelope.

Center for Science in the Public Interest (CSPI)

1875 Connecticut Avenue, N.W., Suite 300
Washington, DC 20009
202–332–9110
Fax: 202–265–4954

A non-profit, membership organization, CSPI conducts research, education and advocacy on nutrition, health, food safety and related issues, and publishes the monthly *Nutrition Action Healthletter* as well as other consumer information materials.

Citizen Action

1730 Rhode Island Avenue, N.W.
Washington, DC 20036
202–775–1580
Fax: 202–296–4054

Citizen Action works on behalf of its 3 million members and 34 state organizations on health care reform, environment, energy, transportation and civil rights issues.

Community Nutrition Institute (CNI)

910 17th Street, N.W.,
Suite 413
Washington, DC 20006
202–776–0595
Fax: 202–776–0599
E-mail: cni@digex.net

An advocate for programs and services to enable consumers to enjoy a diet that is adequate, safe and healthy, CNI also works to increase citizen participation in the state and Federal policy and administrative processes to achieve these goals. CNI publishes *Nutrition Week,* a newsletter covering nutrition and food safety issues, as well as related legislative and regulatory actions.

Congress Watch

215 Pennsylvania Avenue, S.E.
Washington, DC 20003
202–546–4996
Fax: 202–547–7392
E-mail: congresswatch@
citizen.org

An arm of Public Citizen, Congress Watch works for consumer-related legislation, regulation and policies in such areas as trade, health and safety, and campaign financing, and has publications available on the issues with which it deals.

Consumer Action (CA)

116 New Montgomery,
Suite 233
San Francisco, CA 94105
415–777–9635 (consumer complaint hotline, 10 a.m.— 2 p.m., PST)
Fax: 415–777–5267

Consumer Action assists consumers with marketplace problems. An education and advocacy organization specializing in credit, finance and telecommunications issues, Consumer Action offers a multi-lingual consumer complaint hotline, free information on its surveys of banks and long-distance telephone companies, and consumer education materials in as many as eight languages.

Consumer Alert

1001 Connecticut Avenue,
N.W., Suite 1128
Washington, DC 20036
202–467–5809
Fax: 202–467–5814
E-mail: calert@his.com

Consumer Alert is a non-profit, membership organization whose mission is to inform the public about the consumer benefits of competitive enterprise, advancing competition as the best regulator of business. A bimonthly newsletter and other materials are available.

Consumer Federation of America (CFA)

1424 16th Street, N.W.,
Suite 604
Washington, DC 20036
202–387–6121
Fax: 202–265–7989

Made up of more than 240 organizations representing a membership exceeding 50 million consumers, CFA is a consumer advocacy and education organization. Issues on which it currently represents consumer interests before Congress and Federal regulatory agencies include telephone service, insurance and financial services, product safety, indoor air pollution, health care, product liability and utility rates. It develops and distributes studies of various consumer issues, as well as consumer guides in book and pamphlet form. In addition, CFA publishes several newsletters. The National Insurance Consumer Organization (NICO) has merged with CFA and is now known as CFA Insurance Group.

Consumers for World Trade (CWT)

2000 L Street, N.W., Suite 200
Washington, DC 20036
202–785–4835
Fax: 202–416–1734
E-mail: cwt@ids2.idsonline.com

A non-profit organization, CWT supports trade expansion and liberalization to promote economic growth and increase consumer choice and price competition in the marketplace. Various publications are available.

Consumers Union of U.S., Inc. (CU)

101 Truman Avenue
Yonkers, NY 10703–1057
914–378–2000
Fax: 914–378–2900

A non-profit, independent organization, CU researches and tests consumer goods and services and disseminates the results in its monthly magazine, *Consumer Reports,* as well as in other publications and media.

Council of Better Business Bureaus, Inc. (CBBB)

4200 Wilson Boulevard
Arlington, VA 22203
703–276–0100
Fax: 703–525–8277
E-mail: bbb@bbb.org
Website: www.bbb.org

Sponsored by national companies and the nation's Better Business Bureaus, the Council of Better Business Bureaus provides coordination and leadership to the 162 Better Business Bureaus (BBBs) in the United States (see page 34 for the listing), offers a national advertising review program, dispute resolution services, an advisory service that reports on national charities, consumer information services, and voluntary industry guidelines for advertising and selling products and services.

Families USA Foundation

1334 G Street, N.W., Suite 300
Washington, DC 20005
202–628–3030
Fax: 202–347–2417
E-mail: info@familiesusa.org
Website: epn.org/families.html

A national, non-profit membership organization committed to comprehensive reform of health and long–term care, Families USA works to educate and mobilize consumers on health care issues. In addition to its two grassroots advocacy networks— a.s.a.p., a network of health and long-term care reform activists and HealthLink USA, a nationwide health reform computer network for public interest groups—Families USA develops and distributes reports and other materials on health and long-term care issues.

Health Research Group (HRG)

1600 20th Street, N.W.
Washington, DC 20009
202–588–1000

A division of Public Citizen, HRG works for protection against unsafe foods, drugs, medical devices and workplaces, and advocates for greater consumer control over personal health decisions. A monthly Health Letter and other publications are available.

National Association of Consumer Agency Administrators (NACAA)

1010 Vermont Avenue, N.W.
Suite 514
Washington, DC 20005
202–347–7395
Fax: 202–347–2563

An association of the administrators of local, state and Federal Government consumer protection agencies, NACAA provides training programs, public policy studies and conferences, professional publications and other member services.

National Association of State Utility Consumer Advocates (NASUCA)

1133 15th Street, N.W.,
Suite 550
Washington, DC 20005
202–727–3908
Fax: 202–727–3911

A national organization of 41 utility ratepayer advocate offices in 38 states and the District of Columbia, NASUCA members represent millions of consumers served by investor-owned gas, telephone, electric and water companies before Congress, state regulatory commissions, the courts, the Federal Energy Regulatory Commission and the Federal Communications Commission.

National Coalition for Consumer Education (NCCE)

295 Main Street, Suite 200
Madison, NJ 07940
201–377–8987
Fax: 201–377–4828

The coalition brings together people and resources from government, business, education, consumer organizations and the media to educate consumers about such important issues as financial management, health and safety, and the environment. The coalition develops and provides educational materials and resources to consumer educators but does not handle requests from individuals.

National Consumers League (NCL)

1701 K Street, N.W.
Suite 1200
Washington, DC 20006
202–835–3323
Fax: 202–835–0747

Founded in 1899, NCL is America's pioneer consumer advocacy organization. The league is a non-profit, membership organization working for health, safety and fairness in the marketplace and workplace. Current principal issue areas include consumer fraud, food and drug safety, fair labor standards, child labor, health care, the environment, financial services and telecommunications. The league develops and distributes consumer education materials and newsletters.

National Foundation for Consumer Credit, Inc. (NFCC)

8611 2nd Avenue, Suite 100
Silver Spring, MD 20910
301–589–5600
Toll free: 800–388–2227
Fax: 301–495–5623

A membership organization for non-profit community organizations which are often called Consumer Credit Counseling Service agencies and are in more than 1,100 locations in the United States and Canada. The agencies educate and counsel individuals and families on credit issues. Consumers are taught to budget and use credit wisely and may be helped to resolve their credit problems. The 800 number provides the location of the nearest agency.

National Fraud Information Center (NFIC)

P.O. Box 65868
Washington, DC 20035
Toll free: 800–876–7060 (9 a.m.—5 p.m.; TDD available)
Fax: 202–835–0767
E-mail: nfic@internetmci.com
Website: www.fraud.org

NFIC assists consumers with recognizing and filing complaints about telemarketing and Internet fraud. A project of the National Consumers League, the center's toll-free hotline provides consumers with information to help them avoid becoming victims of fraud, referral to appropriate law enforcement agencies and professional associations, and assistance in filing complaints. The center also provides professionals involved in consumer fraud prevention and enforcement with telecommunications systems and data links to improve fraud regulation, prevention and law enforcement.

National Institute for Consumer Education (NICE)

207 Rackham Building
College of Education
Eastern Michigan University
Ypsilanti, MI 48197
313–487–2292
Fax: 313–487–7153
E-mail:
rosella.bannister@emich.edu

A consumer education resource and professional development center for K–12 classroom teachers, business, government, labor and community educators, NICE conducts training programs, develops teaching guides and resource lists, and manages a national clearinghouse of consumer education materials, including videos, software programs, textbooks and curriculum guides.

National Insurance Consumer Organization (NICO) See Consumer Federation of America (CFA)

Project OPEN (Online Public Education Network)

c/o Interactive Services Association
8403 Colesville Road, Suite 865
Silver Spring, MD 20910
301–495–4955
Fax: 301–495–4959
E-mail: project-open@isa.net

Project OPEN is a joint effort of the National Consumers League (NCL), the Interactive Services Association (ISA), and leading online/Internet service companies. Its primary mission is to help consumers understand how to use online and Internet services in an informed and responsible way. Project OPEN's brochure, "How To Get the Most Out of Going Online," provides basic information about going online and describes tools that are available to help parents and educators screen online content for children. Single copies of the brochure are available free by calling 800–466–OPEN. For information about bulk copies, contact ISA at 301–495–4955.

Public Citizen, Inc.

1600 20th Street, N.W.
Washington, DC 20009
202–588–1000

A national, non-profit membership organization representing consumer interests through lobbying, litigation, research and publications, Public Citizen represents consumer interests in Congress, the courts, government agencies and the media. Primary current areas of interest include product liability, health care delivery, safe medical devices and medications, open and ethical government, and safe and sustainable energy use.

Public Voice for Food and Health Policy

1101 14th Street, N.W.
Suite 710
Washington, DC 20005
202–371–1840
Fax: 202–371–1910
E-mail: pvoice@ix.netcom.com
Website:
www.publicvoice.org/pvoice.html

A national research, education and advocacy organization, Public Voice works for food and agriculture policies and practices that improve the safety, health and affordability of the food supply and protect the environment. Public Voice develops and distributes consumer information materials on pesticide reduction, nutrition labeling, seafood safety and inner-city food access.

Society of Consumer Affairs Professionals in Business (SOCAP)

801 North Fairfax Street
Suite 404
Alexandria, VA 22314
703–519–3700
Fax: 703–549–4886
E-mail: socap@aol.com

An international professional organization, SOCAP provides training, conferences and publications to encourage and maintain the integrity of business in transactions with consumers; to encourage and promote effective communication and understanding among business, government and consumers; and to define and advance the consumer affairs profession.

U.S. Public Interest Research Group (U.S. PIRG)

218 D Street, S.E.
Washington, DC 20003–1900
202–546–9707
202–546–2461
E-mail: pirg@pirg.org
Website: www.pirg.org/pirg

The group is the national lobbying office for state public interest research groups, consumer/environmental advocacy groups active in 33 states that lobby and publish reports on issues, including credit bureau errors; bank fees and services; toy, ATV and product safety; toxic chemicals in art supplies and other consumer products; and recycling, overpackaging and green consumerism. U.S. PIRG does not handle individual consumer complaints directly but measures complaint levels to gauge the need for remedial legislation.

Better Business Bureaus

Better Business Bureaus (BBBs) are non-profit organizations supported primarily by local business members. The focus of BBB activities is to promote an ethical marketplace by encouraging honest advertising and selling practices, and by providing alternative dispute resolution. BBBs offer a variety of consumer services. For example, they provide consumer education materials; answer consumer questions; provide information about a company, particularly whether or not there are unanswered or unsettled complaints or other marketplace problems; help resolve buyer/seller complaints against a company, including mediation and arbitration services; and provide information about charities and other organizations that are seeking public donations.

BBBs usually request that a complaint be submitted in writing so that an accurate record exists of the dispute. The BBB will then take up the complaint with the company involved. If the complaint cannot be satisfactorily resolved through communication with the business, a BBB may offer an alternative dispute settlement process, such as mediation or arbitration. BBBs do *not* judge or rate individual products or brands, handle complaints concerning the price of goods or services, handle employer/employee wage disputes or give legal advice.

If you need help with a consumer question or complaint, call your local BBB to ask about its services. Or you can go online to acquire information about the BBB through the Internet, located at http://www.bbb.org. The BBB World Wide Web server features consumer fraud and scam alerts and provides information about BBB programs, services and locations.

The Council of Better Business Bureaus, the umbrella organization for the BBBs, also provides programs and publications for consumers. The Council can assist with complaints about the truthfulness and accuracy of national advertising claims, including children's advertising; provide reports on national soliciting charities; and help to settle disputes with automobile manufacturers through the BBB AUTO LINE program.

In addition to the BBBs listed below, there are 16 BBBs in Canada. The Council of Better Business Bureaus can give you the addresses for Bureaus in Canada.

Council

Council of Better Business Bureaus, Inc.
4200 Wilson Boulevard
Arlington, VA 22203
703–276–0100

Bureaus

Alabama

1210 South 20th Street (35255–5268)
P.O. Box 55268
Birmingham, AL 35205
205–558–2222

1528 Peachtree Lane, Suite 1
Cullman, AL 35057
205–737–0539

118 Woodburn
Dothan, AL 36301
334–794–0492

102 Court Street, Suite 512
Florence, AL 35620
Toll free: 800–239–1642

107 Lincoln Street, N.E.
P.O. Box 383
Huntsville, AL 35804
205–533–1640

100 North Royal Street
Mobile, AL 36602–3295
334–433–5494

60 Commerce Street, Suite 806
Montgomery, AL 36104–3559
334–262–5606

Alaska

2805 Bering Street, Suite 5
Anchorage, AK 99503–3819
907–562–0704

P.O. Box 74675
Fairbanks, AK 99707
907–451–0222

Arizona

4428 North 12th Street
Phoenix, AZ 85014–4585
900–225–5222 ($.95/min.)
602–240–3473 (flat fee of $3.80)

3620 North 1st Avenue, Suite 136
Tucson, AZ 85719
520–888–5353

Arkansas

1415 South University
Little Rock, AR 72204–2605
501–664–7274

California

705 18th Street
Bakersfield, CA 93301
805–322–2074

290 N. 10th Street, Suite 206
Colton, CA 92324–3052
900–225–5222 ($.95/min.)

6101 Ball Road, Suite 309
Cypress, CA 90630–3966
900–225–5222 ($.95/min.)

2519 West Shaw, #106
Fresno, CA 93711
209–222–8111

3727 West Sixth Street, Suite 607
Los Angeles, CA 90020
900–225–5222 ($.95/min.)

510 16th Street, Suite 550
Oakland, CA 94612–1584
510–238–1000

400 S Street
Sacramento, CA 95814–6997
916–443–6843

5050 Murphy Canyon, Suite 110
San Diego, CA 92123
619–496–2131

1530 Meridian, Suite 110
San Jose, CA 95125
408–445–3000

400 South El Camino Real, Suite 350
San Mateo, CA 94402–1706
415–696–1240

213 Santa Barbara Street
Santa Barbara, CA 93102
805–963–8657

11 S. San Joaquin Street
Stockton, CA 95202–3202
209–948–4880

Colorado

3622 North El Paso (80933–5454)
P.O. Box 7970
Colorado Springs, CO 80933–7970
719–636–1155

1780 South Bellaire, Suite 700
Denver, CO 80222–4350
303–758–2100

1730 South College Avenue, Suite 303
Fort Collins, CO 80525–1073
907–484–1348
370–778–2809 (Cheyenne)

119 West 6th Street, Suite 203
Pueblo, CO 81003–3119
719–542–6464

Connecticut

Parkside Building
821 North Main Street Ext.
Wallingford, CT 06492–2420
203–269–2700

Delaware

2055 Limestone Road, Suite 200
Wilmington, DE 19808–5532
302–996–9200

District of Columbia

1012 14th Street, N.W.
9th Floor
Washington, DC 20005–3410
202–393–8000

Florida

5830 142nd Avenue North
Suite B (34620)
P.O. Box 7950
Clearwater, FL 34618–7950
813–842–5459 (Pasco City)
813–535–5522 (Pinellas County)
813–854–1154 (Hills, Tampa)
813–957–0093 (Sarasota, Manatee)
Toll free: 800–525–1447 (Hernando)

2710 Swamp Cabbage Court
Fort Myers, FL 33901–9333
900–225–5222 ($.95/min.)

7820 Arlington Expressway, #147
Jacksonville, FL 32211
904–721–2288

16291 N.W. 57th Avenue
Miami, FL 33014–6709
900–225–5222 ($.95/min.)

4900 Bayou Blvd., Suite 112
Pensacola, FL 32597–1511
904–494–0222

1950 Port St. Lucie Blvd., Suite 211
Port St. Lucie, FL 34952–5579
407–337–2083

580 Village Blvd., Suite 340
West Palm Beach, FL 33409
561–686–2200

1011 North Wymore Road, Suite 204
Winter Park, FL 32789–1736
407–621–3300

Georgia

204 North Jackson
Albany, GA 31706–3241
912–883–0744

100 Edgewood Avenue, Suite 1012
Atlanta, GA 30303–3075
404–688–4910

301 7th Street
P.O. Box 2085
Augusta, GA 30903–2085
706–722–1574

208 13th Street
P.O. Box 2587 (31902–2587)
Columbus, GA 31901–2137
706–324–0712

301 Mulberry Street, Suite 102
Macon, GA 31201
912–742–7999

6606 Abercorn Street, Suite 108–C
Savannah, GA 31405–5817
912–354–7521

Hawaii

1600 Kapiolani Blvd.
Suite 201
Honolulu, HI 96814–3801
808–941–5222

Idaho

1333 West Jefferson
Boise, ID 83702–5320
208–342–4649

1575 South Blvd.
Idaho Falls, ID 83404–5926
208–523–9754

Illinois

330 North Wabash
Chicago, IL 60611
900–225–5222 ($.95/min.)

3024 West Lake
Peoria, IL 61615–3770
309–688–3741

810 East State Street, 3rd Floor
Rockford, IL 61104–1001
900–225–5222 ($.95/min.)

Indiana

722 West Bristol Street
Suite H–2 (46514–2988)
P.O. Box 405
Elkhart, IN 46515–0405
219–262–8996

4004 Morgan Avenue
Suite 201
Evansville, IN 47715–2265
812–473–0202

1203 Webster Street
Fort Wayne, IN 46802–3493
219–423–4433

4189 Cleveland Street
Gary, IN 46408
219–980–1511
219–769–8053

22 E. Washington St., Suite 200
Indianapolis, IN 46204–3584
317–488–2222

207 Dixie Way North, Suite 130
South Bend, IN 46637–3360
219–277–9121

Iowa

852 Middle Road, Suite 290
Bettendorf, IA 52722–4100
319–355–6344

505 5th Avenue, Suite 615
Des Moines, IA 50309–2375
515–243–8137

505 6th Street, Suite 417
Sioux City, IA 51101
712–252–4501

Kansas

501 Southeast Jefferson, Suite 24
Topeka, KS 66607–1190
913–232–0454

328 Laura
P.O. Box 11707–1190
Wichita, KS 67211
316–263–3146

Kentucky

410 West Vine Street, Suite 280
Lexington, KY 40507–1616
606–259–1008

844 South Fourth Street
Louisville, KY 40203–2186
502–583–6546

Louisiana

1605 Murray Street, Suite 117
Alexandria, LA 71301–6875
318–473–4494

2055 Wooddale Blvd.
Baton Rouge, LA 70806–1546
504–926–3010

3038 Park NE, Suite 204
Houma, LA 70360–6354
504–868–3456

100 Huggins Road (70506)
P.O. Box 30297
Lafayette, LA 70593–0297
318–981–3497

3941–L Ryan Street 70605)
P.O. Box 7314
Lake Charles, LA 70606–7314
318–478–6253

141 Desiard Street, Suite 808
Monroe, LA 71201–7380
318–387–4600

1539 Jackson Avenue, Suite 400
New Orleans, LA 70130–5843
504–581–6222

3612 Youree Drive
Shreveport, LA 71105–2122
318–861–6417

Maine

812 Stevens Avenue
Portland, ME 04103–2648
207–878–2715

Maryland

2100 Huntingdon Avenue
Baltimore, MD 21211–3215
900–225–5222 ($.95/min.)

Massachusetts

20 Park Plaza, Suite 820
Boston, MA 02116–4344
617–426–9000

293 Bridge Street, Suite 320
Springfield, MA 01103–1402
413–734–3114

32 Franklin Street (01608–1900)
P.O. Box 16555
Worchester, MA 01608–1900
508–755–2548

Michigan

40 Pearl, N.W., Suite 354
Grand Rapids, MI 49503
616–774–8236

30555 Southfield Road
Suite 200
Southfield, MI 48076–7751
810–644–9100

Minnesota

2706 Gannon Road
St. Paul, MN 55116–2600
612–699–1111

Mississippi

4500 155 N. Suite 287 (39211)
P.O. Box 12745
Jackson, MS 39236–2745
601–987–8282

Missouri

306 E. 12th Street, Suite 1024
Kansas City, MO 64106–2418
816–421–7800

12 Sunnen Drive, Suite 121
St. Louis, MO 63143
314–645–3300

205 Park Central East, Suite 509
Springfield, MO 65806–1326
417–862–4222

Nebraska

3633 O Street, Suite 1
Lincoln, NE 68510–1670
402–476–8855

2237 North 91st Court
Omaha, NE 68134–6022
402–391–7612

Nevada

1022 East Sahara Avenue
Las Vegas, NV 89104–1515
702–735–6900

991 Bible Way (89502)
P.O. Box 21269
Reno, NV 89515–1269
702–322–0657

New Hampshire

410 South Main Street
Suite 3
Concord, NH 03301–3483
603–224–1991

New Jersey

400 Lanidex Plaza
Parsippany, NJ 07054–2797
201–581–1313

1721 Route 37, East
Toms River, NJ 08753–8239
908–270–5577

1700 Whitehorse-Hamilton Square
Suite D–5
Trenton, NJ 08690–3596
609–588–0808

16 Maple Avenue
P.O. Box 303
Westmont, NJ 08108–0303
609–854–8467

New Mexico

2625 Pennsylvania, NE
Suite 2050
Albuquerque, NM 87110–3657
505–884–0500

308 North Locke
Farmington, NM 87401–5855
505–326–6501

201 N. Church, Suite 330
Las Cruces, NM 88001–3548
505–524–3130

New York

346 Delaware Avenue
Buffalo, NY 14202–1899
900–225–5222 ($.95/min.)

266 Main Street
Farmingdale, NY 11735–2618
900–225–5222 ($.95/min.)

257 Park Avenue, South
New York, NY 10010–7384
900–225–5222 ($.95/min.)

847 James Street, Suite 200
Syracuse, NY 13202–2552
900–225–522 ($.95/min.)

30 Glenn Street
White Plains, NY 10603–3213
900–225–5222 ($.95/min.)

North Carolina

1200 BB&T Building
Asheville, NC 28801–3418
704–253–2392

5200 Park Road, Suite 202
Charlotte, NC 28209–3650
704–527–0012

3608 West Friendly Avenue
Greensboro, NC 27410–4895
910–852–4240

3125 Poplarwood Court
Suite 308
Raleigh, NC 27604–1080
919–872–9240

Eden Place
8366 Drena Drive (28673)
P.O. Box 69
Sherrils Ford, NC 28673–0069
704–478–5622

500 West 5th Street, Suite 202
Winston-Salem, NC 27101–2728
910–725–8384

Ohio

222 W. Market Street
Akron, OH 44303–2111
330–253–4590

1434 Cleveland Avenue, N.W. (44703)
P.O. Box 8017
Canton, OH 44711–8017
330–454–9401

898 Walnut Street
Cincinnati, OH 45202–2097
513–421–3015

2217 East 9th Street, Suite 200
Cleveland, OH 44115–1299
216–241–7678

1335 Dublin Street, #30–A
Columbus, OH 43215–1000
614–486–6336

40 West Fourth Street, Suite 1250
Dayton, OH 45402–1828
513–222–5825

112 North West High Street (45801)
P.O. Box 269
Lima, OH 45802–0269
419–223–7010

425 Jefferson Avenue, Suite 909
Toledo, OH 43604–1055
419–241–6276

600 Mahoning Bank Building
P.O. Box 1495
Youngstown, OH 44501–1495
330–744–3111

Oklahoma

17 South Dewey
Oklahoma City, OK 73102–2400
405–239–6081

6711 South Yale, Suite 230
Tulsa, OK 74136–3327
918–492–1266

Oregon

333 SW Fifth Avenue, Suite 300
Portland, OR 97204
503–226–3981

Pennsylvania

528 North New Street
Bethlehem, PA 18018–5789
610–866–8780

29 E. King Street, Suite 322
Lancaster, PA 17602–2852
900–225–5222 ($.95/min.)

1930 Chestnut Street
P.O. Box 2297
Philadelphia, PA 19103–0297
900–225–5222 ($.95/min.)

300 6th Avenue, Suite 100–UL
Pittsburgh, PA 15222–2511
412–456–2700

129 N. Washington Avenue (18503–2204)
P.O. Box 993
Scranton, PA 18501–0993
717–342–9129

Puerto Rico
1608 Bori Street (00927–6100)
San Juan, PR 00927–6100
809–756–5400

Rhode Island

120 Lavan Street
Warwick, RI 02887–1071
401–785–1212

South Carolina

2330 Devine Street (29205)
P.O. Box 8326
Columbia, SC 29202–8326
803–254–2525

307–B Falls Street
Greenville, SC 29601–2829
803–242–5052

1601 North Oak Street
Suite 101
Myrtle Beach, SC 29577–1601
803–626–6881

Tennessee

P.O. Box 1178 TCA
Blountville, TN 37617–1178
423–325–6616

1010 Market Street, Suite 200
Chattanooga, TN 37402–2614
423–266–6144

2633 Kingston Pike, Suite 2 (37919)
P.O. Box 10327
Knoxville, TN 37939–0327
423–522–2552

6525 Quall Hollow, Suite 410 (38120)
P.O. Box 17036
Memphis, TN 38178–0036
901–759–1300

414 Union Street, Suite 1830
Nashville, TN 37219–1778
615–242–4BBB

Texas

3300 S. 14th Street, Suite 307
Abilene, TX 79605–5052
915–691–1533

1000 South Polk (79101–3408)
P.O. Box 1905
Amarillo, TX 79105–1905
806–379–6222

2101 So. IH35, Suite 302
Austin, TX 78741–3854
512–445–2911

476 Oakland Avenue (77701–2011)
P.O. Box 2988
Beaumont, TX 77704–2988
409–835–5348

4346 Carter Creek Parkway
Bryan, TX 77802–4413
409–260–2222

216 Park Avenue
Corpus Christi, TX 78401
512–887–4949

2001 Bryan Street, Suite 850
Dallas, TX 75201–3093
900–225–5222 ($95/min.)

State National Plaza, Suite 1101
El Paso, TX 79901
915–577–0191

1612 Summit Avenue, Suite 260
Fort Worth, TX 76102–5978
817–332–7585

5225 Katz Freeway, Suite 500
Houston, TX 77007
900–225–5222 ($.95/min.))

916 Main Street, Suite 800
Lubbock, TX 79401–3910
806–763–0459

10100 County Road, 118 West
P.O. Box 60206
Midland, TX 79711–0206
915–563–1880

3121 Executive Drive (76904)
P.O. Box 3366
San Angelo, TX 76902–3366
915–949–2986

1800 Northeast Loop 410
Suite 400
San Antonio, TX 78217–5296
210–828–9441

3600 Old Bullard Road, #103–A (75701)
P.O. Box 6652
Tyler, TX 75711–6652
903–581–5704

6801 Sanger Avenue, Suite 125 (76710)
P.O. Box 7203
Waco, TX 76714–7203
817–772–7530

609 International Blvd. (78596)
P.O. Box 69
Weslaco, TX 78599–0069
210–968–3678

4245 Kemp Blvd., Suite 900
Wichita Falls, TX 76308–2830
817–691–1172

Utah

1588 South Main Street
Salt Lake City, UT 84115–5382
801–487–4656

Vermont

(Contact Boston office)
800–4BBB–811 (802–Vermont only)

Virginia

11903 Main Street
Fredericksburg, VA 22408
540–373–9872

3608 Tidewater Drive
Norfolk, VA 23509–1499
804–627–5651

701 East Franklin, Suite 712
Richmond, VA 23219–2332
804–648–0016

31 West Campbell Avenue
Roanoke, VA 24011–1301
540–342–3455

Washington

1401 N. Union, #105
Kennewick, WA 99336–3819
509–783–0892

4800 South 188th Sreet, Suite 222 (98188)
P.O. Box 68926
Sea Tac, WA 98168–0926
900–225–5222 ($4 call)

East 123 Indiana, Suite 106
Spokane, WA 99207–2356
509–328–2100

32 North 3rd Street, Suite 410
P.O. Box 1584
Yakima, WA 98901
509–248–1326

Wisconsin

740 North Plankinton Avenue
Milwaukee, WI 53203–2478
414–273–1600

Corporate Consumer Contacts

This section will help you resolve a complaint about a service or product. First, be sure to go back to the place where you bought the product or service. Try to resolve the complaint with the seller. If that does not work, the next step is to write or call the company's headquarters.

This section lists the names and addresses of more than 650 corporate headquarters and, in many cases, the name of the person to contact. Many listings also include toll free "800" numbers. Additionally, TDD (Telecommunications Devices for the Deaf) numbers, made available by a number of companies, are in **bold type.**

In some cases, you will see a company name or brand name listed with the instructions to see another company listed elsewhere in this section, for example, "Max Factor, see Procter and Gamble." This means that questions about Max Factor products should be directed to the consumer contact at Procter and Gamble. Also, if a company has changed its name recently or is popularly known by another name, you will be directed to the company name listed.

If you do not find the product name in this section, check the product label or warranty for the name and address of the manufacturer. Public libraries also have information that might be helpful. The *Standard & Poor's Register of Corporations, Directors and Executives; Trade Names Directory; Standard Directory of Advertisers; and Dun & Bradstreet Directory* are four sources that list information about most firms. If you cannot find the name of the manufacturer, the *Thomas Register of American Manufacturers* lists the manufacturers of thousands of products.

Remember, to save time, first take your complaint back to where you bought the product. If you contact the company's headquarters first, the consumer contact probably will direct you back to the local store where you made the purchase.

A

Anna Wright
Administrator
AAMCO Transmissions, Inc.
One Presidential Boulevard
Bala Cynwyd, PA 19004–1034
610–668–2900
Toll free: 800–523–0401

Consumer Affairs
AETNA Life and Casualty
151 Farmington Avenue
Hartford, CT 06156
203–273–0123
Toll free outside CT: 800–US–AETNA

AJAY Leisure Products, Inc.
1501 East Wisconsin Street
Delavan, WI 53115
414–728–5521
Fax: 414–728–5521
Toll free: 800–558–3276

Susan Mach
Director of Consumer Affairs
AT&T
295 North Maple Avenue
Basking Ridge, NJ 07920
908–221–5311

Customer Service
Ace Hardware Corp.
2200 Kensington Court
Oak Brook, IL 60521
708–990–6600

**Airwick Industries, Inc.
see Reckitt & Colman, Inc.**

Andrea Cohan, Senior Manager
Customer Response Center
Alamo Rent A Car
P.O. Box 22776
Ft. Lauderdale, FL 33335
305–522–0000
Toll free: 800–445–5664

Manager, Consumer Affairs
Alaska Airlines
P.O. Box 68900
Seattle, WA 98168
206–431–7286 (consumer affairs)
206–431–7428 (cargo/freight claims)
206–431–7425 (baggage claims)
206–431–3753 (refunds/lost ticket applications)

Consumer Relations Department
Alberto Culver Co.
2525 Armitage Avenue
Melrose Park, IL 60160
708–450–3163

Consumer Affairs Department
Allied Van Lines
P.O. Box 4403
Chicago, IL 60680
708–717–3590
Fax: 708–717–3123
Toll Free: 800–470–2851
Internet: alliedvan.net

Customer Relations
Allstate Insurance Co.
2775 Sanders Road
Northbrook, IL 60062
847–402–5448

Denise R. Yates
Manager, Customer Relations
Aloha Airlines
P.O. Box 30028
Honolulu, HI 96820
808–836–4115
Toll free: 800–803–9454

Dixie Trout
Vice President of Consumer Relations
Amana Refrigeration, Inc.
Amana, IA 52204
Toll free: 800–843–0304 (product questions)

Relations—Passenger Services
America West Airlines
4000 East Sky Harbor Boulevard
Phoenix, AZ 85034
Toll free: 800–235–9292

American Airlines, Inc.
P.O. Box 619612 MD 2400
DFW International Airport, TX 75261–9612
817–967–2000

Approved Auto Repair
American Automobile Association
Mailspace 15
1000 AAA Drive
Heathrow, FL 32746–5063
(written complaints only)

**American Cyanamid Co.
see Lederle Consumer Health**

Consumer Relations
American Express Co.
777 American ExpressWay
Fort Lauderdale, FL 33337
Toll free: 800–528–4800 (green card inquiries)
Toll free: 800–327–2177 (gold card inquiries)
Toll free: 800–525–3355 (platinum card inquiries)

Customer Service
American Family Publishers
P.O. Box 62000
Tampa, FL 33662
Toll free: 800–AFP–2400

Sue Holiday
Consumer Correspondent
American Greetings Corp.
One American Road
Cleveland, OH 44144
216–252–7300, ext. 1281
Toll free: 800–321–3040

Consumer Affairs Department
**American Home Food
Products, Inc.**
5 Giralda Farms
Madison, NJ 07940
Toll free: 800–544–5680

Ronald J. Fojtlin, Manager
World Wide Fitting Dept.
American Standard, Inc.
P.O. Box 6820
Piscataway, NJ 08855–6820
Toll free: 800–223–0068
Toll free: 800–980–6170

Judith Barker
Vice President, Public,
Government and Investor Relations
American Stores Co.
P.O. Box 27447
Salt Lake City, UT 84127–0447
801–539–0112
Toll free: 800–541–2863

Anthony L. Fera
Director, Consumer Administration
American Tourister, Inc.
91 Main Street
Warren, RI 02885
401–245–2100
Toll free: 800–635–5505

Operations Department
**America's Favorite
Chicken Co.**
6 Concourse Parkway
Suite 1700
Atlanta, GA 30328–5352
404–391–9500

Ameritech
225 West Randolph Street, Room 30–D
Chicago, IL 60606
312–727–2293
Toll free: 800–244–4444

Richard Smith, Manager
Customer Relations and Consumer Affairs
Amoco Oil Co.
200 East Randolph Drive
Chicago, IL 60601
Toll free: 800–333–3991
Fax: 312–616–0889

Martha Tancil
Director, Customer Satisfaction
Service Center
Amtrak
Washington Union Station
60 Massachusetts Avenue, N.E.
Washington, DC 20002
202–906–2121
Toll free: 800–USA–RAIL
(reservations and information)

Robin Koop
Director, Distributor/Customer Services
Amway Co.
7575 East Fulton Road
Ada, MI 49355
616–787–7717
TDD toll free: 800–548–3878

Greg Hubbard
Manager, Customer and Product Services
Andersen Windows, Inc.
100 Fourth Avenue North
Bayport, MN 55003
612–430–5564

Craig Hetterscheidt
Manager, Consumer Relations
Anheuser–Busch, Inc.
One Busch Place
St. Louis, MO 63118–1852
314–577–2000
Toll free: 800–342–5283 (consumer call
center)

Financial Relations
Aon Corp.
123 North Wacker Drive
Chicago, IL 60606
312–701–3000

Customer Relations Department
Apple Computer, Inc.
20525 Mariani Avenue
Cupertino, CA 95014
Toll free: 800–776–2333
(complaints and questions)
Toll free: 800–538–9696
(dealer information)

**Aramis, Inc.
see Estee Lauder Companies**

Customer Service
Arizona Mail Order
3740 East 34th Street
Tucson, AZ 85713
520–748–8600
Fax: 520–750–6755

**Arm & Hammer
see Church & Dwight Co., Inc.**

Mandy Hamilton
Consumer Relations Administrator
Armorall Products Corp.
6 Liberty
Aliso Viejo, CA 92656
714–362–0600
Toll free: 800–747–4104

Armour Swift Eckrich
2001 Butterfield Road
Downers Grove, IL 60515
708–512–1000
Toll free: 800–325–7424
(Eckrich nutrition)

Fred Fuest
Manager, Consumer Affairs
Armstrong Tire Division
Pirelli/Armstrong Tire Corporation
500 Sargent Drive
New Haven, CT 06536
203–784–2200
Toll free: 800–243–0167

Bonnie Muehling
Manager, Consumer Affairs
Armstrong World Industries
P.O. Box 3001
Lancaster, PA 17604
717–396–4780
Toll free: 800–233–3823

Gary Tramiel
Vice President of Dealer Sales
Atari Video Game Systems
455 S. Milhilda Avenue
Sunnyvale, CA 94086
408–328–0900

April Peterson
Manager, Customer Relations
**Atlantic Richfield Co.
ARCO Products Co.**
1055 W. 7th Street
Los Angeles, CA 90017
213–486–3511
Toll free: 800–322–2726

Glen Dunkerson, Vice President
Customer Service
Atlas Van Lines
P.O. Box 509
Evansville, IN 47703–0509
Toll free: 800–252–8885

**Automobile Magazine
see K–III**

Barbara Pearson
Manager, Customer Service
Avis Rent-A-Car System
4500 S. 129th East Avenue
Tulsa, OK 74134–3802
Toll free: 800–352–7900

**Avon Fashions, Inc.
see Newport News, Inc.**

Lynn Baron, Director
Consumer Information Center
Avon Products, Inc.
9 West 57th Street
New York, NY 10019
212–546–6015
Toll free: 800–367–2866

B 

Frederick J. Wilson, General Counsel
Bacardi-Martini USA, Inc.
2100 Biscayne Boulevard
Miami, FL 33137
305–573–8511
Toll free: 800–BACARDI

Bali/Sara Lee Intimate Apparel
Sara Lee Corporation
3330 Healy Drive
P.O. Box 5100 (23113)
Winston-Salem, NC 27103
Toll free: 800–225–4872

Corporate Communications
Bally Entertainment
8700 West Bryn Mawr
Chicago, IL 60631
312–399–1300

Customer Relations #3538
Bank of America, NT & SA
Box 37000
San Francisco, CA 94137
415–622–6081

Paul J. Layden, Senior Vice President
Public and Investor Relations
**The Bank of New York
Company, Inc.**
48 Wall Street, 16th Floor
New York, NY 10286
212–495–2066

Barnett Banks, Inc.
P.O. Box 40789
Jacksonville, FL 32231
904–791–7720

Bill Pegram
Director of Quality Assurance
R.G. Barry Corp.
8000 IH 10 West
Suite 1500
San Antonio, TX 78230
210–366–1092
Fax: 210–366–1092

Bass Pro Shop
1935 South Campbell
Springfield, MO 65898
Toll free: 800–BASS–PRO
Fax: 417–873–5060
TDD: 800–442–5788

Eddie Bauer Customer Service
P.O. Box 3700
Seattle, WA 98124–3700
Toll free: 800–426–6253

Darla J. Elkin
Manager, Regulatory and Consumer Affairs
**Contact Lens Care Products
OTC Health Care Products
Bausch and Lomb**
Personal Products Division
1400 North Goodman Street
Rochester, NY 14692
Toll free: 800–553–5340

Janice Glerum
Director, Customer Service
**Contact Lenses
Bausch and Lomb**
Contact Lens Division
1400 North Goodman Street
Rochester, NY 14609
Toll free: 800–552–7388

Ethel Killenbeck
Manager, Consumer Affairs
**Eyewear Division
Bausch and Lomb**
P.O. Box 478
Rochester, NY 14692–0478
Toll free: 800–343–5594

Consumer Relations
Bayer Corp.
36 Columbia Road
Morristown, NJ 07962–1910
Toll free: 800–331–4536
(Sterling Health, Glenbrook,
Winthrop Consumer Products)

Customer Service
L.L. Bean, Inc.
Casco Street
Freeport, ME 04033–0001
Toll free: 800–341–4341
TDD toll free: 800–545–0090

Customer Service Department
Bear Creek Corp.
2518 South Pacific Highway
P.O. Box 299
Medford, OR 97501
541–776–2400

Beatrice Cheese, Inc.
Cheese Division
770 North Springdale Road
Waukesha, WI 53186
414–782–2750
Fax: 414–782–5738

Charles F. Baer, President
Consumer Products Division
Becton Dickinson and Co.
One Becton Drive
Franklin Lakes, NJ 07417
201–847–6658
Fax: 201–884–5487

**Beech Holdings Corp.
see Budget Rent-A-Car Corp.**

Beiersdorf, Inc.
P.O. Box 5529
Norwalk, CT 06856–5529
203–853–8008
Toll free outside CT: 800–233–2340

BellSouth Communications
(Southern Bell and South Central Bell)
Consumer Affairs Manager
600 North 19th Street, 24th Floor
Birmingham, AL 35203
205–321–2892
Toll free: 800–346–9000
(Bell South Products)
TDD toll free: 800–251–5325

Keith Card, Director
Marketing and Public Relations
Benihana of Tokyo
8685 Northwest 53rd Terrace
Miami, FL 33166
305–593–0770
Toll free: 800–327–3369

Adair Sampogna
Director, Consumer Communications
Best Foods
CPC International, Inc.
P.O. Box 8000 International Plaza
Englewood Cliffs, NJ 07632
201–894–2324

Peggy Yoder
Manager, Customer Service
Best Western International
P.O. Box 42007
Phoenix, AZ 85080–2007
Toll free: 800–528–1238

Consumer Relations Department
BIC Corp.
500 Bic Drive
Milford, CT 06460
203–783–2000

**Birds Eye
see General Foods**

Floyd Coonce
Manager, Consumer Assistance
and Information
**Black and Decker
Household Products**
6 Armstrong Road
Shelton, CT 06484
Toll free: 800–231–9786

Consumer Services
Black and Decker Power Tools
626 Hanover Pike
Hampstead, MD 21074
410–239–5300
Toll free: 800–762–6672

**Blockbuster Entertainment
Corp.**
One Blockbuster Plaza
Ft. Lauderdale, FL 33301
954–832–3000

Lori Hunt
Customer Affairs Representative
Block Drug Company, Inc.
257 Cornelison Avenue
Jersey City, NJ 07302
201–434–3000
Fax: 201–434–5739
Toll free outside NJ: 800–365–6500

Customer Service Department
Bloomingdale's by Mail, Ltd.
475 Knotter Drive
P.O. Box 593
Cheshire, CT 06410–9933
203–271–1313
Toll free: 800–777–0000 (mail order)
Fax: 203–271–5321

**Blue Bell, Inc.
see Wrangler**

Consumer Affairs
**Blue Cross and
Blue Shield Association**
1310 G Street, N.W., 12th Floor
Washington, DC 20005
202–626–4780
Fax: 202–626–4833

Karen Braswell
Marketing Director
Bojangles
P.O. Box 240239
Charlotte, NC 28224
704–527–2675, ext. 3226
Toll free: 800–366–9921

Consumer Response Department
Borden, Inc.
180 East Broad Street
Columbus, OH 43215
614–225–4511
Fax: 616–225–7680

**Boyle-Midway Household
Products, Inc.
see Reckitt & Colman, Inc.**

Stephanie Whelan
Manager, Consumer Affairs
**Bradlees Discount
Department Stores**
One Bradlees Circle
P.O. Box 9015
Braintree, MA 02184–9015
617–380–5377

**Breck Hair Care Products
see The Dial Corp.**

Consumer Affairs
Bridgestone/Firestone, Inc.
P.O. Box 7988
Chicago, IL 60680–9534
Toll free: 800–367–3872

Customer Service
Brights Creek
5000 City Lane Road
Hampton, VA 23661
804–827–1850

Carla Navello
Manager, Consumer Affairs
Bristol-Myers Products
1350 Liberty Avenue
Hillside, NJ 07205
Toll free: 800–468–7746

Robert Laverty
Director, Public Affairs
**Bristol-Myers Squibb
Pharmaceutical Group**
P.O. Box 4000
Princeton, NJ 08543–4000
609–252–4000
Toll free: 800–332–2056

**Brita, USA
see Clorox Co.**

Customer Relations
British Airways
75–20 Astoria Blvd.
Jackson Heights, NY 11370
718–397–4000

Dianne Hall
Consumer Services Administrator
Brown-Forman Beverage Co.
P.O. Box 1080
Louisville, KY 40201
Toll free: 800–753–1177

Consumer Care Information
Brown Group, Inc.
P.O. Box 354
St. Louis, MO 63166
Toll free: 800–766–6465
Fax: 314–854–4274

Consumer Affairs
Budget Gourmet
P.O. Box 10
Boise, ID 83707
Toll free: 800–488–0050

Customer Relations
Budget Rent-A-Car Corp.
P.O. Box 111580
Carrollton, TX 75011–1580
Toll free: 800–621–2844

Investor Service Center
Bull & Bear Group, Inc.
11 Hanover Square
New York, NY 10005
212–363–1100
Toll free: 800–847–4200

Manager, Customer Relations
Bulova Watch Co.
26–15 Brooklyn Queens Expressway
Woodside, NY 11377
718–204–3300 (consumer relations)
718–204–3222 (service)

Monroe Milstein, President
**Burlington Coat Factory
Warehouse Corp.**
1830 Route 130 North
Burlington, NJ 08016
609–387–7800

**Burlington Hosiery
see Kayser-Roth Corp.**

Public Relations
Burlington Industries
3330 West Friendly Avenue
Greensboro, NC 27420
910–379–2276
Fax: 910–379–4504

Glaxo Wellcome Co.
5 Moore Drive
Research Triangle Park, NC 27709
919–248–3000

C ______________

Ray Faiola, Director
CBS Broadcast Group
Audience Services
524 West 57th Street
New York, NY 10019
212–975–3247

Consumer Affairs Department
CIBA Self-Medication, Inc.
581 Main Street
Woodbridge, NJ 07095
908–602–6800
908–602–6600
Fax: 908–602–6612

CIBA Corp.
Plant Protection
410 Swing Road
Greensboro, NC 27409
919–632–6000
Toll free: 800–334–9481

CIBA Corp.
Pharmaceuticals Division
556 Morris Avenue
Summit, NJ 07901–1398
908–277–5000
TDD: 908–277–3226

CIBA Vision Corp.
11460 Johns Creek Parkway
Duluth, GA 30136
Toll free: 800–227–1524, ext. 4435
(consumer relations)

Customer Service
CIE America
2701 Dow Avenue
Tustin, CA 92580
Toll free: 800–877–1421, ext. 4260

**CIE Terminals
see CIE America**

Mark A. Whiter
Director, Customer Services
**CIGNA Property and
Casualty Companies**
1601 Chestnut Street
Philadelphia, PA 19192
215–761–4555

Consumer Affairs Department
CPC International Inc.
International Plaza
Box 8000
Englewood Cliffs, NJ 07632
201–894–4000
Fax: 201–894–2126

Neil Dinerman
President and Chairman of the Board
C&R Clothiers
8660 Hayden Place
Culver City, CA 90232
310–559–8200
Fax: 310–839–7480

CVN
see QVC Network

Customer Relations Department
CVS
One CVS Drive
Woonsocket, RI 02895–9988
401–765–1500
Fax: 401–762–6949
Toll free: 800–555–4771

Cabela's, Inc.
812 13th Avenue
Sidney, NE 69160–8888
Toll free: 800–237–8888

Cadbury Beverages, Inc,
see Motts, USA

Caloric Modern Maid Corp.
see Amana Refrigeration, Inc.

Holly Masclans
Manager, Consumer Response and
Information
Campbell Soup Co.
Campbell Place
Camden, NJ 08103–1799
609–342–3714
Fax: 609–342–6449
Toll free: 800–257–8443

Susan Read
Quality Control Manager
Winery Operations
Canandaigua Wine Co.
116 Buffalo Street
Canandaigua, NY 14424
716–394–7900
Fax: 716–394–4839

Customer Relations Department
Canon U.S.A., Inc.
One Canon Plaza, Bldg. C
Lake Success, NY 11042
516–488–6700
Toll free: 800–828–4040

Audience Information
Capitol Cities/ABC, Inc.
77 West 66th Street
New York, NY 10023
212–456–7477

Marcia King-Gamble
Director, Guest Relations
Carnival Cruise Lines
3655 Northwest 87th Avenue
Miami, FL 33178–2428
305–599–2600
Toll free: 800–438–6744

James Witz
Customer Relations Manager
Carrier Air Conditioning Co.
P.O. Box 4808
Syracuse, NY 13221
Toll free: 800–227–7437

Bryant Heating and Air Conditioning
Toll free: 800–428–4326
Day & Night Heating and Air Conditioning
Toll free: 800–428–4326

Payne Heating and Air Conditioning
Toll free: 800–428–4326

Carte Blanche
see Diners Club International

Consumer Relations Department
Carter-Wallace Inc.
1345 Avenue of the Americas
New York, NY 10105
212–339–5000

Retail Operations
Carvel Corp.
20 Batterson Park Road
Farmington, CT 06032–2502
(written inquiries only)

Customer Service Department
Casio, Inc.
570 Mount Pleasant Avenue
Dover, NJ 07801
201–361–5400
Toll free: 800–962–2746

Ceridian Contact Center
Ceridian Corp.
8100 34th Avenue South
Bloomington, MN 55425
612–853–8100

Ron Dohr
Customer Service Supervisor
Champion Spark Plug Co.
P.O. Box 910
Toledo, OH 43661
419–535–2002

Suzanne Vallebuona
Coordinator, Consumer Relations
and Training
Chanel, Inc.
9 West 57th Street, 44th Floor
New York, NY 10019–2790
212–688–5055
Fax: 212–752–1851

Chase Manhattan Bank
270 Park Avenue
New York, NY 10017
212–270–9300

Consumer Products Division
Chattem, Inc.
1715 West 38th Street
Chattanooga, TN 37409
Toll free outside TN: 800–745–2429

Walter Dabek
Director, Consumer Information
Cheesebrough-Pond's, USA
55 Merritt Boulevard
Trumbull, CT 06611
203–661–2000
Toll free: 800–243–5804

ChemLawn Services Corp.
see TruGreen Limited
Partnership

W.P. Howell, Supervisor
Dealer and Consumer Affairs
Chevron Products Co.
P.O. Box H
Concord, CA 94524
Toll free: 800–962–1223

Guest Relations
Chi-Chi's, Inc.
10200 Linn Station Road
Louisville, KY 40223
502–426–3900
Fax: 502–429–6243

Chuck E. Cheese
see ShowBiz Pizza Time, Inc.

Nancy Sevinsky
Consumer Professional Relations
Church & Dwight
Company, Inc.
469 North Harrison Street
Princeton, NJ 08540–7648
609–683–5900
Toll free: 800–524–1328

Church's Fried Chicken, Inc.
see America's Favorite
Chicken Co.

Cincinnati Microwave
One Microwave Plaza
Cincinnati, OH 45249–9502
513–489–5400
Toll free: 800–433–3487

Circuit City Stores, Inc.
9950 Mayland Drive
Richmond, VA 23233
804–527–4000
Toll free: 800–627–2274

Dinah Jacobs
Corporate Director of Customer
Satisfaction and Quality
Citicorp/Citibank
599 Lexington Avenue, 24th Floor
New York, NY 10043
212–559–0043

Tina Sherritt, Executive Secretary
Citizen Watch Co.
of America, Inc.
8506 Osage Avenue
Los Angeles, CA 90045
Toll free: 800–321–1023

Jeanne D. Matson
Consumer Affairs Dept.
Clairol, Inc.
300 Park Avenue South
New York, NY 10010
Voice/TDD toll free: 800–223–5800
Voice/TDD toll free: 800–HISPANA
(Spanish)

Clinique Laboratories, Inc.
see Estee Lauder Companies

Sandy Stewart
Manager, Consumer Services
Clopay Building Products Co.
312 Walnut Street, Suite 1600
Cincinnati, OH 45202–4036
Toll free: 800–225–6729

Susan Silva
Consumer Services Manager
Clorox Co.
1221 Broadway
Oakland, CA 94612–1888
510–271–7283
Toll free: 800–292–2200
(laundry brands)
Toll free: 800–537–2823
(charcoal and food brands)
Toll free: 800–227–1860
(household surface cleaners)
Toll free: 800–426–6228
(insecticides)
Toll free: 800–242–7482
(water purification systems)

Consumer Affairs Department
Club Med Sales, Inc.
40 West 57th Street
New York, NY 10019
212–977–2100

Amanda Pace, Director
Industry and Consumer Affairs
The Coca-Cola Co.
P.O. Drawer 1734
Atlanta, GA 30301
Toll free: 800–438–2653
TDD toll free: 800–262–2653

Corporate Office
Coldwell Banker Corp.
339 Jefferson Road
Parsippany, NJ 07054
Toll free: 800–733–6629

Jan M. Guifarro
Associate Director, Consumer Response
Colgate, Palmolive, Mennen Co.
300 Park Avenue
New York, NY 10022
Toll free: 800–228–7408

Corporate Office
Collins & Aikman Products Co.
P.O. Box 32665
Charlotte, NC 28232
704–547–8500

Gregory Barstead
President, Life/Health
Colonial Penn Group, Inc.
399 Market Street, 5th Floor
Philadelphia, PA 19181
215–928–8000
Toll free: 800–523–1700
(auto customer service)
Toll free: 800–523–2800
(homeowner customer service)
Toll free: 800–523–4000
(health customer service)
Toll free: 800–523–9100
(life customer service)

Columbia House
A Division of SONY Music
Entertainment, Inc.
P.O. Box 4450
New York, NY 10101–4450
Toll free: 800–457–0500
(records and tapes)
Toll free: 800–457–0866 (videos)

Teresa C. Infantino
Executive Vice President
Combe Inc.
1101 Westchester Avenue
White Plains, NY 10604–3597
914–694–5454
Toll free: 800–431–2610

Combined Insurance Co. of America
see Aon Corp.

Customer Relations Department
Compaq Computer Corp.
P.O. Box 692000
Houston, TX 77269–2000
Toll free: 800–345–1518

Comprehensive Care Corp.
16305 Swingley Ridge Drive
Suite 100
Chesterfield, MO 63017
314–537–1288
Toll free: 800–678–2273

Brian Quigley
Director of Warranty Administration
and Control
Congoleum Corp.
3705 Quakerbridge Road
P.O. Box 3127
Mercerville, NJ 08619
609–584–3000

Supervisors Department
Contempo Casuals
5433 West Jefferson Boulevard
Los Angeles, CA 90016
213–936–2131

Customer Relations
Continental Airlines, Inc.
3663 North Sam Houston
Suite 500
Houston, TX 77032
713–987–6500

Customer Relations
Converse, Inc.
One Fordham Road
North Reading, MA 01864–2680
Toll free: 800–428–CONS (2667)

Conwood Company, L.P.
813 Ridge Lake Blvd.
Memphis, TN 38120
901–761–2050

Coors Brewing Co.
Consumer Information Center
NH475
Golden, CO 80401
Toll free: 800–642–6116

Coppertone
see Schering-Plough
HealthCare Products, Inc.

Ron Almarode, Supervisor
Corning/Consumer Products
Corning Inc.
1300 Hopeman Parkway
Waynesboro, VA 22980
Toll free: 800–999–3436

Connie J. Shelby
Director, Consumer Affairs
Cosmair, Inc.
P.O. Box 98
Westfield, NJ 07091–9987
Toll free: 800–631–7358

Consumer Relations
Cotter & Company
8600 W. Bryn Mawr
Chicago, IL 60631–3505
312–695–5000

Service Department
Craftmatic Organization, Inc.
2500 Interplex Drive
Trevose, PA 19053–6998
215–639–1310
Toll free: 800–677–8200

Jenny Craig International
445 Marine View Avenue
Del Mar, CA 92014
619–259–7000

Gail Compagnone
Manager, Consumer Relations
A.T. Cross Co.
One Albion Road
Lincoln, RI 02865
Toll free: 800–AT CROSS (282–7677)

Crown Books
3300 75th Avenue
Landover, MD 20785
301–731–1200
Toll free: 800–831–7400

Peter Cammarata
Director, Sales and Marketing Operations
Cuisinarts Corp.
One Cummings Point Road
Stamford, CT 06904
203–975–4600
609–426–1300 (in NJ)
Toll free outside NJ: 800–726–0190

Michelle Soucie
Special Assistant to the President
for Consumer Affairs
Culligan International Co.
One Culligan Parkway
Northbrook, IL 60062
847–205–5757

Marvin E. Eisenstadt, President
Cumberland Packing Corp.
Two Cumberland Street
Brooklyn, NY 11205
718–858–4200

Customer Relations
Cunard Line
555 Fifth Avenue
New York, NY 10017
Toll free: 800–528–6273
Fax: 718–786–2350

Don Roth
Department Head, Customer Service
Current, Inc.
P.O Box 2559
Colorado Springs, CO 80901
Toll free: 800–525–7170

D ___________

**d–Con
see Reckitt & Colman, Inc.**

Cheryl Beck
Manager, Customer Service
DHL Corp.
1900 West University
Tempe, CA 85282
800–225–5345

**Dairy Queen
see International Dairy Queen**

Eileen O'Gorman
Director, Consumer Relations
Dannon Co., Inc.
1111 Westchester Avenue
White Plains, NY 10604
(written inquiries only)

N. Shelby
Consumer Division
Danskin
P.O. Box 15016
York, PA 17405–7016
Toll free: 800–288–6749

Terry Pitra, Manager
Guest Relations
**Dayton's, Hudson's,
Marshall Field's Dept. Stores**
Box 1197
700 Nicollet Mall
Minneapolis, MN 55402
612–375–3382

Shareholder Services
Dean Witter, Discover & Co.
2 World Trade Center, 66th Floor
New York, NY 10048
Toll free: 800–733–2307

**Dearfoam
see R.G. Barry Corp.**

Deere & Co.
John Deere Road
Moline, IL 61265–8098
309–765–8000

Consumer Relations Department
Del Laboratories, Inc.
565 Broad Hollow Road
Farmingdale, NY 11735
516–293–7070

Consumer Affairs
Del Monte Foods
P.O. Box 193575
San Francisco, CA 94119–3575
Toll free: 800–543–3090

**Del Pharmaceuticals, Inc.
see Del Laboratories, Inc.**

Public Relations
**Delphi Auto Systems
General Motors Corp.**
2401 Columbus Avenue
Mail Code 18–109
Anderson, IN 46016
317–646–3000

Consumer Affairs
Delta Air Lines
Hartsfield Atlanta International Airport
Atlanta, GA 30320
404–715–1402

Barbara Ashley, Assistant Manager
Product Service
Delta Faucets
P.O. Box 40980
Indianapolis, IN 46280
317–848–1812

Operations
Denny's, Inc.
203 East Main Street
Spartanburg, SC 29319–0001
864–597–8000

George Andrassy, Vice President
Research and Development
Dep Corp.
2101 East Via Arado
Rancho Dominguez, CA 90220–6189
213–604–0777
Toll free: 800–367–2855

Julie Jason
Manager, Customer Service
DeVry, Inc.
1 Tower Lane
Oakbrook Terrace, IL 60181
708–571–7700
Toll free: 800–225–8000

Marie Shubin
Consumer Information Center
The Dial Corp.
15101 N. Scottsdale Road
Scottsdale, AZ 85254
602–207–5518
Toll free: 800–528–0849
(foods division)
Toll free: 800–45–PUREX
(household and laundry division)
Toll free: 800–258–DIAL
(personal care division)

Customer Relations
Diet Center, Inc.
395 Springdale Drive
Akron, OH 44333
330–665–5861

Customer Relations Department
Digital Equipment Corp.
111 Powder Mill Road
Maynard, MA 01754
508–493–5111
Toll Free: 800–332–4636

Customer Relations
Dillard Department Stores, Inc.
1600 Cantrell Road
Little Rock, AR 72201
501–376–5200

Jim Scherman
Vice President, Customer Service
Diners Club International
183 Inverness Drive West
Englewood, CO 80112
303–799–9000
Toll free: 800–234–6377
TDD: 303–643–2155

**Discover
see Dean Witter, Discover & Co.**

Helen Robinson
Manager, Consumer Response
Dole Packaged Foods
ATTN: Consumer Response Department
5795 Lindero Canyon Road
Westlake Village, CA 91362–4013
Toll free: 800–232–8888

Thomas S. Monaghan
President and CEO
Domino's Pizza, Inc.
P.O. Box 997
Ann Arbor, MI 48106–0997
313–930–3030

Robert J. Posch, Jr.
Vice President, Legal Affairs
**Doubleday Book &
Music Clubs, Inc.**
401 Franklin Avenue
Garden City, NY 11530–5806
516–873–4628

Sharon Clark
Manager, Consumer Affairs
DowBrands
P.O. Box 68511
Indianapolis, IN 46268–0511
Toll free: 800–428–4795

Jim Ball, Vice President
Corporate Communications
Wynema Hamilton, Coordinator
Consumer Affairs
**Dr Pepper/Cadbury
North America, Inc.**
P.O. Box 655086
Dallas, TX 75265–5086
214–360–7000

Customer Service Department
Walter Drake & Sons Inc.
Drake Building
Colorado Springs, CO 80940–0001
719–596–3140

Jane Lagusch
Vice President
Drug Emporium, Inc.
155 Hidden Ravines Drive
Powell, OH 43065
614–548–7080, ext. 104

Dulcolax
CIBA Consumer Pharmaceuticals
581 Main Street
Woodbridge, NJ 07095
908–602–6780

Robert M. Rosenberg
Chairman of the Board
**Dunkin Donuts of
America/Baskin Robbins**
P.O. Box 317
Randolph, MA 02368
617–961–4000

Steven Wyanacek, Manager
Consumer Affairs and OE Service
Dunlop Tire Corp.
P.O. Box 1109
Buffalo, NY 14240–1109
Toll free: 800–548–4714

Customer Information Center
DuPont Co.
BMP/Reeves Mill
Wilmington, DE 19880–0010
Toll free: 800–548–4714

Consumer Affairs Department
Duracell USA
Division of Duracell, Inc.
Duracell Drive
Bethel, CT 06801
203–796–4500
Toll free: 800–551–2355

**Durkee-French Foods
see Reckitt & Colman, Inc.**

 **E** ________________________

John Vaeth
Eastman Kodak Co.
343 State Street
Rochester, NY 14650–0811
Toll free: 800–242–2424

Nancy J. Avino
Customer Service Representative
Eckerd Drug Co.
8333 Bryan Dairy Road
P.O. Box 4689
Clearwater, FL 34618
813–399–6000

Customer Service
Edmund Scientific Co.
101 East Gloucester Pike
Barrington, NJ 08007–1380
609–573–6260

Electrolux Corp.
2300 Windy Ridge Parkway
Suite 900
Marietta, GA 30067
404–933–1000
Toll free: 800–243–9078

Customer Relations
**Emery Worldwide
A CF Company**
One Lagoon Drive
Redwood City, CA 94065
415–596–9600
Toll free: 800–227–1981

Sonia Franklin
Director of Consumer Affairs
**Encore Marketing
International, Inc.**
4501 Forbes Boulevard
Lanham, MD 20706
301–459–8020
Toll free: 800–638–0930

Norman Braun
Vice President, Public Affairs
Encyclopaedia Britannica, Inc.
310 South Michigan Avenue
Chicago, IL 60604–4293
312–347–7200

Labat R. Yancey
Vice President, Office of Consumer Affairs
Equifax
P.O. Box 105139
Atlanta, GA 30348
770–612–2899
Toll free: 800–685–1111

Carolann V. Mathews
Vice President, Customer Relations
**Equitable Life
Assurance Society**
787 7th Avenue
New York, NY 10020
212–554–1749

Retail Customer Service Department
Esprit de Corps
900 Minnesota Street
San Francisco, CA 94107–3000
415–648–6900
Fax: 415–550–3960

Theresa Sullivan
Vice President, Consumer Relations
Estee Lauder Companies
767 Fifth Avenue
New York, NY 10153–0003
212–572–4200

Francine Recine-Quinn
Corporate Manager, Consumer Affairs
Ethan Allen, Inc.
Ethan Allen Drive
Danbury, CT 06813
203–743–8668
Fax: 203–743–8354
E-mail: ethanadv@ethanallen.com

Rick Gremer
Consumer Relations Manager
The Eureka Co.
1201 East Bell Street
Bloomington, IL 61701–6902
309–823–5735
Toll free: 800–282–2886
(warranty center)

Bob Evans Farms, Inc.
3776 South High Street
Columbus, OH 43207
614–491–2225
Toll free outside OH: 800–272–7675
Fax: 614–492–4949

Sharon L. Plummer
Consumer Assistance Manager
Exxon Company U.S.A.
P.O. Box 2180
Houston, TX 77252–2180
713–656–2111
Toll free: 800–243–9966
Fax: 713–656–9745

F ________________________

Shawn McCormac
Family Circle Magazine
110 Fifth Avenue
New York, NY 10011
212–463–1124

Consumer Affairs Department
**Faultless Starch/
Bon Ami Co.**
1025 West Eighth Street
Kansas City, MO 64101–1200
816–842–1230

**Fayva Shoe Stores
see Morse Shoe, Inc.**

Jean H. Ward-Jones, Manager
Quality and Procsss Improvement
Federal Express Corp.
P.O Box 727, Department 1845
Memphis, TN 38194–1845
901–395–4539
Toll free: 800–238–5355
Fax: 901–395–4511

Paula S. Coffey
Consumer Affairs Assistant
Federated Department Stores
7 West Seventh Street
Cincinnati, OH 45202
513–579–7000
Fax: 513–579–7185

Joan Garrison
Manager, Consumer Relations
Fieldcrest Cannon, Inc.
1271 Avenue of the Americas
New York, NY 20020
212–957–2500
Toll free: 800–841–3336
(Fieldcrest Stores)
Toll free: 800–237–3209
(Cannon Stores)
Fax: 212–957–2533

Susan Alcorn, Director
Consumer, Government and Media Center
Finast
17000 Rockside Road
Cleveland, OH 44137–4390
216–587–7100
Fax: 216–518–6188

Mary Luethmers
Customer Relations Manager
Fingerhut Corp.
11 McLeland Road
St. Cloud, MN 56395
612–259–2500
Fax: 320–654–4858

L.A. Mann, Sr.
Director, Quality Assurance
First Brands Corp.
88 Long Hill Street
East Hartford, CT 06108
203–728–6000
Toll free: 800–835–4523

Consumer Affairs Department
**First Interstate Bank
of California**
707 Wilshire Blvd., W35–13
Los Angeles, CA 90017
213–614–3103

Thomas J. Metz
Senior Vice President, Customer Services
Customer Relationship Center
First Union National Bank
100 Constitution Drive
Upper Darby, PA 19082–4603
610–734–5090
Toll free: 800–225–5332
TDD: 610–734–5599
TDD toll free: 800–835–7721

Customer Service
**First Union National Bank
of Florida**
P.O. Box 2870
Jacksonville, FL 32231–0010
904–361–6996
Toll free: 800–735–1012

**Fisher
see SFS Corp.**

Jeff Ortel
Director, Consumer Affairs
Fisher Price
636 Girard Avenue
East Aurora, NY 14052
Toll free: 800–432–5437
TDD toll free: 800–382–7470
Fax: 716–687–3494

Tamara Arenson
Special Consumer Services Manager
Florida Power and Light Co.
P.O. Box 029100
Miami, FL 33102–9100
305–552–4653
Toll free: 800–397–6544
TDD toll free: 800–432–6554
Fax: 304–552–3792

April Reynolds
Customer Service Planning
**Florist Transworld Delivery
Associates (FTD)**
29200 Northwestern Highway
P.O. Box 2227
Southfield, MI 48037–4077
810–355–9300
Toll free: 800–669–1000

Phil Hurwitz
Customer Service
Florsheim Shoe Co.
130 South Canal Street
Chicago, IL 60606–3999
312–559–2549
Toll free: 800–633–4988

Heeth Varnedoe, President
Flowers Industries, Inc.
P.O. Box 1338
Thomasville, GA 31799–1338
912–226–9110
Fax: 912–226–1318

Scott R. Yablon
Vice President, Finance Administration
Forbes Inc.
60 Fifth Avenue
New York, NY 10011
212–620–2409
Fax: 212–620–5199

George McKittrick
Customer Relations Manager
Foster & Gallagher, Inc.
6523 North Galena Road
Peoria, IL 61632
309–691–4610
(Mon.-Fri., 8:30 a.m.–5 p.m.)
309–691–3633
(Mon.—Fri. after 5:15 p.m.)

Rosemary Myers, Vice President
Customer Service/Operations
The Franklin Mint
U.S. Route One
Franklin Center, PA 19091
610–459–6000
Toll free: 800–523–7622

Linda Yocum
Customer Service
Frank's Nursery and Crafts, Inc.
6501 East Nevada
Detroit, MI 48234
313–300–8400
Fax: 313–366–5386

Customer Assistance Center
The Frigidaire Co.
P.O. Box 7181
Dublin, OH 43017–0781
Toll free: 800–451–7007

Joyce Wolfe
Office of Consumer Affairs
Friskies PetCare Co.
800 N. Grand Blvd.
Glendale, CA 91203
818–543–7749

Janet Rosati
Director, Consumer Services
Fruit of the Loom, Inc.
One Fruit of the Loom Drive
Bowling Green, KY 42102–9015
502–781–6400
502–782–5400 (customer service)
Fax: 502–781–0903

Marianne Salimbene
Associate Manager
Customer Service Department
Fuji Photo Film U.S.A., Inc.
400 Commerce Blvd.
Carlstadt, NJ 07072–3009
Toll free: 800–659–3854, ext. 2571 (toll free)
Fax: 201–507–2591

Customer Resource Center
Fuller Brush Co.
P.O. Box 1247
Great Bend, KS 67530–0729
Toll free: 800–523–3794
Fax: 316–793–4523

 **G**

Customer Service
GTE Corp.
One Stamford Forum
Stamford, CT 06904
203–965–2000
Toll free: 800–548–2389

Teddi Burris
Manager, Consumer Relations
Ernest & Julio Gallo Winery
P.O. Box 1130
Modesto, CA 95353
209–579–3161
Fax: 209–579–8993

Jeannine Deming
Manager, Consumer Service Department
Lewis Galoob Toys, Inc.
500 Forbes Blvd.
San Francisco, CA 94080
415–952–1678
Fax: 415–583–4996

Sheila Gibbons
Director, Public Affairs
Gannett Co., Inc.
1100 Wilson Blvd.
Arlington, VA 22234
703–284–6048

General Electric Co.
For information on GE consumer products
and services, call: GE ANSWER CENTER ®
service
Toll free: 800–626–2000

Giselle Simmons
Manager, Consumer Response and
Information Center
General Foods Corp.
250 North Street
White Plains, NY 10625
Toll free: 800–431–1001

(General Foods products)
General Host Corp.
P.O. Box 10045
Stamford, CT 06904
203–357–9900

Sandy Weisenburger
Assistant Manager, Consumer Services
General Mills, Inc.
P.O. Box 1113
Minneapolis, MN 55440–1113
612–540–4295
Toll free: 800–328–6787 (bakery products)
Toll free: 800–328–1144 (cereals)
Toll free: 800–222–6846 (Gorton's)
Toll free: 800–231–0308 (snacks)

Bob Dann
Customer Relations Manager
**General Motors Acceptance
Corp. (GMAC)**
3044 West Grand Blvd., Room AX348
Detroit, MI 48202
313–556–0510
Toll free: 800–441–9234
TDD toll free: 800–TDD–GMAC

Joyce Bowman
Customer Service
General Tire Inc.
One General Street
Akron, OH 44329–0007
Toll free: 800–847–3349

Donna Leggate
Vice President
Customer Service
Generra
316 Occidental Avenue, South
Suite 410
Seattle, WA 98104
206–728–6888

Sales Department
Genesee Brewing Co., Inc.
445 St. Paul Street
Rochester, NY 14605
716–546–1030

Georgia-Pacific Corp.
P.O. Box 105605
Atlanta, GA 30348–5605
Denise Irish (paper products)
404–652–4000
Kathy Ziprik (building products)
770–953–7000

Van Windes, Director
Gerber Products Co.
445 State Street
Fremont, MI 49413–1056
616–928–2000
Toll free: 800–4–GERBER
(24 hour breast feed advice)
Toll free: 800–828–9119 (baby formula)
Fax: 616–928–2723

Odonna Mathews
Vice President for Consumer Affairs
Giant Food Inc.
P.O. Box 1804
Department 597
Washington, DC 20013
301–341–4365
TDD: 301–341–4327
Fax: 301–618–4968

**Gibson Appliances
see The Frigidaire Co.**

Beverly Smart
Manager, Consumer Affairs
Gillette Co.
P.O. Box 61
Boston, MA 02199
617–463–3337

James Sainsbury
Manager, Product Regulation
The Glidden Co.
925 Euclid Avenue
Cleveland, OH 44115
216–344–8818

Golden Grain Co.
4576 Willow Road
Pleasanton, CA 94588
Toll free: 800–421–2444

A.L. Finley, Director
Consumer Relations
Goodyear Tire & Rubber Co.
1144 East Market Street
Akron, OH 44316
330–796–3909
TDD: 216–796–6055
Fax toll free: 800–321–2136

Michael Legrand
Senior President of Operations
Gordon's Jewelers
A Subsidiary of Zale Corporation
901 West Walnut Hill Lane
Irving, TX 75038–1003
214–580–4924
Fax: 214–580–5286

Christine Cusumano
Consumer Affairs Specialist
Greensweep
P.O. Box 50108
San Ramon, CA 94583–0808
510–355–3431
Toll free: 800–225–2883
Fax: 510–355–3535

Julie Churchill
Manager, Customer Relations
Greyhound Lines, Inc.
P.O. Box 660362
Dallas, TX 75266–0362
214–849–8000

Gabby Rios
Customer Services
Guess? Inc.
1444 South Alameda Street
Los Angeles, CA 90021
213–765–3100
Toll free: 800–394–8377

Guinness Import Co.
Six Landmark Square
Stamford, CT 06901–2704
203–323–3311
Toll free: 800–521–1591
Fax: 203–847–4109

H ___________

Marti Johnson
Director of Client Relations
H&R Block, Inc.
4410 Main Street
Kansas City, MO 64111–9986
816–753–6900
Toll free: 800–829–7733

**HVR Co.
see Clorox Co.**

Don Freberg
Manager of Consumer Affairs
Hallmark Cards, Inc.
P.O. Box 419034
Kansas City, MO 64141–6034
Toll free: 800–425–6275

John Schultz
Manager, Customer Services
Halston Borghese, Inc.
767 5th Avenue, 49th Floor
New York, NY 10153
212–572–3100

**Hanes
see L'eggs**

Cathy Teixeira
Customer Services
Hanover-Direct Inc.
340 Poplar Street
Hanover, PA 17333–9989
717–637–6000
Fax: 717–633–3199

Consumer Relations Department
Hartz Mountain Corp.
400 Plaza Drive
Secaucus, NJ 07094
201–271–4800

Bonnie Fisher
Supervisor, Consumer Affairs
Hasbro, Inc.
P.O. Box 200
Pawtucket, RI 02862–0200
Toll free: 800–255–5516
Toll free: 800–242–7276

**Hathaway Shirts
see Warnaco Men's Apparel**

Tom Wise
Marketing Manager
Heath Co.
Benton Harbor, MI 49022
616–925–6000
Fax: 616–925–2898

Donna Elliott
Manager, Consumer Affairs
Heinz U.S.A.
P.O. Box 57
Pittsburgh, PA 15230
412–237–5740
Fax: 412–237–5922

Paula Cisar
Manager, Consumer Affairs Department
Helene Curtis, Inc.
325 North Wells Street
Chicago, IL 60610–4713
312–661–0222
Toll free: 800–682–8301
Fax: 312–661–2787

Mindy Soleman
Manager, Consumer Relations
Hershey Foods Corp.
100 Crystal A Drive
Hershey PA 17033
717–534–6799

Frank Gonzalez, Manager
Manager, Customer Relations
Hertz Corp.
225 Brae Blvd.
Park Ridge, NJ 07656–0713
201–307–2000

Toll free: 800–654–3131 (reservations)
TDD toll free: 800–654–2280
Fax: 201–307–2644

Doug Moore, Manager
Direct Marketing Organization
Hewlett-Packard Co.
19310 Prune Ridge Avenue
Mail Stop 49AU25
Copertino, CA 95014–0604
Toll free: 800–752–0900
Fax: 408–345–8178

Daniel Dinell
Director, Staff Service
Hilton Hotels Corp.
9336 Civic Center Drive
Beverly Hills, CA 90209–5567
310–278–4321

Mike Rudman
Vice President, Human Resources
Hit or Miss
100 Campanelli Parkway
Stoughton, MA 02072
617–344–0800
Fax: 617–297–7268

Bruce Schoenogge
Director of Marketing
**Hitachi Home Electronics
(America), Inc.**
3890 Steve Reynolds Blvd.
Norcross, GA 30093
404–279–5600
Toll free: 800–241–6558

Mary Briend
Customer Information Manager
Hoechst Marion Roussel
North American Headquarters
P.O. Box 9627
Kansas City, MO 64134–0627
Toll free: 800–552–3656

Randall Smith
Manager, Worldwide Sales
Holiday Inn Worldwide
Three Ravenia Drive
Suite 2000
Atlanta, GA 30346
404–604–2000

Bill Sanders
Director, Consumer Affairs
Home Depot Inc.
2727 Paces Ferry Road, N.W.
Atlanta, GA 30339
404–433–8211
Toll free: 800–553–3199

Corporate Communications Manager
Home Shopping Network
P.O. Box 9090
Clearwater, FL 34618–9090
813–572–8585
Toll free: 800–284–3900
Fax: 813–572–5801

Ray Gwin, Manager
Consumer Affairs
Residential Division–MN 272164
Honeywell, Inc.
Honeywell Plaza
P.O. Box 524
Minneapolis, MN 55440–0524
612–951–1000
Toll free: 800–468–1502

Larry Calder
Manager of Consumer Response Center
Hoover Co.
101 East Maple
North Canton, OH 44720
330–499–9499
Toll free: 800–944–9200

Terry Gradite
Customer Service Division
The Horchow Collection
111 Customer Way
Irving, TX 75039
214–401–6300
Toll free: 800–395–5397

Cheryl Cook
Director, Consumer Affairs
Hormel Foods Co.
One Hormel Place
Austin, MN 55912–9989
507–437–5940
Toll free: 800–523–4635

Kevin koesters
Consumer Relations
Huffy Bicycle Co.
P.O. Box 1204
Dayton, OH 45401
513–866–6251
Toll free: 800–872–2453
Fax: 513–865–2835

Customer Relations
Humana Inc.
500 West Main Street
P.O. Box 1438
Louisville, KY 40201–1438
502–580–1000

Hunt-Wesson, Inc.
P.O. Box 4800
Fullerton, CA 92634–4800
714–680–1431

Chris Buzanis
Director, Quality Assurance
Hyatt Hotels & Resorts
200 West Madison Street
39th Floor
Chicago, IL 60606
312–750–1234
Toll free: 800–228–3336

**IBM International Services
Center**
300 East Valencia
Tucson, AZ 85706
Toll free: 800–426–3333

Illinois Bell
see Ameritech

Stephen Powell
Government Affairs Manager
Indiana Bell
251 North Illinois Street
Room 1680
Indianapolis, IN 46204
317–265–5965

Integra International
5200 Keller Springs Road
Suite 1131
Houston, TX 75248
214–233–0966

Dean Peters
Communications Department Manager
International Dairy Queen, Inc.
P.O. Box 39286
7505 Metro Blvd.
Minneapolis, MN 55439–0286
612–830–0200

J 

Michael Bomba
Customer Service Manager
JRT
5000 City Line Road
Hampton, VA 23661
804–827–6000

Jim Bennett
Customer Relations Manager
JVC Company of America
107 Little Falls Road
Fairfield, NJ 07004
201–808–2100
Toll free: 800–252–5722
Fax: 201–808–3351

Carolyn Calkins
Manager, Customer Service
Jackson & Perkins
Nursery Stock
2518 South Pacific Highway
Medford, OR 97501
541–776–2400
Toll free: 800–348–3222
Fax: 800–242–0329

Ophelia R. Millon
Manager of Consumer Affairs
James River Corp.
P.O. Box 6000
Norwalk, CT 06856–6000
203–854–2458
Toll free: 800–243–5384

Consumer Relations
Jockey International, Inc.
2300 60th Street
Kenosha, WI 53140
414–658–8111
Fax: 414–658–4740

Public Relations
John Hancock
Financial Services
P.O. Box 111
Boston, MA 02117
617–572–6272
TDD: 619–572–9986

Virginia Mellace
Johnny Appleseed's, Inc.
30 Tozer Road
Beverly, MA 01915
Toll free: 800–767–6666

Johnson & Johnson
Consumer Products, Inc.
199 Grandview Road
Skillman, NJ 08558
908–874–1000

Claudia Hunter
Subscription Department
Johnson Publishing Co., Inc.
820 South Michigan Avenue
Chicago, IL 60605
312–322–9200
(written complaints only)

Tom Conrardy
Director, Consumer Resource Center
S.C. Johnson and Sons
1525 Howe Street
Racine, WI 53403
Toll free: 800–558–5252

Howard Johnson, Inc.
3400 N.W. Grand Avenue
Phoenix, AZ 85017
602–264–9164

Kaaryn Denig
Vice President
Advertising and Marketing
Jordache Enterprises, Inc.
1411 Broadway
New York, NY 10018
212–944–1330
Toll free: 800–289–5326

K

Brian Beckwith
President of Special Interest Magazine Group
K–III
717 5th Avenue
New York, NY 10022
212–447–4700

Lisa Brown
Manager, Customer Service
K-mart Corp.
3100 West Big Beaver Road
Troy, MI 48084
810–643–1643

Wayne Wilson
Manager, Customer Relations
Karastan Rugmill
Division of Mohawk Industries, Inc.
P.O. Box 129
Eden, NC 27289
800–476–7113

Rory J. Murphy
Senior Vice President, Operations
Carl Karcher Enterprises
1200 North Harbor Blvd.
P.O. Box 4349
Anaheim, CA 92803
714–774–5796

Consumer Services
Kawasaki Motor Corp., U.S.A.
P.O. Box 25252
Santa Ana, CA 92799–5252
714–770–0400

Consumer Relations Manager
Kayser-Roth Corp.
612 South Main Street
Burlington, NC 27215
910–229–2224

Consumer Communications
Keebler Co., Inc.
One Hollow Tree Lane
Elmhurst, IL 60126
708–833–2900

Linda J. Pell
Director, Consumer Affairs
Kellogg Co.
P.O. Box CAMB
Battle Creek, MI 49016
Toll free: 800–962–1413

Robert A. Shower
Manager, Product Service
Kelly Springfield Tire Co.
12501 Willow Brook Road, S.E.
Cumberland, MD 21502–2599
301–777–6635
301–777–6017

Kelvinator Appliance Co.
see The Frigidaire Co.

Nancy Brebmar
Supervisor, Consumer Relations
Kemper National Insurance Co.
1 Kemper Drive
Long Grove, IL 60049–0001
708–320–2522
Toll free: 800–833–0355

Bonnie Bolduc
Supervisor, Consumer Affairs
Kenner Products
P.O. Box 200
Pawtucket, RI 02862–0200
401–431–8697
Toll free: 800–327–8264

Cindy Van Grinsven
Director, Consumer Services
Kimberly-Clark Corp.
P.O. Box 2020
Neenah, WI 54957–2020
414–721–8000
Toll free: 800–544–1847

Kinetico, Inc.
10845 Kinsman Road
Newbury, OH 44065
216–564–9111

**Kingsford Products Co.
see Clorox Co.**

Consumer Assistance Center
KitchenAid
2000 M–63 North
Benton Harbor, MI 49022
616–923–4500
Toll free: 800–422–1230

Denise Feglar
Assistant to the Senior Vice President
Public Relations and Communications
Calvin Klein Industries, Inc.
205 West 39th Street, 10th Floor
New York, NY 10018
212–326–6800

**Kodiak Smokeless Tobacco
see Conwood Co., L.P.**

Kohler Co.
Mark Grunow
Manager, Consumer Affairs
Plumbing and Specialty Products
Alan Wilson
Manager, Sales Administration
Paul Schoelten
Manager, Service and Technical
Publications
Kohler, WI 53044
414–457–4441

ATTN: Consumer Response Center
Kraft, Inc.
Kraft Court
Glenview, IL 60025
Toll free: 800–323–0768

Judy Holland
Customer Relations Manager
Kroger Co.
1014 Vine Street
Cincinnati, OH 45202
513–762–1589
Toll free: 800–632–6900

Rody Davenport, IV
President and C.O.O.
Krystal Co.
One Union Square
Chattanooga, TN 37402
453–757–1550

L

Customer Service Department
LA Gear
2850 Ocean Park Blvd.
Santa Monica, CA 90405
310–452–4327
Toll free: 800–786–7800

**L&F Products
see Reckitt & Colman, Inc.**

Customer Service
L.W.I. Holding Inc.
23279 Thomas Park
Beachwood, OH 44122
216–831–6191
Toll free: 800–654–7817

**LaCoupe
see Playtex Family Products
Group**

Ann P. Gallaher
Manager of Consumer Services
La-Z-Boy Chair Co.
1284 North Telegraph Road
Monroe, MI 48162–3309
313–242–1444

Lydie Botham
Director of Test Kitchens and
Consumer Affairs
Land O'Lakes, Inc.
P.O. Box 116
Minneapolis, MN 55440–0116
612–481–2222
Toll free: 800–328–4155

Customer Service
Land's End
Two Land's End Lane
Dodgeville, WI 53595
Toll free: 800–332–4700; 800–356–4444

Bill West
Vice President, Customer Service
Lane Furniture
East Franklin Avenue
P.O. Box 151
Altavista, VA 24517
804–369–5641

Lechmere
275 Wildwood Street
Woburn, MA 01801
617–476–1404
Toll free: 800–733–4666

Carol Manley/White Hall/Robins
Manager, Consumer Affairs
Lederle Consumer Health
1407 Cumming Drive
Richmond, VA 23220
Toll free: 800–282–8805

Tim Kellerman
Customer Service Team
Lee Apparel
9001 West 67th Street
Merriam, KS 66202
913–384–4000

L'eggs Products
5660 University Parkway
Winston-Salem, NC 27105
910–768–9540

**Leichtung, Inc.
see L.W.I. Holding Inc.**

Lennox Industries
P.O Box 799900
Dallas, TX 75379–9900
214–497–5000

Consumer Services Dept.
Lever Brothers Co.
390 Park Avenue
New York, NY 10022–4698
Toll free: 800–598–1223

Levi Strauss & Co.
1155 Battery Street
San Francisco, CA 94111
Toll free: 800–USA–LEVI

Eleanor Eckardt
Vice President, Consumer Relations
Levitz Furniture Corp.
6111 Broken Sound Parkway, N.W.
Boca Raton, FL 33487–2799
Toll free: 000–031–4001

Customer Service
Levolor Home Fashion
4110 Premier Drive
High Point, NC 27265
910–812–8181
Toll free: 800–LEVOLOR

David Hoffman
Assistant Vice President
Director of Corp. and Public Affairs
**Liberty Mutual
Insurance Group**
175 Berkeley Street
Boston, MA 02117
617–357–9500
Toll free: 800–225–2390

Customer Service
Lillian Vernon Corp.
2600 International Parkway
Virginia Beach, VA 23452
804–430–1500
Toll free: 800–285–5555

Consumer Communications
Eli Lilly & Co.
Lilly Corporate Center
Indianapolis, IN 46285
317–276–8588

Vice President
Financial and Public Relations
The Limited, Inc.
Three Limited Parkway
Columbus, OH 43230
614–479–7000

Long John Silver's
315 S. Broadden
Lexington, KY 40508
606–388–6000

**L'Oreal
see Cosmair, Inc.**

Mike Loy
Customer Relations Manager
Lorillard Tobacco Co.
2525 East Market Street
P.O. Box 21688
Greensboro, NC 27420–1688
910–373–6669 (complaints)

Communications Department
Los Angeles Times
Times Mirror Square
Los Angeles, CA 90053
213–237–5000

Judith Decker
Communications Manager
Lucky Stores, Inc.
P.O. Box 5008
San Leandro, CA 94577
510–678–5444

M ___________________

Customer Services
MAACO, Inc.
381 Brooks Road
King of Prussia, PA 19406
Toll free: 800–523–1180; 800–521–6282

Corporate Communications and Public Affairs
MCA Inc.
100 Universal City Plaza
Universal City, CA 91608–1085
818–777–3591

Jane King
Senior Manager, Consumer Affairs
MCI Communications
1200 South Hayes Street, 11th Floor
Arlington, VA 22202
Toll free: 800–677–6580

Consumer Affairs Department
M&M/Mars, Inc.
High Street
Hacketstown, NJ 07840
908–852–1000

**MTV Networks
see Viacom International Inc.**

Vice President
Customer Service
R.H. Macy & Co., Inc.
151 West 34th Street
New York, NY 10001
212–695–4400

Consumer Services Manager
Mannington Mills, Inc.
P.O. Box 30
Salem, NJ 08079
609–935–3000
Toll free: 800–356–6787

Professional Services Office
Manor Care Corp.
10770 Columbia Pike
Silver Spring, MD 20901
301–681–9400
Toll free: 800–833–7696

Manville Corporation/Schuller International, Inc.
P.O. Box 5108
Denver, CO 80217–5108
303–978–2000
Toll free: 800–654–3103

Corporate Customer Relations
Marine Midland Bank, N.A.
One Marine Midland Center
Buffalo, NY 14203
716–841–1000

**Marion Merrell Dow Inc.
see Hoechst Marion Roussel**

Attention: Department 921.60
Consumer Affairs
Marriott Corp.
One Marriott Drive
Washington, DC 20058
301–380–3000

Karen Filler, CLU
Director of Customer Relations
Massachusetts Mutual Insurance Co.
1295 State Street
Springfield, MA 01111
413–788–8411
Toll free: 800–828–4902

MasterCard International
(contact issuing bank)
Toll free: 800–826–2181
(lost or stolen cards or questions about the MasterCard system)

Anthony Lopes, President
Matsushita Services Co.
50 Meadowlands Parkway
Secaucus, NJ 07094
201–348–7000

Gail Carpentar
Director, Consumer Affairs
Mattel Toys, Inc.
333 Continental Blvd.
El Segundo, CA 90245–5012
310–252–2000
Toll free: 800–524–TOYS

**Max Factor
see Procter & Gamble Co.**

Consumer Affairs
Maxicare Health Plans, Inc.
1149 South Broadway
Los Angeles, CA 90015
213–742–0900

**Maxwell House
see General Foods**

James F. Harner
Senior Vice President
Customer Service and Operations
May Department Stores Co.
611 Olive Street
St. Louis, MO 63101
314–342–6300

Lori L. Wren
Manager, Consumer Relations
Maybelline Inc.
P.O. Box 372
Memphis, TN 38101–0372
901–320–2166
Toll free: 800–944–0730

Customer Service Department
Mayflower Transit, Inc.
P.O. Box 107
Indianapolis, IN 46206
317–875–1000
Toll free: 800–428–1234

Mary Randisi
Director, Consumer Affairs
McCormick & Co., Inc.
211 Schilling Circle
Hunt Valley, MD 21031
301–527–6273
Toll free: 800–632–5847

McCrory Stores, Inc.
2955 East Market Street
York, PA 17402
717–757–8181

Beth Petersohn
Manager, Customer Satisfaction Department
McDonald's Corp.
Kroc Drive
Oak Brook, IL 60521
708–575–6198

Customer Service Manager
McGraw-Hill, Inc.
1221 Avenue of the Americas
New York, NY 10020
Toll free: 800–262–4729

Consumer Services
McKee Foods Corp.
P.O. Box 750
Collegedale, TN 37315
Toll free: 800–522–4499

Vice President Manufacturing/TSO
McKesson Water Products Co.
3280 E. Foothill Blvd. #400
Pasadena, CA 91107
818–585–1000

Consumer Affairs
**McNeil Consumer Products Co.—
Johnson & Johnson**
7050 Camp Hill Road
Fort Washington, PA 19034
215–233–7000

Marshall Morton
Senior Vice President
Media General, Inc.
333 East Grace Street
Richmond, VA 23219
804–649–6000

Nancy Little
Customer Service Representative
Meineke Discount Muffler
128 South Tryon Street, Suite 900
Charlotte, NC 28202
704–377–3070

Yvette Harris
Manager, Customer Relations
Melitta USA, Inc.
17757 U.S. Highway 19 North
Suite 600
Clearwater, FL 34624
Toll free: 888–635–4882

Paul S. Videman
Executive Vice President
(Retail Bank)
Mellon Bank Corp.
One Mellon Bank Center
Room 5135
Pittsburgh, PA 15258–0001
412–234–8552

Consumer Affairs
Melville Corporation
1 Theall Road
Rye, NY 10580
914–925–4000

Consumer Relations
Mem Company, Inc.
Union Street
Northvale, NJ 07647
201–767–0100

**Mennen Co.
see Colgate, Palmolive,
Mennen Co.**

Mentholatum Co., Inc.
1360 Niagara Street
Buffalo, NY 14213
716–882–7660

Patricia Royer
Vice President, Consumer Affairs
Merck Medco Manage Care, Inc.
100 Summit Avenue
Montvale, NJ 07645
201–358–5530
Fax: 201–358–5793

Service Department
Mercruiser
3003 North Perkins Road
Stillwater, OK 74075
405–377–1200

Service Department
Mercury Marine
P.O. Box 1939
Fond Du Lac, WI 54936–1939
414–929–5000

M. J. Mosiniak
Manager, Customer Support
Merillat Industries
5353 West U.S. 223
Adrian, MI 49221
517–263–0771

Customer Service Dept.
**Merrill Lynch Pierce
Fenner & Smith**
265 Davidson Avenue, 4th Floor
Somerset, NJ 08873
908–563–8777

Colleen Dahle-Hong
Consumer Affairs Analyst
Mervyn's
22301 Industrial Blvd.
Hayward, CA 94541
510–727–3000

Bruce C. Hemer
Director, Consumer Affairs
Metropolitan Life Insurance Co.
One Madison Avenue
Area 1–Z
New York, NY 10010–3690
212–578–2544

Consumer Relations Dept.
Michelin Tire Corp.
P.O. Box 19001
Greenville, SC 29602
Toll free: 800–847–3435

**Michigan Bell Telephone Co.
see Ameritech**

Cindy Rosenbrook
Customer Service Manager
Michigan Bulb Co.
1950 Waldorf, N.W.
Grand Rapids, MI 49550
616–771–9500
Fax: 616–435–9208

Louis Gergits
Manager, Consumer Relations
Midas International Corp.
225 North Michigan Avenue
Chicago, IL 60601
Toll free: 800–621–8545

Mid-Michigan Surgical Supply
595 North Avenue
Battle Creek, MI 19017
616–962–9541
Toll free: 800–445–5820
Fax: 616–926–9650

Customer Service
Miles Kimball
41 West 8
Oshkosh, WI 54906
(written inquiries only)

Debra K. Wood
Consumer Service Coordinator
Milton Bradley Co.
443 Shaker Road
East Long Meadow, MA 01028
413–525–6411, ext. 2288
Fax: 413–525–1767

Charles Hoppe
National Manager, Consumer Service
Minolta Corp.
101 Williams Drive
Ramsey, NJ 07446
201–825–4000
Fax: 201–825–7605

Help Line
Minwax, Inc.
10 Mountain View Road
Upper Saddle River, NJ 07458–1934
Toll free: 800–523–9299

**Miracle Gro Products, Inc.
see Scotts Miracle Gro
Products, Inc.**

Consumer Relations
**Mitsubishi Electronics
America, Inc.**
6100 Atlantic Blvd.
P.O. Box 5025
Norcross, GA 30071–1305
Toll free: 800–332–2119

Otis Williams
Customer Relations Manager
Mobil Oil Corp.
3225 Gallows Road
Fairfax, VA 22037
Toll free: 800–662–4592

R.D. Bahr
Credit Services Manager
Mobil Oil Credit Corp.
11300 Corporate Avenue
Lenexa, KS 66219–1385
Toll free: 800–225–9547

Customer Service
**Monet Group Inc.
Crystal Brand Jewelry Group**
Number Two Lonsdale Avenue
Pawtucket, RI 02860
401–728–9800

General Information
Monsanto Co.
800 North Lindbergh Boulevard
St. Louis, MO 63167
314–694–1000

Cindy Mace
Customer Relations Manager
Montgomery Ward
One Montgomery Ward Plaza, 9–S
Chicago, IL 60671
Toll free: 800–695–3553

Mark T. Beaudouin
Sr. Vice President and General Counsel
Morse Shoe Inc.
A Subsidiary of J. Baker, Inc.
555 Turnpike Street
Canton, MA 02021
617–828–9300

Fax: 617–821–0614

Consumer Affairs
Morton International
Morton Salt Division
100 North Riverside Plaza
Chicago, IL 60606
312–807–2694

Corporate Communications
Motorola, Inc.
1303 East Algonquin Road
Schaumburg, IL 60196
847–576–2108
Fax: 708–576–7653

Darlene Stovall-Hendricks
Supervisor, Consumer Affairs
Motts, USA
6 High Ridge Park
Stamford, CT 06905
203–968–7673
Fax: 203–968–5757
Toll free: 800–426–4891

George Smedley
Plant Manager
Murphy-Phoenix Co.
31900 Solon Road
P.O. Box 39670
Solon, OH 44139
216–248–2411

**Mutual Life Insurance
Company of New York (MONY)**
Glenpoint Center West
500 Frank W. Burr Blvd.
Teaneck, NJ 07666
401–342–7600

Elizabeth Powell
Manager, Customer Relations
Mutual of Omaha Insurance Co.
Mutual of Omaha Plaza
Omaha, NE 68175
402–342–7600
Fax: 402–351–2775

N _______________

Audience Services
NBC
30 Rockefeller Plaza
New York, NY 10112
212–664–2333

Linda Middleton
Customer Service Manager
NEC Technologies Inc.
1255 Michael Drive
Wood Dale, IL 60191–1094
708–238–7982
Toll free: 800–366–9500

Sandra Lowe, Manager
Consumer Information Services
Nabisco Foods Group
100 DeForest Ave.
East Hanover, NJ 07936
201–503–2617
Toll free: 800–NABISCO
Fax: 201–503–2202

William Towey
Senior Vice President, Theater Operations
National Amusements Inc.
200 Elm Street
Dedham, MA 02026
617–461–1600
Fax: 617–329–4670

Mary McElroy-Mullvain
Manager, Consumer Affairs
**National Car Rental
System, Inc.**
7700 France Avenue South
Minneapolis, MN 55435
612–830–2936
Toll free: 800–468–3334

National Media Corp.
1700 Walnut Street
Philadelphia, PA 19103
215–772–5000
Fax: 215–772–5018

James Jensen, Controller
National Presto Industries, Inc.
3925 North Hastings Way
Eau Claire, WI 54703–3703
715–839–2121
Fax: 715–839–2122

Glenn W. Soden
Customer Relations Officer
**Nationwide Insurance
Companies**
One Nationwide Plaza, 1–22–01
Columbus, OH 43215–2220
614–249–6985
TDD toll free: 800–622–2421

Near East Food Products
797 Lancaster Street
Leominster, MA 01453
Toll free: 800–822–7423

Customer Service Department
Neiman-Marcus
P.O. Box 729080
Dallas, TX 75372
Toll free: 800–685–6695
Fax: 214–761–2650

Consumer Relations Department
Nestlé Beverage Co.
345 Spear Street
San Francisco, CA 94105

Office of Consumer Affairs
Nestlé Food Co.
P.O. Box 29055
Glendale, CA 91209–9055

Consumer Information Center
**Nestlé Frozen, Refrigerated
& Ice Cream Companies, Inc.**
P.O. Box 39487
Solon, OH 44139–0487

Office of Consumer Affairs
Nestlé USA, Inc.
P.O. Box 29055
Glendale, CA 91209–9055

Alene Lain
Consumer Affairs
Neutrogena Corp.
5760 West 96th Street
Los Angeles, CA 90045
310–642–1150
Toll free outside CA: 800–421–6857
Fax: 310–337–5564

External Affairs
Nevada Bell
645 East Plumb Lane
Reno, NV 89520
702–333–4339
TDD toll free: 800–356–4040

Edward C. Hall
President, New England
Service Administration
The New England
501 Boylston Street
Boston, MA 02116
617–578–2000

George Ittner
Chairman, CEO
New Hampton, Inc.
5000 City Line Road
Hampton, VA 23661
804–827–7010

Customer Service
Newport News, Inc.
(formerly AVON Fashions)
5000 City Line Road
Hampton, VA 23661
804–827–7010
Fax: 804–825–4161

Customer Service
News America Publishing, Inc.
Four Radnor Corporate Center
Radnor, PA 19088
610–293–8500
Toll free: 800–866–1400
Fax: 610–687–6965

Customer Service Representative
Newsweek, Inc.
P.O. Box 403
Livingston, NJ 07039
212–316–2000
Toll free: 800–631–1040 (subscriber service)
Fax: 201–335–5971

**New Woman Magazine
see K–III**

Barbara Fagnano
Assistant Vice President
**New York Life
Insurance Co.**
51 Madison Avenue
New York, NY 10010
212–576–5081 (collect calls accepted)
Fax: 212–447–4180

**New York Magazine
see K–III**

Robert P. Smith, Manager
Advertising Acceptability Department
New York Times Co.
229 West 43rd Street
New York, NY 10036
212–556–7171

Customer Service
Nexxus Products Co.
P.O. Box 1274
Santa Barbara, CA 93116–9976
805–968–6900

Lynda Danovitz
Manager, Customer Advocacy
Niagara Mohawk Power Corp.
Dey's Centennial Plaza
401 South Salina Street
Syracuse, NY 13202
315–460–7015
Fax: 315–460–7009

Consumer Services
Nike, Inc.
Nike/World Campus
1 Bowerman Drive
Beaverton, OR 97005
Toll free: 800–344–6453

**Nine West Group
Corporate Headquarters**
9 West Broad Street
Stamford, CT 06902
203–324–7567

Nine West—Easy Spirit
One Eastwood Drive
Cincinnati, OH 45227–1197
Toll free: 800–285–9955

Nine West—Selby
One Eastwood Drive
Cincinnati, OH 45227–1197
Toll free: 800–284–9949

Nile Spice Foods
P.O. Box 20581
Seattle, WA 98102
Toll free: 800–265–6453

Consumer Services
Nintendo of America Inc.
4820 150th Avenue NE
Redmond, WA 98052
Toll free: 800–255–3700
TDD toll free: 800–422–4281

Julie Brown, Manager
Consumer Relations Department
Norelco Consumer Products Co.
A division of Philips Electronics
North America Corp.
1010 Washington Boulevard
P.O. Box 120015
Stamford, CT 06912–0015
Toll free: 800–243–7884
Fax: 203–975–1812

Roslyn DeTasquale
Marketing Servicing Manager
North American Watch Corp.
125 Chubb Avenue
Lyndhurst, NJ 07071
201–460–4800
Fax: 201–460–3305

Customer Relations
Northwest Airlines
C6590
5101 Northwest Drive
St. Paul, MN 55111–3034
612–726–2046
**TDD toll free: 800–328–2298
(reservations)**

Thomas W. Towers
Associate Director, Public Relations
**Northwestern Mutual
Life Insurance Co.**
720 East Wisconsin Avenue
Milwaukee, WI 53202
414–299–7179
Fax: 414–299–2463

Alice Kain-Moore
Manager, Customer Relations
Norwegian Cruise Line
95 Merrick Way
Coral Gables, FL 33134
305–460–2796
Toll free: 800–327–7030
305–567–9173

Mike Walsh
Director of Consumer Relations
Nu Tone, Inc.
Madison and Redbank Roads
Cincinnati, OH 45227
513–527–5231

The NutraSweet Co.
Consumer Affairs
The Merchandise Mart, Suite 900
200 World Trade Center
Chicago, IL 60654
Toll free: 800–321–7254 (NutraSweet)
Toll free: 800–323–5316 (Equal)
Fax: 708–405–7790

Nutri/System Inc.
410 Horsham Road
Horsham, PA 10944
215–445–5300

President's Help Line
Nynex/New York Telephone
1095 Avenue of the Americas
New York, NY 10036
Toll free in NY: 800–722–2300
TDD toll free in NY: 800–342–4181

O ___________

Linda Compton
Manager, Consumer Affairs
Ocean Spray Cranberries Inc.
One Ocean Spray Drive
Lakeville/Middleboro, MA 02349
508–946–7407
Toll free: 800–662–3263
Fax: 508–946–7720

**Ohio Bell Telephone Co.
see Ameritech**

**O'Keefe & Merit Appliances
see The Frigidaire Co.**

Mark Hartline
Director, Customer Service
Olan Mills, Inc.
4325 Amnicola Highway
P.O. Box 23456
Chattanooga TN 37422–3456
615–622–5141
Toll free: 800–251–6323
Fax: 615–499–3864

Barbara Abe
Manager, Customer Support
Olympus America
2 Corporate Center Drive
Melville, NY 11747
516–844–5000
Toll free: 800 622 6372
Fax: 516–844–5262

Denise Armstrong
Consumer Relations Supervisor
Oneida, Ltd.
The Telemarketing Center
Sherrill, NY 13461
315–361–3000
Toll free: 800–877–6667

Merine Heberger
Manager, Consumer Affairs
Ore-Ida Foods, Inc.
P.O. Box 10
Boise, ID 83707
Toll free: 800–842–2401

**Orkin
see Rollins, Inc.**

**OSCO Drugs
see American Stores Co.**

Henry Hegel
Director, Corporate Service
Outboard Marine Corp.
100 Sea Horse Drive
Waukegan, IL 60085
847–689–6200
Fax: 847–689–5489

**Owens Corning
World Headquarters**
Fiberglas Tower
Toledo, OH 43659–0001
419–248–8000

P ___________

Customer Appeals Group
Pacific Bell
140 New Montgomery Street
San Francisco, CA 94105
Toll free in Ca: 800–791–6661
Toll free outside CA: 800–697–6547

Corporate Communications
Pacific Enterprises
555 W. 5th Street
Los Angeles, CA 90013
213–244–1200
Fax: 213–244–8253

**Pacific Telesis Group
see Pacific Bell**

Robert Karem
Senior Vice President
Client Relations
PaineWebber Inc.
1000 Harbor Blvd., 8th Floor
Weehawken, NJ 07087
201–902–4936
Toll free: 800–354–9103
Fax: 201–902–5795

**Panasonic
see Matsushita Services Co.**

Rick Bates
Vice President, Customer Operations
Paramount Publishing
200 Old Tappan Road
Old Tappan, NJ 07675
201–767–5000
Fax: 201–767–4017

**Parke-Davis
see Warner-Lambert Co.**

Noreen MacConchic
Manager, Customer Relations
Pathmark Stores Inc.
301 Blair Road
Woodbridge, NJ 07095
908–499–3500
Fax: 908–499–3072

**Peidmont Airlines
see USAir**

Customer Service
Pella Corp.
102 Main Street
Pella, IA 50219
515–628–1000

Jane Cooper
Consumer Relations Manager
J.C. Penney Co., Inc.
P.O. Box 10001
Dallas, TX 75301–8212
214–431–8500
Fax: 214–431–8792

Bill Hover
Manager, Customer Service
Pennzoil Products Co.
P.O. Box 2967
Houston, TX 77252–2967
Toll free: 800–990–9811

**Peoples Drug Stores, Inc.
see CVS**

Ellie Eng
Manager, Consumer Affairs
Pepperidge Farm, Inc.
595 Westport Avenue
Norwalk, CT 06851
203–846–7276
Fax: 203–846–7278

Christine Jones
Manager, Public Affairs
Pepsi-Cola Co.
1 Pepsi Way
Somers, NY 10589–2201
Toll free: 800–433–2652
Fax: 914–767–7761

Lisa Nowak
Manager of Consumer Relations
Perdue Farms
P.O. Box 1537
Salisbury, MD 21802
410–543–3000
Toll free outside MD: 800–442–2034
Fax: 410–543–3292

Lisa Druker
Marketing Division
The Perrier Group
777 West Putnam Avenue
Greenwich, CT 06830
203–531–4100
Fax: 203–863–0256

Mark E. Wooley
Manager, Consumer Affairs
Pet Inc.
P.O. Box 66719
St. Louis, MO 63166–6719
314–622–6695
Toll free: 800–325–7130

Pfizer Inc.
235 East 42nd Street
New York, NY 10017
212–573–2323
Fax: 212–573–7851

Pharmacia and UpJohn Corp.
Consumer Products Division (over the counter)
Patient Information (prescriptions)
7000 Portage Road
Kalamazoo, MI 49001
Toll free: 800–253–8600

Susan A. Strausser
Supervisor, Consumer Affairs
Philip Morris Companies, Inc.
120 Park Avenue
New York, NY 10017
212–880–3366
Toll free: 800–343–0975

Toni J. Honkisz
Corporate Quality Administrator
Philips Lighting Co.
200 Franklin Square Drive
P.O. Box 6800
Somerset, NJ 08875–6800
908–563–3081

Public Relations
Phillips Petroleum Co.
16 Phillips Building
Bartlesville, OK 74004
918–661–1215
Fax: 918–662–2075

**Piaget
see North American Watch Corp.**

Pillsbury Co.
Consumer Response
P.O. Box 550
Minneapolis, MN 55440
Toll free: 800–767–4466

Al Segal, Division Manager
Customer Service
**Pioneer Electronics
Service, Inc.**
P.O. Box 1760
Long Beach, CA 90810
Toll free: 800–421–1404
Fax: 301–952–2821

Bonnie Bolduc
Supervisor, Consumer Affairs
Playskool
Consumer Affairs Dept.
P.O. Box 200
Pawtucket, RI 02862–0200
Toll free: 800–752–9755
Fax: 401–431–8464

Theresa B. Thomas
Manager, Consumer Affairs
Playtex Apparel, Inc.
P.O. Box 631
MS 1526
Dover, DE 19903–0631
302–674–6000
Toll free: 800–537–9955

Playtex Family Products Corp.
215 College Rd.
P.O. Box 728
Paramus, NJ 07652
Toll free in NJ: 800–624–0825
Toll free outside NJ: 800–222–0453
Fax: 201–265–0630

Customer Care Center
Polaroid Corp.
201 Burlington Road
Bedford, MA 01730
617–386–2000
(collect calls accepted within MA)
Toll free outside MA: 800–343–5000
Fax: 617–386–5605

Daisy Modernel
Consumer Relations Manager
Polo/Ralph Lauren Corp.
4100 Beechwood Drive
Greensboro, NC 27410
Toll free: 800–775–7656
Fax: 910–632–9097

Popeye's
see America's Favorite
Chicken Co.

Premiere Magazine
see K–III

Prescriptives, Inc.
see Estee Lauder Companies

Princess Marcella
see Halston Borghese, Inc.

Princeton Pharmaceutical
Products
see Bristol-Myers Squibb
Pharmaceutical Group

Kathleen Fitzsimmons Braun
Manager, Consumer Services
Cosmetic and Fragrance Division
Procter & Gamble Co.
11050 York Road
Hunt Valley, MD 21030–2098
410–785–4411
Toll free: 800–426–8374

Patti Shively
Associate Director, Consumer Relations
Procter & Gamble Co.
P.O. Box 599
Cincinnati, OH 45201–0599
513–945–8787
(toll free numbers appear on all
Procter & Gamble product labels)

Progresso
see Pet Inc.

Diane Koken
General Counsel
Provident Mutual
Life Insurance
1600 Market Street
P.O. Box 7378
Philadelphia, PA 19101
215–636–5000
Toll free: 800–523–4681
Fax: 215–636–8166

Prudential Insurance Co. of
America
Executive Offices
Prudential Plaza, 24th Floor
Newark, NJ 07101
201–802–6000
Fax: 201–622–4729

Prudential Property &
Casualty Co.
23 Main Street
P.O. Box 419
Holmdel, NJ 07733
908–946–6000
Toll free: 800–437–5556

Patricia Lucey
Vice President, Client Relations
Prudential Securities Inc.
One New York Plaza
New York, NY 10292
Toll free: 800–367–8701
Fax: 212–778–2899

Patricia Kaufman
Director, Customer Operations
Publishers Clearing House
382 Channel Drive
Port Washington, NY 11050
516–883–5432
Toll free: 800–645–9242
TDD toll free: 800–248–8670
Fax: 800–453–0272

Q ______________________

QVC Incorporated
Goshen Corporate Park
1365 Enterprise Drive
West Chester, PA 19380
610–701–1000
Toll free: 800–367–9444 (customer service)
Fax: 610–701–1138

Quaker Oats Co.
Consumer Response
P.O. Box 049003
Chicago, IL 60604–9003
Check product package for toll–free num-
ber or call:
312–222–7111

Steven Blum
Vice President, Corporate Relations
Quaker State Corp.
P.O. Box 989
Oil City, PA 16301
814–676–7676
Toll free: 800–759–2525
Fax: 814–676–7030

Quasar
see Matsushita Services Co.

R ______________________

Radio Shack
see Tandy Corp.

Office of Consumer Affairs
Pet Products Group
Ralston Purina Co.
Checkerboard Square
St. Louis, MO 63164
Toll free: 800–778–7462

Patricia Rosafort
Supervisor, Customer Services
Readers Digest Association,
Inc.
Pleasantville, NY 10570–7000
Toll freeL 800–431–1246
TDD toll free: 800–735–4327
Fax: 914–238–4559

Donna Carr
Consumer Relations Manager
Reckitt & Colman, Inc.
225 Summit Avenue
Montvale, NJ 07645–1575
201–573–5898
Toll free: 800–232–9665

Orville Redenbacher
see Hunt-Wesson, Inc.

Consumer Relations
Reebok International, Ltd.
100 Technology Center Drive
Stoughton, MA 02072
Toll free: 800–843–4444

Richard Jones
Customer Service Manager
The Regina Co.
P.O. Box 638
Long Beach, MS 39560
Toll free: 800–847–8336
Fax: 800–235–8750

Cass Carroll
Director of Consumer Relations
Reliance Insurance Co.
Four Penn Center Plaza
Philadelphia, PA 19103
215–864–4445
Toll free: 800–441–1652
Fax: 215–864–4640

Consumer Affairs
Remco America, Inc.
8200 Thorn Drive
Wichita, KS 67226
316–646–7389

Remington Arms
see DuPont Co.

Customer Relations Department
Remington Products Co.
60 Main Street
Bridgeport, CT 06004
203–367–4400
Toll free: 800–736–4648

Customer Service
(Renaissance Hotels, Ramada outside the
United States and
New World Hotels in Asia)
Renaissance Hotels
International
29800 Bainbridge Road
Cleveland, OH 44139
216–498–9090

Linda H. Porter, Director
Revlon Consumer
Information Center
P.O. Box 6113
Oxford, NC 27565
Toll free: 800–473–8566
Fax: 919–603–2953

Carol Owen, Director
Consumer Services
Reynolds Metals Co.
6603 West Broad Street
Richmond, VA 23230
Toll Free: 800–433–2244
Fax: 804–281–4530

**Rhône-Poulenc Rorer
Pharmaceuticals Inc.
see Ciba Self-Medication, Inc.**

**Richardson-Vicks, Inc.
see Procter & Gamble Co.**

Rockport
220 Donald Lynch Blvd.
Marlboro, MA 01752
Toll free: 800–343–9255
Fax: 508–624–4299

Jeanne Dorney
Customer Satisfaction Call Center Manager
Rodale Press, Inc.
33 East Minor Street
Emmaus, PA 18048
Toll free: 800–848–4735
Fax: 610–967–8964

Michael Baviello
Service Manager
Rolex Watch U.S.A. Inc.
665 Fifth Avenue
New York, NY 10022
212–758–7700
Fax: 212–980–2166

Lawrence Beverley, Jr.
Manager, Customer Service
Rollins, Inc.
2170 Piedmont Road, N.E.
Atlanta, GA 30324
404–888–2151
800–346–7546
Fax:404–888–2912

Joanne Taddeo
Manager, Customer Relations
Ross Laboratories
625 Cleveland Avenue
Columbus, OH 43215
614–624–7900
Toll free: 800–227–5767
Fax: 614–624–7919

Larry Rothman, Director
Franchise Administration
Roto-Rooter Corp.
300 Ashworth Road
West Des Moines, IA 50265
515–223–1343
Toll free: 800–575–7737
Fax: 515–223–4420

**Roundup Lawn and Garden
see Greensweep**

Dana Pillsbury, Marketing Secretary
Royal Oak Enterprises, Inc.
900 Ashwood Parkway, Suite 800
Atlanta, GA 30338
404–393–1430
Toll free: 800–241–3955
Fax: 404–393–0313

Deborah Poole
Customer Service Manager
Royal Silk
800–A 31st Street
Union City, NJ 07087
Toll free: 800–962–6262

**Royal Viking Line
see Cunard Line**

Ruth A. Chambers
Supervisor, Consumer Services
Rubbermaid, Inc.
1147 Akron Road
Wooster, OH 44691–0800
330–264–6464, ext. 2619
Fax: 330–287–2751

**Rustler Jeans
see Wrangler**

Carol Yannone
Group Manager, Customer Service
Ryder Truck Rental
P.O. Box 020816
Miami, FL 33102–0816
Toll free: 800–327–7777
Fax: 305–593–4463

S

**7 Eleven Food Stores
see The Southland Corp.**

Customer Information Center
SFS Corp.
1200 West Artesia Blvd.
Compton, CA 90220
Toll free: 800–421–5013

Debra Lambert
Public Affairs Department Manager
Safeway Inc.
Oakland, CA 94660
510–891–3267

Donna Lane Swaap
Manager of Corporate Customer Relations
Saks Fifth Avenue
12 East 49th Street, 3rd Floor
New York, NY 10021
212–940–5027
Toll free: 800–239–3089
Fax: 212–940–5031

Sandoz Co.
Sandoz Pharmaceuticals Corp.
59 Route 10
East Hanover, NJ 07936
201–503–7500

**Sanyo Electric Inc.
see SFS Corp.**

Sara Lee Corp.
Three First National Plaza
70 West Madison Street
Chicago, IL 60602–4260
312–726–2600
Toll free: 800–621–5235
Fax: 312–726–0712

Watson Brooks
Manager, Consumer Relations
**Schering-Plough
HealthCare Products, Inc.**
3030 Jackson Avenue
Memphis, TN 38151–0001
901–320–2998
Toll free: 800–842–4090
Fax: 901–320–2954

**Scholl
see Schering-Plough
HealthCare Products, Inc.**

Penny Sass, Manager
Consumer Relations
Scott Paper Co.
Scott Plaza One
Philadelphia, PA 19113–1510
610–522–5143
Toll free: 800–835–7268

Rose B. Zosuls, Consumer Affairs
**Scotts Miracle Gro Products,
Inc.**
800 Port Washington Boulevard
Port Washington, NY 11050
516–883–6550
Fax: 516–883–6563

Scudder Investor Information
Scudder Investor Services Inc.
160 Federal Street
Boston, MA 02110
Toll free: 800–225–5163
Fax: 800–821–6234

Jerri Stuckey
Alice Bauer
Consumer Relations
Joseph E. Seagram & Sons, Inc.
800 3rd Avenue
New York, NY 10022
212–572–7335
Fax: 212–572–7946

Customer Service
**Sealy Mattress
Manufacturing Co.**
1228 Euclid Avenue, 10th Floor
Cleveland, OH 44115
216–522–1310
Fax: 216–522–1366

Donald Leibowitz
Customer Affairs Director
Seamans Furniture Co., Inc.
300 Crossways Park Dr.
Woodbury, NY 11797
516–682–1563
Toll free: 800–445–2503

Customer Service
**G.D. Searle and Co.
Pharmaceuticals**
P.O. Box 5110
Chicago, IL 60680
Toll free: 800–323–1603
Fax: 847–470–6633

Jerry Hauber
National Customer Relations Manager
Sears Merchandise Group
3333 Beverly Road—731CR
Hoffman Estates, IL 60179
847–286–5188
Fax: 800–427–3049

Coserv
Seiko Corporation of America
27 McKee Drive
Mahwah, NJ 07430
201–529–3311

President
Select Restaurants, Inc.
30050 Chagrin Blvd.
Cleveland, OH 44124
216–464–6606
Fax: 216–464–8565

Customer Service
Serta, Inc.
325 Spring Lake Drive
Itasca, IL 60143
708–285–9300
Toll free: 800–426–0371
Fax: 708–285–9330

**Seventeen Magazine
see K–III**

**Seven-Up
see Dr Pepper/Seven-Up
Companies, Inc.**

Greg Vanzandt, General Manager
Customer Service
Sharp Electronics Corp.
1300 Naperville Drive
Romeville IL 60441

Customer Relations
The Sharper Image
650 Davis Street
San Francisco, CA 94111
Toll free: 800–344–5555
Fax: 415–391–1584

Manager
Credit Card Marketing Programs
Shell Oil Co.
Box 4650
Houston, TX 77252
Toll free: 800–248–4257

Product Information Department
**Sherwin-Williams Co.
Paint Stores Group**
101 Prospect Avenue, N.W.
Cleveland, OH 44115–1075
216–566–2151

Shoppers Department
Shoney's Inc.
1717 Elm Hill Pike, Suite B3A
Nashville, TN 37210
615–391–5201
Fax: 615–231–2604

Sue Oram
Assistant to the President
ShowBiz Pizza Time, Inc.
4441 W. Airport Freeway
Irving, TX 75062
214–258–8507
Fax: 214–258–8545

**Showtime Networks Inc.
see Viacom International Inc.**

Deborah Slaughter
Manager, Consumer/Marketing Services
Simmons Co.
6424 Warren Drive
P.O. Box 2768
Norcross GA 30093
Toll free: 800–654–9258

Consumer Affairs Department
Sewing Products Division
Singer Sewing Co.
P.O. Box 1909
Edison, NJ 08818–1909
908–225–8844
Toll free: 800–877–7762

**Skaggs Co.
see American Stores Co.**

**Skoal Moist Smokeless
Tobacco
see UST**

Consumer Services Department
Slim•Fast Foods Co.
777 S. Flager Drive
West Tower, Suite 1400
West Palm Beach, FL 33401
Toll free: 800–223–1248

Law and Compliance Department
Smith Barney
388 Greenwich Street
New York, NY 10013
212–816–6000
Toll free: 800–421–8609
Fax: 212–723–2184

Snapper Power Equipment
McDonough, GA 30253

Snapple Beverages
Consumer Response Center
333 W. Merrick Road
Valley Stream, NY 11580
Toll Free: 800–Snapple (762–7753)

**Soap Opera Digest
Soap Opera Weekly
see K–III**

**Solar Nutritionals
see Thompson Medical Co., Inc.**

Steffanie Sonnabend, President
**Sonesta International
Hotels Corp.**
200 Clarendon Street
Boston, MA 02116
617–421–5432
Fax: 617–421–5402

National Customer Relations
Sony Corp. of America
Sony Service Co.
One Sony Drive
Park Ridge, NJ 07656
Toll free: 80 0–282–2848

**South Central Bell see
BellSouth Telecommunications**

**Southern Bell Corp. see
BellSouth Telecommunications**

Janey Camacho
Manager, Customer Relations
The Southland Corp.
P.O. Box 711
Dallas, TX 75221–0711
214–841–6585
Toll free: 800–255–0711
Fax: 904–636–1237

Jim Ruppel, Director
Customer Relations
Southwest Airlines
Love Field
P.O. Box 36611
Dallas, TX 75235–1611
214–904–4223
**TDD toll free: 800–533–1305
(reservations)**

Corporate Communications
Southwestern Bell Corporation
175 East Houston
San Antonio, TX 78205
210–351–2604
Fax: 210–351–2198

Shirley Brisbois
Manager, Consumer Relations
Spalding & Evenflo, Inc.
425 Meadow Street
P.O. Box 901
Chicopee, MA 01021–0901
413–536–1200
Toll free: 800–225–6601
Fax: 413–536–1404

**Speed Queen Co.
see Amana Refrigeration, Inc.**

Customer Service Department
Spencer Gifts
6826 Black Horse Pike
Egg Harbor Township, NJ 08234
609–645–3300
Toll free: 800–762–0419

Judith P. Luken
Director of Customer Satisfaction
Spiegel, Inc.
P.O. Box 927
Oak Brook, IL 60522–0927
708–986–8800

Springs Industries Inc.
Springmaid/Performance
787 7th Avenue
New York, NY 10019
212–903–2100
Toll free: 800–537–0115
Fax: 212–903–2115

David Thornhill
Executive Consumer Services
Sprint
1603 LBJ Freeway, Suite 300
Dallas, TX 75234
Toll free: 800–347–8988
Fax: 214–405–6114

Squibb
see Bristol-Myers Squibb
Pharmaceutical Group

Jack Gauthier, Marketing Manager
Stanley Hardware
Division Stanley Works
480 Myrtle Street
New Britain, CT 06050
203–225–5111
Toll free: 800–622–4393

Jim Stahly
Public Relations Director
State Farm Mutual Automobile
Insurance Co.
One State Farm Plaza
Bloomington, IL 61710
309–766–2714
Fax: 309–766–6169

Sterling Health
see Bayer Corp.

J.P. Stevens
see WestPoint Stores

Consumer Relations
Stokley USA, Inc.
1055 Corporate Center Drive
P.O. Box 248
Oconomowoc, WI 53066–0248
414–569–1800
800–872–1110

Terry Vandewater
Director, Public Affairs
Stop & Shop Supermarket Co.,
Inc.
P.O. Box 1942
Boston, MA 02105
617–770–6040

Matthew Cook
Director, Customer Relations
Strawbridge & Clothier
801 Market Street, 7th Floor
Philadelphia, PA 19107
215–629–6722
Fax: 215–629–6475

Consumer Complaints
The Stroh Brewery Co.
9399 West Higgins Road
Rosemont, IL 60018
847–292–2100

Consumer Affairs
Sunbeam/Oster
Household Products
P.O. Box 247
Laurel, MS 39441–0247
(written inquiries only)

Donna Samelson
Manager, Consumer Affairs
Sun-Diamond Growers
of California
P.O. Box 1727
Stockton, CA 95201
209–467–6267
Fax: 209–467–6257

Subscriber Service
Sunset Magazine
P.O. Box 56656
Boulder, CO 80322
Toll free: 800–777–0117
Fax: 303–661–1994

Supermarket General Corp.
see Pathmark Stores Inc.

Doug Williams, Customer Service
Swatch Watch USA
1817 William Penn Way
Lancaster, PA 17604
717–394–5288
Toll free: 800–937–9282
Fax: 717–394–8580

The Swiss Colony
Customer Service
1112 Seventh Avenue
Monroe, WI 53566
608–324–4000
Fax: 608–242–1001

T ___________________

Nancy Sperling, Supervisor
Consumer Affairs
3M
3M Center, Building 225–5N–04
St. Paul, MN 55144–1000
612–733–1871
Toll free: 800–364–3577
Fax: 612–736–3094

TJX Companies (T.J. Maxx)
Customer Service
770 Cochituate Road
Framingham, MA 01701
508–390–1000
Toll free: 800–926–6299

National Consumer Assistance Center
TRW Information Services
P.O. Box 949
Allen, TX 75002–0949
214–235–1200

TV Guide
see News America Publishing,
Inc.

Customer Service
Talbots
175 Beal Street
Hingham, MA 02043
Toll free: 800–992–9010
TDD toll free: 800–624–9179

Cindy Nothe
Manager, Consumer Services
TAMBRANDS, Inc.
P.O. Box 271
Palmer, MA 01069
413–289–3450
Toll free: 800–523–0014
Fax: 800–289–3510

Lucille Frey
Director, Customer Relations
Tandy Corp./
Radio Shack
600 One Tandy Center
Fort Worth, TX 76102
817–390–3218
Fax: 817–390–3292

Tappan Appliance Co., Inc.
see The Frigidaire Co.

Guest Relations and Quality Assurance
Target Stores
33 South 6th Street
P.O. Box 1392
Minneapolis, MN 55440–1392
612–304–4996

Technics
see Matsushita Services Co.

George White
Director, Consumer Affairs
Teledyne Water Pik
1730 East Prospect Road
Fort Collins, CO 80553–0001
970–484–1352
Toll free: 800–525–2774
Fax: 970–221–8292

Cathy Laffin
Director, Customer Service
Teleflora
12233 West Olympic, Suite 140
Los Angeles, CA 90064–0780
310–826–5253
Toll free: 800–421–2815
Fax: 310–207–5197

Corporate Communications
Tenneco, Inc.
1275 King Street
Greenwich, CT 06831
203–863–1000

Consumer Affairs Department
Tetley, Inc.
100 Commerce Drive
P.O. Box 856
Shelton, CT 06484–0856
203–929–9341
Toll free: 800–732–3027
Fax: 203–926–0876

W.D. Kistler
Manager, Customer Relations
Texaco
P.O. Box 790001
Houston, TX 77094
713–647–1500

Customer Service
Texas Instruments, Inc.
P.O. Box 6118
Temple, TX 76503–6118
817–774–6827 (technical support)
Toll free: 800–842–2737
Fax: 817–774–6074

Customer Service
Thom McAn Shoe Co.
67 Millbrook Street
Worcester, MA 01606–2804
508–791–3811
Fax: 508–792–2908

Consumer Service
Thompson & Formby, Inc.
825 Crossover Lane, Suite 240
Memphis, TN 38117
Toll free: 800–FORMBYS
901–682–5245

Consumer Services Department
Thompson Medical Co., Inc.
223 Lakeview Avenue
West Palm Beach, FL 33401–6112
407–820–9900
Fax: 407–832–2297

Customer Service
Thrift Drug, Inc.
615 Alpha Drive
Pittsburgh, PA 15238
412–963–6600
Toll free: 800–284–8212
Fax: 412–967–8992

Customer Service
Time Inc.
3000 University Drive Center
Tampa, FL 33612
813 878 6100
Toll free: 800–541–1000
Fax: 813–979–6615

Time Warner Inc.
75 Rockefeller Plaza
New York, NY 10019
212–484–8000

Customer Service
Timex Corp.
P.O. Box 2740
Little Rock, AR 72203–2740
501–372–1111
Toll free: 800–448–4639
Fax: 570–370–5747

Barb Pendergast, Paul Hayles,
Mike Benning, Dave Barsantee
Golf Division
National Consumer Relations
Titleist
P.O. Box 965
Fairhaven, MA 02719
Toll free: 800–225–8500
Fax: 508–979–3910

Bonnie Fisher
Supervisor, Consumer Affairs
Tonka Products
P.O. Box 200
Pawtucket, RI 02861–0200
Toll free: 800–248–6652

Mary Elliott, Director
Communications and Public Affairs
The Toro Co.
8111 Lyndale Avenue South
Minneapolis, MN 55420
612–887–8900

Customer Service
Toshiba America
Consumer Products, Inc.
82 Totowa Road
Wayne, NJ 07470
201–628–1000
Toll free: 800–631–3811

Helen Baur
Consumer Affairs Manager
Totes, Inc.
10078 East Kemper Road
Loveland, OH 45140
513–583–2300
Fax: 513–583–9948

Tourneau, Inc.
488 Madison Avenue
New York, NY 10022
212–758–3265
Toll free outside NY: 800–223–1288

Carol Fuller
Corporate Spokesperson
Toys "R" Us
461 From Road
Paramus, NJ 07652
201–599–7897
Fax: 201–262–8919

Bob Thomas
Manager, Control Center
Trak Auto
3300 75th Avenue
Landover, MD 20785
301–731–1200
Toll free: 800–835–7300
Fax: 301–731–1470

Trane/CAC, Inc.
903581–3200 (residential)
608–787–2000 (commercial)

Trans Union Corp.
Regional Consumer Relations Centers
Fullerton, CA
1561 East Orangethorpe
Fullerton, CA 92631

Wichita, KS
8200 East 32nd Street, N
Wichita, KS 67226

Springfield, PA
760 West Sproul Road
Springfield, PA 19064

National Disclosure Center
P.O. Box 390
Springfield, PA 19064

S. Ahl
Staff Vice President, Customer Relations
Trans World Airlines, Inc.
110 South Bedford Road
Mt. Kisco, NY 10549
314–589–3600
TDD toll free: 800–421–8480
(reservations)
Fax: 314–589–3626

J. David Dwyer
Second Vice President
Consumer Affairs
The Travelers Companies
One Tower Square Central Row East
Hartford, CT 06183–9079
203–277–3198 (executive line)
203–954–2382 (if executive line is busy)
Fax: 203–954–3956

**True Value Hardware Stores
see Cotter & Co.**

Barbara Catalano
Consumer Affairs Coordinator
Tsumara International, Inc.
300 Lighting Way
Secaucus, NJ 07096
201–223–8169
Fax: 201–223–8282

Penny Lake
Supervisor, Consumer Services
Tupperware
P.O. Box 2353
Orlando, FL 32802–2353
Toll free: 800–858–7221
Fax: 407–847–1897

Terri Tingle
Vice President of Public Affairs
**Turner Entertainment
Networks**
One CNN Center
P.O. Box 105366
Atlanta, GA 30348–5366
404–827–1632

Patricia Arvidson
Consumer Correspondence Representative
Turtle Wax, Inc.
5655 West 73rd Street
Chicago, IL 60638–6211
708–563–3600
Toll free: 800–323–9883
Fax: 708–563–4302

Judy Rowley
Director, Customer Service
Tyco Toys
P.O. Box 490
Portland, OR 97207
503–644–1181
Toll free: 800–367–8926
Fax: 503–641–7736

Willie D. Barber
Manager, Consumer Relations
Tyson Foods
P.O. Box 2020
Springdale, AR 72765–2020
501–290–4714
Toll free: 800–233–6332
Fax: 501–290–7930

U _______________

Mary Kaup
Senior Supervisor, Customer Service
U–Haul International
Phoenix, AZ 85036–1120
Toll free: 800–528–0463
Fax: 602–263–6984

Alan Kaiser, Director
Corporate Communications
UST
100 West Putnam Avenue
Greenwich, CT 06830
203–661–1100

**Union Fidelity Life Insurance Co.
see Aon Corp.**

Jim Wilkins
Manager, Consumer Relations
Uniroyal Goodrich Tire Co.
P.O. Box 19001
Greenville, SC 29602–9001
Toll free: 800–521–9796
Fax: 864 458–6650

UNISYS Corp.
P.O. Box 500
Blue Bell, PA 19424–0001
Toll free: 800–328–0440

Customer Relations
United Airlines
P.O. Box 66100
Chicago, IL 60666
847–700–6796
Toll free: 800–323–0710

Customer Relations
**United Parcel Service of
America, Inc.**
55 Glenlake Parkway
Atlanta, GA 30328
404–828–6000

**United States Fidelity &
Guarantee Co. (USF&G)**
100 Light Street
Baltimore, MD 21202
410–547–3000

Shirley Stewart
Director, Customer Service
United Van Lines, Inc.
One United Drive
Fenton, MO 63026
Toll free: 800–325–9980 (customer service)
Toll free: 800–325–9970 (claims)

Dawn Windholz
Supervisor, Customer Service
Unocal Corp.
17700 Castleton Street, Suite 500
City of Industry, CA 91748
818–854–7063
Toll free: 800–527–5476 (problems with service stations)
Toll free: 800–944–7676 (credit cards)
Fax: 818–854–7100

**The Upjohn Co.
see Pharmacia and UpJohn
Corp.**

Deborah Thompson
Director, Consumer Affairs
USAir
P.O. Box 1501
Winston–Salem, NC 27102–1501
910–661–0061
Fax: 910–661–8187

**U.S. Shoe Corp.
see Nine West**

**U.S. Sprint
see Sprint**

US WEST, Inc.
Customer Response Center
Toll free: 800–255–6920
TDD toll free: 800–955–5833

V _______________

Michael Cornett
Director, Customer Service
Valvoline Oil Co.
3499 Dabney Drive
P.O. Box 14000
Lexington, KY 40512
606–357–7777
Toll free: 800–354–9061
Fax: 606–352–7918

Pat Jordan
Van Camp Seafood Co.
4510 Executive Drive, Suite 300
San Diego, CA 92121
619–597–4275

Van Heusen Co.
1001 Frontier Road
Bridgewater, NJ 08807
908–685–0050

Vanity Fair
640 Fifth Avenue
New York, NY 10019
Toll free: 800–366–8334

Hilary E. Condit
Vice President, Corporate Relations
Viacom, Inc.
1515 Broadway, 52nd Floor
New York, NY 10036
212–258–6346

Vicorp Restaurants, Inc.
400 West 48th Avenue
Denver, CO 80216
303–296–2121
Fax: 303–672–2673

Customer Relations
Visa USA, Inc.
P.O. Box 8999
San Francisco, CA 94128–8999
415–432–3200
Fax: 415–432–4153
(Cardholders should always call issuing
bank first.)

Consumer Affairs
Vons Companies, Inc.
P.O. Box 3338
Los Angeles, CA 90051
818–821–7000

W _______________

Customer Service Representative
Wagner Spray Tech Corp.
1770 Fernbrook Lane
Plymouth, MN 55447
612–553–7000
Toll free: 800–328–8251

Customer Relations
Walgreen Co.
200 Wilmot Road
Deerfield, IL 60015
847–940–2500
Toll free: 800–289–2273

Customer Relations
Wal-Mart Stores, Inc.
702 S.W. Eighth Street
Bentonville, AR 72716–0117
501–273–4000

Rebecca Pierce
Consumer Affairs Manager
Wamsutta Pacific
1285 Avenue of the Americas
34th Floor
New York, NY 10019
212–903–2000
Toll free: 800–344–2142

Wang Laboratories, Inc.
600 Technology Park Drive
Billerca, MA 01821–4130
508–967–5000
Toll free: 800–639–9264
Fax: 508–967–0829

Daniel Pruolx
Manufacturing Vice President
Warnaco Men's Apparel
10 Water Street
Waterville, ME 04901
207–873–4241

Mitch Rosalsky, Director
Consumer Affairs Division
Warner-Lambert Co.
201 Tabor Road
Morris Plains, NJ 07950
201–540–2459
Toll free: 800–223–0182
Toll free: 800–524–2624 (Parke Davis products/over-the-counter)
Toll free: 800–742–8377 (Schick razor)
Toll free: 800–562–0266 (EPT)
Toll free: 800–223–0182 (Warner-Lambert products)
Toll free: 800–524–2854 (Trident)
TDD toll free: 800–343–7805

Customer Service
Weider Health and Fitness
21100 Erwin Street
Woodland Hills, CA 91367
818–884–6800
Fax: 818–704–5734

Consumer Affairs
Weight Watchers Food
P.O. Box 10
Boise, ID 83707
Toll free: 800–651–6000

**Welch's
see Dr Pepper/Seven-Up
Companies, Inc.**

Karen Wegmann
Executive Vice President
Corporate Community Development Group
Wells Fargo & Co.
420 Montgomery Street
MAC 0101–121
San Francisco, CA 94163
415–396–3832
TDD: 916–322–1700

Susan Kosling
Consumer Relations Manager
Wendy's International, Inc.
P.O Box 256
Dublin, OH 43017–0256
614–764–6800

Joanne Turchany
Manager of Consumer Information
West Bend Co.
400 Washington Street
West Bend, WI 53095
414–334–2311

Karen Walters
Senior Operations Manager
Customer Service
**Western Union Financial
Services, Inc.**
13022 Hollenberg Drive
Bridgeton, MO 63044
314–291–8000

Jackie McWhorter
Consumer Affairs Coordinator
WestPoint Stores
P.O. Box 609
West Point, GA 31833–0609
Toll free: 800–533–8229

Customer Relations Department
Whirlpool Corp.
2303 Pipestone Road
Benton Harbor, MI 49022–2427
616–926–5000
Toll free: 800–253–1301

**White Westinghouse Appliances
see The Frigidaire Co.**

Marc Seim
Manager, Consumer Affairs
Whitehall-Robins Health Care
1405 Cummings Drive
Richmond, VA 23261–6609
804–257–2000
Toll free: 800–762–4672

Customer Service
Williams-Sonoma
100 North Point Street
San Francisco, CA 94133
Toll free: 800–541–1262

C.H. McKellar
Executive Vice President
Winn Dixie Stores Inc.
Box B
Jacksonville, FL 32203
904–783–5000

Steven R. Evenson
Service Operations Manager
Winnebago Industries
P.O. Box 152
Forest City, IA 50436–0152
515–582–6939

**Winthrop Consumer Products
see Bayer Corp.**

Corporate Communications
Wisconsin Bell
722 North Broadway, 13th Floor
Milwaukee, WI 53202–4396
414–678–0681
Toll free: 800237–8576
TDD toll free in WI: 800–242–9393

Customer Service
F.W. Woolworth Co.
233 Broadway
New York, NY 10279–0001
212–553–2000

Customer Service
**World Book Educational
Products**
101 Northwest Point Blvd.
Elk Grove Village, IL 60007–1192
Toll free: 800–621–8202

Pam Daugherty
Consumer Relations
Wrangler
P.O. Box 21488
Greensboro, NC 27420
910–332–3564

Barbara Zibell
Consumer Affairs Administrator
Wm. Wrigley Jr. Co.
410 North Michigan Avenue
Chicago, IL 60611
312–644–2121

X

Customer Relations
Xerox Corp.
100 Clinton Avenue South
Rochester, NY 14644
716–423–5490

Y

Lindsey Foster
Manager, Customer Relations
Yamaha Motor Corp.
6555 Katella Avenue
Cypress, CA 90630–5101
714–761–7439
Fax: 714–761–7559

Lori L. Wren
Manager, Consumer Relations
The Yardley Limited Co.
P.O. Box 372
Memphis, TN 38101–0372
901–320–2166
Fax: 901–320–5132

Z

Laura Moore
Vice President
Zale Corp.
901 West Walnut Hill Lane
Irving, TX 75038–1003
214–580–5104
Fax: 214–580–5523

Consumer Affairs
Zenith Electronics Corp.
1000 Milwaukee Avenue
Glenview, IL 60025–2493
847–391–8100
Toll free: 800–488–8129

Penny Flanagen
Customer Service Supervisor
Zenith Packard Bell
8285 West 3500 South
Magna, UT 84044
Toll free: 800–227–3360
Fax: 708–808–4468

Car Manufacturers

If you have a problem with a car purchased from a local dealer, first try to work it out with the dealer. If the problem is not resolved, contact the manufacturer's regional or national office. Many of these are listed in this section.

If you still cannot resolve your problem, contact one of the third-party dispute resolution programs. The list of these programs begins on page 68. Be sure to contact your local or state consumer agency to see if your state offers state-run dispute resolution programs.

If you suspect you have a vehicle problem that might fall under your state's lemon law, call your local or state consumer agency to find out about your rights under the lemon law.

Be sure to review the automobile tips beginning on page 9.

If you have a safety problem with your vehicle, you can report it to the Auto Safety Hotline at the National Highway Traffic Safety Administration (see page 110). Also contact NHTSA to obtain recall and crash test information. (Note: no complaint handling is provided.)

Acura

Customer Relations Department
Acura
1919 Torrance Blvd.
Torrance, CA 90501–2746
Toll free: 800–382–2238

Alfa-Romeo Distributors of North America, Inc.

Owner Relations Manager
Alfa-Romeo Distributors of North America, Inc.
6220 S. Orange Blossom Trail
Suite 209
Orlando, FL 32809
407–856–5000

American Honda Motor Co., Inc.

Corporate Office:
American Honda Motor Co., Inc.
Consumer Affairs Department
1919 Torrance Blvd.
Torrance, CA 90501–2746
310–783–3260

For recall/campaign information, write or fax:
Customer Information Service
1919 Torrance Blvd.
Torrance, CA 90501–2746
Fax: 310–783–3785

California
Customer Relations Department
American Honda Motor Co., Inc.
Western Zone
700 Van Ness Blvd.
Torrance, CA 90509–2260
213–781–4565

Utah, Arizona, Colorado, New Mexico, Nebraska, Kansas, Oklahoma, Nevada, Texas (El Paso)
Customer Relations Department
American Honda Motor Co., Inc.
West Central Zone
1600 South Abilene Street, Suite D
Aurora, CO 80012–5815
303–696–3935

Maine, Vermont, New Hampshire, New York State (excluding NY City, its five boroughs, Long Island, Westchester County), Connecticut (excluding Fairfield County), Massachusetts, Rhode Island
Customer Relations Department
American Honda Motor Co., Inc.
New England Zone
555 Old County Road
Windsor Locks, CT 06096–0465
860–623–3310

Tennessee, Alabama, Georgia, Florida
Customer Relations Department
American Honda Motor Co., Inc.
Southeastern Zone
1500 Morrison Parkway
Alpharetta, GA 30201–2199
404–442–2045

Minnesota, Iowa, Missouri, Wisconsin, Illinois, Michigan (Upper Peninsula)
Customer Relations Department
American Honda Motor Co., Inc.
North Central Zone
601 Campus Drive, Suite A–9
Arlington Heights, IL 60004–1407
847–870–5600 (Honda automobiles only)

West Virginia, Maryland, Virginia, North Carolina, South Carolina, District of Columbia
Customer Relations Department
American Honda Motor Co., Inc.
Mid-Atlantic Zone
902 Wind River Lane, Suite 200
Gaithersburg, MD 20878–1974
301–990–2020

Ohio (Steubenville), West Virginia (Wheeling), Pennsylvania, New Jersey, Delaware, New York (NY City, its five boroughs, Long Island, Westchester County), Connecticut (Fairfield County)
Customer Relations Department
American Honda Motor Co., Inc.
Northeast Zone
115 Gaither Drive
Moorestown, NJ 08057–0337
609–235–5533

Michigan (except for Upper Peninsula), Indiana, Ohio, Kentucky
Customer Relations Department
American Honda Motor Co., Inc.
Central Zone
101 South Stanfield Road
Troy, OH 45373–8010
513–332–6250

Washington, Oregon, Idaho, Montana, Wyoming, North Dakota, South Dakota, Hawaii, Alaska
Customer Relations Department
American Honda Motor Co., Inc.
Northwest Zone
12439 N.E. Airport Way
Portland, OR 97220–0186
503–256–0943

Texas (excluding El Paso), Arkansas (excluding Fayetteville, Bentonville, Fort Smith, Jonesboro), Oklahoma (Lawton, Ardmore), Louisiana, Mississippi
Customer Relations Department
American Honda Motor Co., Inc.
South Central Zone
4529 Royal Lane
Irving, TX 75063–2583
214–929–5481

American Isuzu Motors, Inc.

Headquarters:
American Isuzu Motors, Inc.
Customer Relations Department
2300 Pellisier Place
P.O. Box 995
Whittier, CA 90608
310–699–0500
Toll free: 800–255–6727

California, Alaska, Hawaii, Idaho (northern), Nevada, Oregon, Washington
Regional Customer Relations Manager
American Isuzu Motors, Inc.
One Autry Street
Irvine, CA 92718–2785
714–770–2626

Alabama, Florida, Georgia, Mississippi, North Carolina, South Carolina
Regional Customer Relations Manager
American Isuzu Motors, Inc.
Southeastern Region
205 Hembree Park Drive
P.O. Box 6250
Roswell, GA 30076
404–475–1995

Illinois, Indiana, Iowa, Michigan, Minnesota, Missouri (except Kansas City Metro Area), North Dakota, Ohio, Wisconsin, South Dakota, Nebraska
Regional Customer Relations Manager
American Isuzu Motors, Inc.
Central Region
695 Tollgate Road
Elgin, IL 60123
847–931–8050

Connecticut, Maine, Massachusetts, New Hampshire, New Jersey (north of Toms River), New York, Rhode Island, Vermont
Regional Customer Relations Manager
American Isuzu Motors, Inc.
Northeast Region
3 Stewart Court
P.O. Box 3015
Denville, NJ 07834
201–328–3000

Arizona, Arkansas, Kansas (Kansas City Metro Area), Louisiana, Nevada (southern), New Mexico, Oklahoma, Texas, Colorado, Wyoming, Utah, Montana, Idaho (southern), Missouri (Kansas City Metro area)
Regional Customer Relations Manager
American Isuzu Motors, Inc.
Southwest Region
1150 Isuzu Parkway
Grand Prairie, TX 75050
214–647–2911

New Jersey (south of Toms River), Pennsylvania, Maryland, Delaware, Kentucky, Tennessee, Virginia, West Virginia
Regional Customer Relations Manager
American Isuzu Motors, Inc.
1 Isuzu Way
Glen Burnie, MD 21061
410–761–2121

American Motors Corp. see Chrysler Corp. Zone and Corporate Offices

American Suzuki Motor Corp.

American Suzuki Motor Corp.
P.O. Box 1100
Brea, CA 92822–1100
Attn: Customer Relations Department
714–996–7040, ext. 380 (motorcycles)
Toll free: 800–934–0934 (automotive only)

Audi of America, Inc.

Customer Relations—2F02
Audi of America, Inc.
3800 Hamlin Road
Auburn Hills, MI 48326
Toll free: 800–822–2834 (general assistance and customer relations)
Toll free: 800–955–5100 (replacement and repurchase assistance)

BMW of North America, Inc.

Corporate Office:
National Customer Relations Manager
BMW of North America, Inc.
P.O. Box 1227
Westwood, NJ 07675–1227
Toll free: 800–831–1117

Chrysler Corporation

Corporate Office:
Chrysler Customer Center
Chrysler Corp.
P.O. Box 21–8004
Auburn Hills, MI 48321–8004
Toll free: 800–992–1997
Toll free: 800–763–8422

Phoenix Zone Office
Customer Relations Manager
Chrysler Corp.
11811 N. Tatum Blvd., Suite 4025
Phoenix, AZ 85028–1627
602–494–6820

Los Angeles Zone Office
Customer Relations Manager
Chrysler Corp.
7700 Irvine Center Drive, 3rd Floor
Irvine, CA 92618–2924
714–450–5200
Toll free: 800–207–3025

San Francisco Zone Office
Customer Relations Manager
Chrysler Corp.
6150 Stoneridge Mall Road
Suite 200
P.O. Box 5009
Pleasanton, CA 94566–0509
Toll free: 800–987–9809

Denver Zone Office
Customer Relations Manager
Chrysler Corp.
12225 East 39th Avenue
Denver, CO 80239
303–373–8888

Orlando Zone Office
Customer Relations Manager
Chrysler Corp.
8000 South Orange Blossom Trail
Orlando, FL 32809
407–888–5430

Chicago Zone Office
Customer Relations Manager
Chrysler Corp.
650 Warrenville Road, Suite 502
Lisle, IL 60532
630–515–2450

Kansas City Zone Office
Customer Relations Manager
Chrysler Corp.
P.O. Box 25745
Overland Park, KS 66225–5745
913–469–3000

New Orleans Zone Office
Customer Relations Manager
Chrysler Corp.
One Galleria Blvd.
Metairie, LA 70004
504–833–4800

Washington, D.C. Zone Office
Customer Relations Manager
Chrysler Corp.
P.O. Box 1900
Bowie, MD 20717–1900
301–464–4000
Toll free: 800–763–8422

Minneapolis Zone Office
Customer Relations Manager
Chrysler Corp.
13005 Highway 55 (zip 55441)
Minneapolis, MN 55441–3805
612–553–2546

Syracuse Zone Office
Customer Relations Manager
Chrysler Corp.
5788 Widewaters Parkway
Dewitt, NY 13214–0603
315–445–6954

New York Zone Office
Customer Relations Manager
Chrysler Corp.
500 Route 303
Tappan, NY 10983–1592
914–578–2221

Portland Zone Office
Customer Relations Manager
Chrysler Corp.
10030 S.W. Allen Blvd.
Beaverton, OR 97005
503–526–5555

Philadelphia Zone Office
Customer Relations Manager
Chrysler Corp.
Valley Brook Corporate Center
101 Lindenwood Drive
Malvern, PA 19355–0725
610–251–2990

Pittsburgh Zone Office
Customer Relations Manager
Chrysler Corp.
Penn Center West 3, Suite 420
Pittsburgh, PA 15276–0198
412–788–7070

Memphis Zone Office
Customer Relations Manager
Chrysler Corp.
P.O. Box 18050
Memphis, TN 38181–0050
901–797–3870

Dallas Zone Office
Customer Relations Manager
Chrysler Corp.
P.O. Box 110162
Carrollton, TX 75011–0162
214–418–4600

Houston Zone Office
Customer Relations Manager
Chrysler Corp.
363 North Sam Houston Parkway East
Suite 590
Houston, TX 77060–2404
713–820–7067

Milwaukee Zone Office
Customer Relations Manager
Chrysler Corp.
20935 Swenson Drive
Suite 400
P.O. Box 1634
Waukesha, WI 53187–1634
414–798–3750

Daihatsu America, Inc.

4422 Corporate Center Drive
Los Alamitos, CA 90720
Toll free: 800–777–7070

Ferrari North America, Inc.

Corporate Office:
Umberto Masoni
Director of Service and Parts
Ferrari North America, Inc.
250 Sylvan Avenue
Englewood Cliffs, NJ 07632
201–816–2684

Ford Motor Co.

Customer Relations Manage
Ford Motor Co.
300 Renaissance Center
P.O. Box 43360
Detroit, MI 48243
Toll free: 800–392–3673 (all makes)
Toll free: 800–521–4140 (Lincoln and Merkur only)
Toll free: 800–241–3673 (towing and dealer location service)
TDD toll free: 800–232–5952

General Motors Corp.

Customer Assistance Center
Chevrolet/Geo Motor Division
General Motors Corp.
P.O. Box 7047
Troy, MI 48007–7047
Toll free: 800–222–1020
TDD toll free: 800–TDD–CHEV
Toll free: 800–243–8872 (roadside assistance)

Customer Assistance Center
Pontiac Division
General Motors Corp.
One Pontiac Plaza
Pontiac, MI 48340–2952
Toll free: 800–762–2737
TDD toll free: 800–TDD–PONT

Customer Assistance Network
Oldsmobile Division
General Motors Corp.
P.O. Box 30095
Lansing, MI 48909–7595
Toll free: 800–442–6537
TDD toll free: 800–TDD–OLDS

Customer Assistance Center
Buick Motor Division
General Motors Corp.
902 East Hamilton Avenue
Flint, MI 48550
Toll free: 800–521–7300
TDD toll free: 800–832–8425

Consumer Assistance Center
Cadillac Motor Car Division
General Motors Corp.
P.O. Box 9025
Warren, MI 48090–9025
Toll free: 800–458–8006
TDD toll free: 800–TDD–CMCC

Consumer Assistance Center
GMC Truck Division
General Motors Corp.
31 Judson Street
Pontiac, MI 48342–2230
Toll free: 800–462–8782
TDD toll free: 800–462–8583

Saturn Assistance Center
Saturn Corp.
General Motors Corp.
100 Saturn Parkway
Spring Hill, TN 37174
Toll free: 800–553–6000
TDD toll free: 800–TDD–6000

Honda
see American Honda Motor Co., Inc.

Hyundai Motor America

Consumer Affairs
Hyundai Motor America
10550 Talbert Avenue
P.O. Box 20850
Fountain Valley, CA 92728–0850
Toll free: 800–633–5151

Isuzu
see American Isuzu Motors, Inc.

Jaguar Cars Inc.

U.S. National Headquarters:
Customer Relations Department
Jaguar Cars Inc.
555 MacArthur Boulevard
Mahwah, NJ 07430–2327
201–818–8500
Toll free: 800–452–4827

Jeep/Eagle Division of Chrysler Corp.
see Chrysler Corp. Zone and Corporate Offices

Kia Motor America, Inc.

Owner Relationa Manager
6220 S. Orange Blossom Trail
Suite 209
Orlando, FL 32809
407–856–5000

Mazda Motor of America, Inc.

Corporate Headquarters:
Customer Relations Manager
Mazda Motor of America, Inc.
P.O. Box 19734
Irvine, CA 92713–9734
Toll free: 800–222–5500

Mercedes Benz of North America, Inc.

Customer Assistance Center
1 Glenview Road
Montvale, NJ 07645
Toll free: 800–222–0100
Toll free: 800–367–6372 (800–FOR–MERC)

Mitsubishi Motor Sales of America, Inc.

Corporate Office:
Attn.: Customer Relations
National Consumer Relations Manager
Mitsubishi Motor Sales of America, Inc.
6400 West Katella Avenue
Cypress, CA 90630–0064
Toll free: 800–222–0037

Nissan Motor Corp. in USA

Nissan Motor Corp. in USA
P.O. Box 191
Gardena, CA 90248–0191
Toll free: 800–647–7261 (all consumer inquiries)

Peugeot Motors of America, Inc.

William J. Atanasio
National Customer Relations Manager
Peugeot Motors of America, Inc.
P.O. Box 607
One Peugeot Plaza
Lyndhurst, NJ 07071–3498
201–935–8400
Toll free: 800–345–5549

Porsche Cars North America, Inc.

Manager, Owner Relations
Porsche Cars North America, Inc.
100 West Liberty Street
P.O. Box 30911
Reno, NV 89520–3911
800–545–8039

Saab Cars USA, Inc.

Customer Assistance Center
Saab Cars USA, Inc.
4405–A Saab Drive
P.O. Box 9000
Norcross, GA 30091
Toll free: 800–955–9007

Subaru of America, Inc.

National Customer Service Center
Subaru of America, Inc.
Subaru Plaza
P.O. Box 6000
Cherry Hill, NJ 08034–6000
Toll free: 800–782–2783

Hawaii
Schuman Carriage Co.
1234 S. Beretania Street
P.O. Box 2420
Honolulu, HI 96804
808–553–6211

Suzuki
see American Suzuki Motor Corp.

Toyota Motor Sales, Inc.

Customer Assistance Center
Toyota Motor Sales USA, Inc.
Department A102
19001 South Western Avenue
Torrance, CA 90509–2991
Toll free: 800–331–4331
TDD toll free: 800–443–4999
Fax: 310–618–7814

Volkswagen United States, Inc.

Customer Relations—2F02
Volkswagen United States, Inc.
3800 Hamlin Road
Auburn Hills, MI 48326
Toll free: 800–822–8987 (general assistance and customer relations)

Volvo Cars of North America

Corporate Office.
Customer Service
Volvo Cars of North America
P.O. Box 914
Rockleigh, NJ 07647–0914
201–767–4760
Toll free: 800–458–1552

Trade Associations' and Other Dispute Resolution Programs

Companies that manufacture similar products or offer similar services often belong to industry associations. These associations help resolve problems between their member companies and consumers. Depending on the industry, you might have to contact an association, service council or consumer action program.

If you have a problem with a company and cannot get it resolved with that firm, ask if the company is a member of an association. Then, check this section to see if the association is listed. If the name of the association is not included here, check with a local library.

This list includes the names and addresses of the associations' and other dispute resolution programs that handle consumer complaints for their members. In some cases, the national organizations listed here can refer you to dispute resolution programs near you.

These programs are usually called alternative dispute resolution programs. Generally, there are three types: arbitration, conciliation and mediation. All three methods of dispute resolution vary. Ask for a copy of the rules of the program before you file your case. Generally, the decisions of the arbitrators are binding and must be accepted by both the customer and the business. However, in other forms of dispute resolution, only the business is required to accept the decision. In some programs, decisions are not binding on either party.

Remember, before contacting one of these programs, try to resolve the complaint with the company.

Accrediting Council for Independent Colleges and Schools (ACICS)
750 First Street, N.E., Suite 980
Washington, DC 20002
202–336–6780
Association of accredited career schools training in business and business-related subjects.

Joan McNeal, Director
Member and Industry Relations
American Apparel Manufacturers Association
2500 Wilson Boulevard, Suite 301
Arlington, VA 22201
703–524–1864
Membership: Manufacturers of clothing.

Toni L. Griffin
Director of Public Relations
American Arbitration Association
140 West 51st Street
New York, NY 10020–1203
212–484–4006
A non-profit public service organization with 37 regional offices across the country. Provides consumer information on request. Check local telephone directory for listing. If there is no office in your area, write or call the office listed above.

American Bar Association
Section on Dispute Resolution
740 15th Street, N.W.
Washington, DC 20005
202–662–1680
Publishes a directory of state and local alternative dispute resolution programs. Provides consumer information on request.

Gary Rippentrop, CEO
American Collectors Association
P.O. Box 39106
Minneapolis, MN 55439–0106
612–926–6547
Membership: Collection services handling overdue accounts for retail professional and commercial credit grantors.

American Council of Life Insurance
1001 Pennsylvania Avenue, N.W.
Suite 500 South
Washington, DC 20004–2599
202–624–2000
Membership: Legal reserve life insurance companies authorized to do business in the United States.

American Health Care Association
1201 L Street, N.W.
Washington, DC 20005–4014
202–842–4444
Toll free: 800–321–0343 (publications only)
Membership: State associations of long-term health care facilities. Also, associate business membership program for health related businesses.

Herbert A. Finkston, Director
Professional Ethics Division
American Institute of Certified Public Accountants
Harborside Financial Center
201 Plaza III
Jersey City, NJ 07311–3881
201–938–3175
Membership: Professional organization of accountants certified by the states and territories.

American Orthotic and Prosthetic Association
1650 King Street, Suite 500
Alexandria, VA 22314–1885
703–836–7116
Represents member companies that custom fit or manufacture components for patients with prostheses or orthoses.

Ray Greenly, Vice President
Consumer Affairs
American Society of Travel Agents, Inc.
1101 King Street, Suite 200
Alexandria, VA 22314
703–739–2782
Membership: Travel agents.

Gail A. Raiman, Director
Communications Division
American Textile Manufacturers Institute
1130 Connecticut Avenue, N.W., Suite 1200
Washington, DC 20006
202–862–0552
Membership: Textile plants which produce a variety of textile products, including fabrics for apparel and home furnishings and industrial fabrics.

Automotive Consumer Action Program (AUTOCAP)
8400 Westpark Drive
McLean, VA 22102
703–821–7144
Third-party dispute resolution program administered through the National Automobile Dealers Association. Consumer information available on request.

BBB AUTO LINE
Council of Better Business Bureaus, Inc.
4200 Wilson Boulevard, Suite 800
Arlington, VA 22203–1804
Toll free: 800–955–5100
Third-party dispute resolution program for automobile manufacturers.

Better Hearing Institute (BHI)
P.O. Box 1840
Washington, DC 20013
703–642–0580
Toll free: 800–EAR–WELL
A non-profit educational organization, BHI informs persons with impaired hearing and the general public about hearing loss and available help through medicine, surgery, amplification and other rehabilitation. Membership: professionals and others who help persons with impaired hearing.

Consumer Affairs
Blue Cross and Blue Shield Association
1310 G Street, N.W., 12th Floor
Washington, DC 20005
202–626–4780
Membership: Local Blue Cross and Blue Shield plans in the United States, Canada and Jamaica.

Caroline C. Ajootian
Director, Consumer Protection Bureau
Boat Owners Association of The United States Boat/U.S.
880 South Pickett Street
Alexandria, VA 22304–0730
703–823–9550
The Consumer Protection Bureau serves as a mediator in disputes between boat owners and the marine industry. BOAT/U.S. also works closely with the U.S. Coast Guard to monitor safety defect problems.

Career College Association (CCA)
750 First Street, N.E., Suite 900
Washington, DC 20002
202–336–6700
Membership: Proprietary and trade institutions.

Kathryn Wise
Director of Public Relations
Carpet and Rug Institute
Box 2048
Dalton, GA 30722
Toll free: 800–882–8846
Membership: Manufacturers of carpets, rugs, bath mats; suppliers of raw materials and services to the industry.

Robert M. Fells, Assistant Secretary
Cemetery Consumer Service Council
P.O. Box 2028
Reston, VA 20195–0028
703–391–8407
Industry-sponsored dispute resolution program. Other consumer information about cemetery practices and rules available on request.

Children's Advertising Review Unit (CARU)
Council of Better Business Bureaus, Inc.
845 Third Avenue
New York, NY 10022
212–705–0124
Website: www.bbb.org
Handles consumer complaints about truth and accuracy of advertising directed to children under 12 years of age.

Chrysler Corporation
Chrysler Customer Center
P.O. Box 21–8004
Auburn Hills, MI 48321–8004
Toll free: 800–992–1997

Credit Union National Association (CUNA)
5710 Mineral Point Road
Madison, WI 53705
608–231–4000
Toll free: 800–356–9655
Toll free: 800–358–5710 (to find out if you are eligible to join a credit union)
Website: www.cuna.org (for consumer information and information about credit unions)
Serves more than 90% of credit unions through credit union leagues in all 50 states and the District of Columbia. Credit unions are cooperative non-profit financial institutions owned and controlled by members; they belong to credit union leagues, which belong to CUNA.

Direct Marketing Association (DMA)
1111 19th Street, N.W., Suite 1100
Washington, DC 20036
(written complaints only)
Membership: Members who market goods and services directly to consumers using direct mail, catalogs, telemarketing, magazine and newspaper ads, and broadcast advertising.

DMA operates the Mail Order Action Line, Mail Preference Service and Telephone Preference Service.

For problems with a mail order company, write:
Mail Order Action Line
1111 19th Street, N.W., Suite 1100
Washington, DC 20036

To remove your name and home address from national mailing lists, write:
Mail Preference Service
P.O. Box 9008
Farmingdale, NY 11735–9008

To remove your name from telephone solicitation lists, write:
Telephone Preference Service
P.O. Box 9014
Farmingdale, NY 11735–9014

William Rogal
Code Administrator
Direct Selling Association
1666 K Street, N.W., Suite 1010
Washington, DC 20006–2387
202–293–5760
Membership: Manufacturers and distributors selling consumer products door-to-door and through home-party plans.

Cindy Donahue
Assistant to Executive Director
Distance Education and Training Council
1601 18th Street, N.W.
Washington, DC 20009
202–234–5100
Membership: Home study (correspondence) schools.

Ford Dispute Settlement Board
P.O. Box 5120
Southfield, MI 48086–5120
Toll free: 800–392–3673

Carole M. Rogin, President
Hearing Industries Association
515 King Street, Suite 420
Alexandria, VA 22314
703–684–5744
Membership: Companies engaged in the manufacture and/or sale of hearing aids, their components, parts, and related products and services.

Jeanne Salvatore
Director, Public Relations & Consumer Affairs
Insurance Information Institute
110 William Street
New York, NY 10038
Toll free: 800–942–4242
National Insurance Consumer Helpline is a resource for consumers with automobile, homeowners and life insurance questions. The Helpline is open Monday through Friday from 8 a.m. to 8 p.m., eastern time.

National Headquarters
International Association for Financial Planning (IAFP)
5775 Glenridge Drive, N.E., Suite B–300
Atlanta, GA 30328–5364
404–845–0011
Membership: Individuals involved in financial planning.

Major Appliance Consumer Action Program (MACAP)
20 North Wacker Drive, Suite 1500
Chicago, IL 60606
312–984–5858
Third-party dispute resolution program of the major appliance industry.

Greg Patzer
Executive Vice President
Monument Builders of North America
3158 South River Road, Suite 224
Des Plaines, IL 60018
708–803–8800
Membership: Cemetery monument retailers, manufacturers and wholesalers; bronze manufacturers and suppliers. Consumer brochures available on request.

Shirlene Datcher
Media Relations Coordinator/Consumer Affairs
Mortgage Bankers Association of America
1125 15th Street, N.W., 7th Floor
Washington, DC 20005
202–861–6565
Membership: Mortgage banking firms, commercial banks, life insurance companies, title companies, and savings and loan associations.

National Advertising Division (NAD)

A Division of the Council of Better Business Bureaus, Inc.
845 Third Avenue
New York, NY 10022
212–754–1320
Handles consumer complaints about the truth and accuracy of national advertising.

William Young, Director
Consumer Affairs/Public Liaison

National Association of Home Builders

1201 15th Street, N.W.
Washington, DC 20005
202–822–0409
Toll free: 800–368–5242 (outside DC)
Membership: Single and multi-family home builders, commercial builders and others associated with the building industry.

Diane Callis, President

National Association of Personnel Services (NAPS)

3133 Mt. Vernon Avenue
Alexandria, VA 22305
703–684–0180
Membership: Private employment agencies.

David L. Fox
Director of Public Relations
Ted Besesparis
Public Relations Associate

National Association of Professional Insurance Agents

400 North Washington Street
Alexandria, VA 22314
703–836–9340
Provides consumers practical advice on personal insurance buying through its national outreach program.

Arbitration and Mediation Department

National Association of Securities Dealers, Inc.

33 Whitehall Street, 8th Floor
New York, NY 10004
212–858–4400
Third-party dispute resolution for complaints about over-the-counter stocks and corporate bonds.

Brian Folkerts, Director
Government Affairs and Communications

National Food Processors Association

1401 New York Avenue, N.W.
Washington, DC 20005
202–639–5939
Membership: Commercial packers of such food products as fruit, vegetables, meat, poultry, seafood, and canned, frozen, dehydrated, pickled and other preserved food items.

Laura M. Oatney
Director, Public Affairs & Education

National Futures Association

200 West Madison Street
Chicago, IL 60606–3447
312–781–1370
Toll free: 800–621–3570 (outside IL)
Membership: Futures commission merchants; commodity trading advisers; commodity pool operators; and introducing brokers and associated individuals.

National Tire Dealers and Retreaders Association (NTDRA)

1250 I Street, N.W., Suite 400
Washington, DC 20005
202–789–2300
Toll free: 800–876–8372
Membership: Independent tire dealers and retreaders.

Department of Public Relations

National Turkey Federation

1225 New York Avenue, N.W., Suite 400
Washington, DC 20005
202–898–0100
Membership: Turkey growers, turkey hatcheries, turkey breeders, processors, marketers, and allied industry firms and poultry distributors.

Craig Halverson
Assistant Executive Director

Photo Marketing Association

3000 Picture Place
Jackson, MI 49201
(written complaints only)
Membership: Retailers of photo equipment, film and supplies; firms developing and printing film.

Jane Meyer
Director of Consumer Education

The Soap and Detergent Association

475 Park Avenue South
New York, NY 10016
212–725–1262
Membership: Manufacturers of soap, detergents, fatty acids and glycerine; raw materials suppliers.

Tele-Consumer Hotline

901 15th Street, N.W., Suite 230
Washington, D.C. 20005
Toll free: 800–332–1124
Voice/TDD: (800) 347–7208
Provides information on special telephone products and services for persons with disabilities, selecting a long distance company, money saving tips for people on low income, reducing unsolicited phone calls, telemarketing fraud, dealing with the phone company, pay phones and other issues. All telephone assistance and publications are free of charge, and Spanish-speaking counselors are available.

Marisa Cascio-Gordon
Communications Associate

Toy Manufacturers of America

200 Fifth Avenue, Room 740
New York, NY 10010
212–675–1141
Membership: American toy manufacturers.

Robert E. Whitley, President

U.S. Tour Operators Association (USTOA)

211 East 51st Street, Suite 12–B
New York, NY 10022
212–750–7371
Membership: Wholesale tour operators, common carriers, suppliers and providers of travel services.

State, County and City Government Consumer Protection Offices

City, county and state consumer protection offices provide consumers with important services. They might mediate complaints, conduct investigations, prosecute offenders of consumer laws, license and regulate a variety of professionals, promote strong consumer protection legislation, provide educational materials and advocate in the consumer interest.

City and county consumer offices are familiar with local businesses and local ordinances and state laws. If there is no local consumer office in your area, contact your state consumer office. State offices, sometimes in a separate department of consumer affairs or the attorney general's or governor's office, are familiar with state laws and look for statewide patterns of problems. Consumer protection offices in the U.S. territories also are included.

To save time, call the office before sending in a written complaint. Ask if the office handles the type of complaint you have or if complaint forms are provided.

Many offices distribute consumer alerts on a variety of consumer issues. Call to obtain available educational information on your problem.

This list is arranged in alphabetical order by state name. State, county and city jurisdictions and TDD numbers are in **bold type**.

Alabama

State Office
Dennis Wright, Chief Director
Consumer Affairs Division
Office of Attorney General
11 South Union Street
Montgomery, AL 36130
334–242–7334
Toll free in AL: 800–392–5658
Fax: 334–242–2433

Alaska

The Consumer Protection Section in the Office of the Attorney General has been closed. Consumers with complaints are being referred to the Better Business Bureau (see page 34), small claims court and private attorneys.

American Samoa

Jennifer Joneson
Assistant Attorney General
Consumer Protection Bureau
P.O. Box 7
Pago Pago, AS 96799
011–684–633–4163
Fax: 011–684–633–1838

Arizona

State Offices
Sydney K. Davis, Chief Counsel
Consumer Protection
Office of the Attorney General
1275 West Washington Street, Room 259
Phoenix, AZ 85007
602–542–3702
602–542–5763
(consumer information and complaints)
Toll free in AZ: 800–352–8431
TDD: 602–542–5002
Fax: 602–542–4377

Noreen Matts
Assistant Attorney General
Consumer Protection
Office of the Attorney General
400 West Congress South Building, Suite 315
Tucson, AZ 85701
602–628–6504

County Offices
Stephen Udall, County Attorney
Apache County Attorney's Office
P.O. Box 637
St. Johns, AZ 85936
520–337–4364, ext. 240
Fax: 520–337–2427

Alan Polley, County Attorney
Cochise County Attorney's Office
P.O. Drawer CA
Bisbee, AZ 85603
520–432–9377
Fax: 520–432–4208

Terence C. Hance, County Attorney
Coconino County Attorney's Office
Coconino County Courthouse
100 East Birch
Flagstaff, AZ 86001
520–779–6518
Fax: 520–779–5618

Jerry B. DeRose, County Attorney
Gila County Attorney's Office
1400 East Ash Street
Globe, AZ 85501
520–425–3231
Fax: 520–425–3720

Jack M. Williams, County Attorney
Graham County Attorney's Office
Graham County Courthouse
800 West Main
Safford, AZ 85546
520–428–3620
520–428–7200

Dennis L. Lusk, County Attorney
Greenlee County Attorney's Office
P.O. Box 1717
Clifton, AZ 85533
520–865–4108
Fax: 520–865–4665

Steven P. Suskin, County Attorney
La Paz County Attorney's Office
1320 Kofa Avenue
P.O. Box 709
Parker, AZ 85344
520–669–6118
Fax: 520–669–2019

William Ekstrom, County Attorney
Mohave County Attorney's Office
315 North 4th Street
P.O. Box 7000
Kingman, AZ 86402–7000
520–753–0719
Fax: 520–753–2669

Melvin Bowers, County Attorney
Navajo County Attorney's Office
P.O. Box 668
Holbrook, AZ 86025
520–524–4026
Fax: 520–524–4244

Stephen D. Neely, County Attorney
Pima County Attorney's Office
1400 Great American Tower
32 North Stone
Tucson, AZ 85701
520–740–5733
Fax: 520–791–3946

Robert Carter Olson
Pinal County Attorney
P.O. Box 887
Florence, AZ 85232
520–868–6271
Fax: 520–868–6521

Jan Smith Florez, County Attorney
Santa Cruz County Attorney's Office
2100 N. Congress Drive, Suite 201
Nogales, AZ 85621
520–287–2468

Charles Hastings, County Attorney
Yavapai County Attorney's Office
Yavapai County Courthouse
Prescott, AZ 86301
520–771–3344
Fax: 520–771–3110

David S. Ellsworth, County Attorney
Yuma County Attorney's Office
168 South Second Avenue
Yuma, AZ 85364
520–329–2270
Fax: 520–329–2284

City Office
Ronald M. Detrick
Deputy City Attorney
Consumer Affairs Division
Tucson City Attorney's Office
110 East Pennington Street, 2nd Floor
P.O. Box 27210
Tucson, AZ 85726–7210
520–791–4886

Arkansas
State Office
Kay Dewitt, Director
Consumer Protection Division
Office of Attorney General
200 Catlett Prien
323 Center Street
Little Rock, AR 72201
501–682–2341
TDD: 501–682–2014
Voice/TDD toll free in AR:
800–482–8982

California
State Offices
Marjorie Berte, Director
California Department of Consumer Affairs
400 R Street, Suite 3000
Sacramento, CA 95814
916–445–4465
TDD: 916–322–1700
Toll free in CA: 800–952–5200

Office of Attorney General
Public Inquiry Unit
P.O. Box 944255
Sacramento, CA 94244–2550
916–322–3360
TDD: 916–324–5564
Toll free in CA: 800–952–5225

Marty Keller, Chief
Bureau of Automotive Repair
California Department of Consumer Affairs
10240 Systems Parkway
Sacramento, CA 95827
916–445–1254
TDD: 916–322–1700
Toll free in CA: 800–952–5210
(auto repair only)

County Offices
Aldene Croswell, Commissioner
Alameda County Consumer Affairs
Commission
4400 MacArthur Boulevard
Oakland, CA 94619
510–535–6444

Gary Yancey, District Attorney
Contra Costa County District Attorney's Office
725 Court Street, 4th Floor
P.O. Box 670
Martinez, CA 94553
510–646–4500
Fax: 510–646–2116

Alan Yengoyan
Senior Deputy District Attorney
Business Affairs Unit
Fresno County District Attorney's Office
1250 Van Ness Avenue, 2nd Floor
Fresno, CA 93721
209–488–3156
Fax: 209–495–1315

Edward R. Jagels, District Attorney
Criminal Division
Kern County District Attorney's Office
1215 Truxtun Avenue, 4th Floor
Bakersfield, CA 93301
805–861–2421
Fax: 805–861–2797

Monty H. Hopper, Director
Kern County Department of Weights
and Measures
1116 E. California Avenue
Bakersfield, CA 93307
805–861–2418
Fax: 805–324–0668

Pastor Herrera, Jr., Director
Los Angeles County Department
of Consumer Affairs
500 West Temple Street, Room B–96
Los Angeles, CA 90012
213–974–1452 (Public)
213–974–9750 (Private)

Marin County Mediation Services
4 Mount Lassen Drive
San Rafael, CA 94903
415–499–7454
Fax: 415–499–6978

Robert Nichols
Deputy District Attorney
Consumer Protection Division
Marin County District Attorney's Office
Hall of Justice, Room 183
3501 Civic Center Drive, Room 183
San Rafael, CA 94903
415–499–6450
Fax: 415–499–3719

Susan Massini, District Attorney
Mendocino County District Attorney's Office
P.O. Box 1000
Ukiah, CA 95482
707–463–4211
Fax: 707–463–4687

Dean D. Flippo
Monterey County District Attorney
Consumer Protection Division
P.O. Box 1369
Salinas, CA 93902
408–755–5073
Fax: 408–755–5608

Daryl A. Roberts
Deputy District Attorney
Consumer Affairs Division
Napa County District Attorney's Office
931 Parkway Mall
P.O. Box 720
Napa, CA 94559
707–253–4211
Fax: 707–253–4041

Robert C. Gannon, Jr.
Supervising Deputy District Attorney
Consumer/Environmental Protection Unit
405 W. 5th Street, Suite 606
Santa Ana, CA 92701
714–568–1240
Fax: 714–568–1250

Jay Orr
Deputy District Attorney
Economic Crime Division
Riverside County District Attorney's Office
4075 Main Street
Riverside, CA 92501
909–275–5400
Fax: 909–275–5470

M. Scott Prentice
Supervising Deputy District Attorney
Consumer and Environmental
Protection Division
Sacramento County District Attorney's Office
P.O. Box 749
Sacramento, CA 95812–0749
916–440–6174

Anthony Samson, Director
Consumer Fraud Division
San Diego County District Attorney's Office
P.O. Box X–1011
San Diego, CA 92112–4192
619–531–3507 (fraud complaint
message line)

Consumer Protection Unit
San Francisco County District
Attorney's Office
732 Brannan Street
San Francisco, CA 94103
415–552–6400 (public inquiries)
415–553–1814 (complaints)
Fax: 415–552–7038

Lorrie Rogers
Consumer Mediator
San Joaquin County District Attorney's Office
222 East Weber, Room 412
P.O. Box 990
Stockton, CA 95202
209–468–2481
Fax: 209–468–0314

Leigh Lawrence
Director, Economic Crime Unit
Consumer Fraud Department
County Government Center
1050 Monterey Street, Room 235
San Luis Obispo, CA 93408
805–781–5856

John E. Wilson, Deputy in Charge
Consumer Fraud and Environmental
Protection Unit
San Mateo County District Attorney's Office
401 Marshall Street
Hall of Justice and Records
Redwood City, CA 94063
415–363–4656
Fax: 415–363–4873

Allan Kaplan, Senior Deputy
District Attorney
Consumer Protection Unit
Santa Barbara County District
Attorney's Office
1105 Santa Barbara Street
Santa Barbara, CA 93101
805–568–2300
Fax: 805–568–2398

Al Bender
Deputy District Attorney
Consumer Fraud Unit
Santa Clara County District Attorney's Office
70 West Hedding Street, West Wing
San Jose, CA 95110
408–299–8478
Fax: 408–279–8742

Patricia McRae, Coordinator
Santa Clara County Consumer
Protection Unit
70 West Hedding Street
West Wing, Lower Level
San Jose, CA 95110–1705
408–299–4211

Robin McFarland Gysin
Coordinator, Division of Consumer Affairs
Santa Cruz County District Attorney's Office
701 Ocean Street, Room 200
Santa Cruz, CA 95060
408–454–2050
Fax: 408–454–2227

Criselda B. Gonzalez
Deputy District Attorney
Consumer Affairs Unit
Solano County District Attorney's Office
600 Union Avenue
Fairfield, CA 94533
707–421–6860
Fax: 707–421–7986

Thomas Quinlan
Deputy District Attorney
Consumer Fraud Unit
Stanislaus County District Attorney's Office
P.O. Box 442
Modesto, CA 95353–0442
209–525–5550
Fax: 209–525–5545

Greg Brose, Deputy District Attorney
Consumer and Environmental
Protection Division
Ventura County District Attorney's Office
800 South Victoria Avenue
Ventura, CA 93009
805–654–3110

Mark Jerome Jones
Chief Deputy District Attorney
Special Services Unit–
Consumer/Environmental
Yolo County District Attorney's Office
P.O. Box 245
Woodland, CA 95776
916–666–8424
Fax: 916–666–8423

City Offices
Donald Kass
Supervising Deputy City Attorney
Consumer Protection Division
Los Angeles City Attorney's Office
200 North Main Street
1600 City Hall East
Los Angeles, CA 90012
213–485–4515
Fax: 213–237–0402

Kimery A. Shelton
Deputy City Attorney
Teresa Bransfield
Consumer Affairs Specialist
Consumer Protection, Fair Housing
& Public Rights Unit
1685 Main Street, Room 310
Santa Monica, CA 90401
310–458–8336
310–458–8370 (Spanish hotline)
Fax: 310–395–6727

Colorado
State Office
Consumer Protection Unit
Office of Attorney General
1525 Sherman St., 5th Floor
Denver, CO 80203–1760
303–866–5189

County Offices
Sarah Law, District Attorney
Archuleta, LaPlata and San Juan Counties
District Attorney's Office
P.O. Drawer 3455
Durango, CO 81302
970–247–8850
Fax: 970–259–0200

Alex Hunter, District Attorney
Boulder County District Attorney's Office
P.O. Box 471
Boulder, CO 80306
303–441–3700
Fax: 303–441–4703

Phillip A. Parrott, Chief
Deputy District Attorney
Lisa Curtis, Director of Consumer Services
Denver District Attorney's Economic
Crimes Division
303 West Colfax Avenue, Suite 1300
Denver, CO 80204
303–640–5956 (administration)
303–640–3557 (complaints)
Fax: 303–640–2592

David Zook
Chief Deputy District Attorney
Economic Crime Division
El Paso and Teller Counties District
Attorney's Office
105 East Vermijo, Suite 205
Colorado Springs, CO 80903–2083
719–520–6002
Fax: 719–520–6006

Gus Sandstrom, District Attorney
Pueblo County District Attorney's Office
201 West 8th Street, Suite 801
Pueblo, CO 81003
719–583–6030
Fax: 719–583–6666

A.M. Dominguez, Jr., District Attorney
Tony Molocznik, Chief Investigator
Weld County District Attorney's Office
P.O. Box 1167
Greeley, CO 80632
970–356–4010
Fax: 970–352–8023

Connecticut
State Offices
Mark A. Shiffrin, Commissioner
Department of Consumer Protection
165 Capitol Avenue
Hartford, CT 06106
860–566–2534
Toll free in CT: 800–842–2649
Fax: 860–566–1531

Steven M. Rutstein
Assistant Attorney General
Antitrust/Consumer Protection
Office of Attorney General
110 Sherman Street
Hartford, CT 06105
860–566–5374
Fax: 860–523–5536

City Office
Philip P. Cacciola, Director
Middletown Office of Consumer Protection
City Hall
245 DeKoven Drive
P.O. Box 1300
Middletown, CT 06457
860–344–3491
TDD: 860–344–3521
Fax: 860–344–0136

Delaware
State Offices
Mary McDonough, Director
Consumer Protection Unit
Department of Justice
820 North French Street
Wilmington, DE 19801
302–577–3250
Fax: 302–577–6499

Eugene M. Hall, Deputy Attorney General
Fraud and Consumer Protection Unit
Office of Attorney General
820 North French Street
Wilmington, DE 19801
302–577–2500
Fax: 302–577–6499

District of Columbia
Hampton Cross, Director
Department of Consumer and
Regulatory Affairs
614 H Street, N.W.
Washington, DC 20001
202–727–7120
Fax: 202–727–8073
Fax: 202–727–7842

Florida
State Offices
James P. Kelly, Director
Department of Agriculture and
Consumer Services
Division of Consumer Services
407 South Calhoun Street
Mayo Building, 2nd Floor
Tallahassee, FL 32399–0800
904–488–2221
Fax: 904–487–4177
Toll free in FL: 800–435–7352

Jack A. Norris, Jr., Chief
Consumer Litigation Section
110 S.E. 6th Street
Fort Lauderdale, FL 33301
954–712–4600
Fax: 954–712–4706

Cecile Dykas
Assistant Deputy Attorney General
Economic Crimes Division
Office of Attorney General
110 S.E. 6th Street
Fort Lauderdale, FL 33301
954–712–4600
Fax: 954–712–4658

County Offices
Mona Fandel, Director
Broward County Consumer Affairs Division
115 S. Andrews Avenue
Annex Room A460
Fort Lauderdale, FL 33301
305–765–5355
Fax: 305–765–5199

Leonard Elias, Consumer Advocate
Metropolitan Dade County
Consumer Protection Division
140 West Flagler Street, Suite 902
Miami, FL 33130
305–375–4222

Frederic A. Kerstein, Chief
Dade County Economic Crime Unit
Office of State Attorney
1350 N.W. 12th Avenue, 5th Floor
Graham Building
Miami, FL 33136–2111
305–547–0671

Harold Delk, Director
Hillsborough County Commerce Dept.
Consumer Protection Unit
P.O. Box 1110
Tampa, FL 33601
813–272–6750

Larry F. Blalock, Chief
Orange County Consumer Fraud Unit
250 North Orange Avenue
P.O. Box 1673
Orlando, FL 32802
407–836–2490

Citizens Intake
Office of the State Attorney
401 N. Dixie Highway, Suite 1600
West Palm Beach, FL 33401
407–355–7108
Fax: 561–355–7192

Lawrence Breeden, Director
Palm Beach County Division of
Consumer Affairs
50 South Military Trail, Suite 201
West Palm Beach, FL 33415
561–233–4820
Fax: 561–233–4838

George Mangrum
Consumer Affairs/Code Compliance Manager
Pasco County Consumer Affairs Division
7530 Little Road, Suite 140
New Port Richey, FL 34654
813–847–8110
Fax: 813–847–8969

Sheryl Lord, Director
Pinellas County Office of Consumer
Protection
P.O. Box 17268
Clearwater, FL 34622–0268
813–464–6129
Fax: 813–464–6200

City Offices
Dana A. Fernety
Chief of Consumer Affairs
City of Jacksonville
Division of Consumer Affairs
421 W. Church Street, Suite 404
Jacksonville, FL 32202
904–630–3667
Fax: 904–630–3638

Katherine Bryant
Department Secretary
Lauderhill Consumer Protection Board
1176 N.W. 42nd Way
Lauderhill, FL 33313
954–321–2456
TDD: 954–321–2455

Georgia
State Office
Barry W. Reid, Administrator
Governor's Office of Consumer Affairs
2 Martin Luther King, Jr. Drive, S.E.
Suite 356
Atlanta, GA 30334
404–656–3790
Toll free in GA: 800–869–1123
Fax: 404–651–9018

Hawaii

State Offices

JoAnn M. Uchida, Executive Director
Office of Consumer Protection
Department of Commerce and
Consumer Affairs
235 South Beretania Street, Room 801
P.O. Box 3767
Honolulu, HI 96813–3767
808–586–2636
Fax: 808–586–2640

Gene Murayama, Investigator
Office of Consumer Protection
Department of Commerce and
Consumer Affairs
75 Aupuni Street
Hilo, HI 96720
808–974–6230

Janice Borngraber, Investigator
Office of Consumer Protection
Department of Commerce and
Consumer Affairs
54 High Street
P.O. Box 1098
Wailuku, HI 96793
808–984–8244

Idaho

State Office

Brett De Lange, Deputy Attorney General
Office of the Attorney General
Consumer Protection Unit
650 West State Street
Boise, ID 83720–0010
208–334–2424
Toll free in ID: 800–432–3545
Fax: 208–334–2830

Illinois

State Offices

Jim Ryan, Attorney General
Governors Office of Citizens Assistance
222 South College
Springfield, IL 62706
217–782–0244
Toll free in IL: 800–642–3112
(handles problems related to state
government)

Patricia Kelly, Chief
Consumer Protection Division
Office of Attorney General
100 West Randolph, 12th Floor
Chicago, IL 60601
312–814–3000
TDD: 312–793–2852

Charles Gil Fergus, Bureau Chief
Consumer Fraud Bureau
100 West Randolph, 13th Floor
Chicago, IL 60601
312–814–3580
TDD: 312–814–3374
Toll free in IL: 800–386–5438

Regional Offices

Assistant Attorney General
Carbondale Regional Office
Office of Attorney General
1001 E. Main Professional Park East
Carbondale, IL 62901
618–457–3505
TDD: 618–457–4421

Bruce Ratcliffe
Assistant Attorney General
Champaign Regional Office
34 East Main Street
Champaign, IL 61820
Voice/TDD: 217–333–7691
Toll free: 800–243–0618
Fax: 217–244–0022

Deborah Hagan
Assistant Attorney General and Chief
Consumer Fraud Bureau
Office of Attorney General
500 South Second Street
Springfield, IL 62706
217–782–9020
Toll free in IL: 800–252–8666
Toll free in Chicago: 800–386–5438

County Offices

Raymond Threlkeld, Supervisor
Consumer Fraud Division–303
Cook County Office of State's Attorney
303 Daley Center
Chicago, IL 60602
312–345–2400

William Haine, State's Attorney
Madison County Office of State's Attorney
157 N. Main, Suite 402
Edwardsville, IL 62025
618–692–6280
Fax: 618–656–7312

City Offices

Caroline O. Shoenberger
Commissioner
Chicago Department of Consumer Services
121 North LaSalle Street, Room 808
Chicago, IL 60602
312–744–4006
TDD: 312–744–9385
Fax: 312–744–9089

Sharon Carter, Administrator
Consumer Protection Office
City of Des Plaines
1420 Miner Street
Des Plaines, IL 60016
847–391–5006
Fax: 847–391–5378

Indiana

State Office

Lisa Hayes
Chief Counsel and Director
Consumer Protection Division
Office of Attorney General
Indiana Government Center South, 5th Floor
402 West Washington Street
Indianapolis, IN 46204
317–232–6330
Toll free in IN: 800–382–5516

County Office

Scott C. Newman
Marion County Prosecuting Attorney
560 City-County Building
200 East Washington Street
Indianapolis, IN 46204–3363
317–327–5338
Fax: 317–327–5409

Iowa

State Office

William Branch
Assistant Attorney General
Consumer Protection Division
Office of Attorney General
1300 East Walnut Street, 2nd Floor
Des Moines, IA 50319
515–281–5926
Fax: 515–281–6771

Kansas

State Office

C. Steven Rarrick
Deputy Attorney General
Consumer Protection Division
Office of Attorney General
301 West 10th
Kansas Judicial Center
Topeka, KS 66612–1597
913–296–3751
Toll free in KS: 800–432–2310
Fax: 913–291–3699

County Office

Consumer Fraud Division
Johnson County District Attorney's Office
Johnson County Courthouse
P.O. Box 728
Olathe, KS 66051
913–764–8484, ext. 5287
Fax: 913–791–5011

City Office

City Attorney's Office
215 Southeast 7th Street
Topeka, KS 66603
913–368–3885
Fax: 913–368–3901

Kentucky
State Offices
Todd Leatherman, Director
Consumer Protection Division
Office of Attorney General
1024 Capital Center Drive
P.O. Box 2000
Frankfort, KY 40601–2000
502–573–2200

Robert L. Winlock, Administrator
Consumer Protection Division
Office of Attorney General
107 South 4th Street
Louisville, KY 40202
502–595–3262
Fax: 502–595–4627

Louisiana
State Office
Tamera R. Velasquez, Chief
Consumer Protection Section
Office of Attorney General
1 America Place
P.O. Box 94095
Baton Rouge, LA 70804–9095
504–342–9638
Fax: 504–342–9637

County Office
Albert H. Olsen, Chief
Consumer Protection Division
Jefferson Parish District Attorney's Office
Gretna Courthouse Annex, 5th Floor
Gretna, LA 70053
504–364–3644
Fax: 504–364–3636

Maine
State Offices
William N. Lund, Director
Office of Consumer Credit Regulation
State House Station
Augusta, ME 04333–0035
207–624–8527
Toll free in ME: 800–332–8529
Fax: 207–582–7699

Stephen Wessler, Chief
Consumer and Antitrust Division
Office of Attorney General
State House Station No. 6
Augusta, ME 04333
207–626–8849

Maryland
State Offices
William Leibovici, Chief
Consumer Protection Division
Office of Attorney General
200 St. Paul Place, 16th Floor
Baltimore, MD 21202–2021
410–528–8662 (consumer hotline)
TDD: 410–576–6372 (Baltimore area)
Fax: 410–576–6566

Jack Joyce, Director
Licensing & Consumer Services
Motor Vehicle Administration
6601 Ritchie Highway, N.E.
Glen Burnie, MD 21062
410–768–7535
Fax: 410–768–7167

Emalu Myer
Consumer Affairs Specialist
Eastern Shore Branch Office
Consumer Protection Division
Office of Attorney General
201 Baptist Street, Suite 30
Salisbury, MD 21801–4976
410–543–6642

Larry Munson, Director
Western Maryland Branch Office
Consumer Protection Division
Office of Attorney General
138 East Antietam Street, Suite 210
Hagerstown, MD 21740–5684
301–791–4780

County Offices
Stephen D. Hannan, Administrator
Howard County Office of Consumer Affairs
6751 Columbia Gateway Drive
Columbia, MD 21046
410–313–6420
TDD: 410–313–6401
Fax: 410–313–6424

Joseph T. Giloley, Acting Director
Montgomery County Office
of Consumer Affairs
100 Maryland Avenue, 3rd Floor
Rockville, MD 20850
301–217–7373
Fax: 301–217–7367

Sandra Peaches
Prince George's County Office of
Business and Regulatory Affairs
County Administration Building, Suite L15
Upper Marlboro, MD 20772
301–952–5323
TDD: 301–925–5167
Fax: 301–952–4709

Massachusetts
State Offices
George Weber, Chief
Consumer and Antitrust Division
Department of Attorney General
1 Ashburton Place
Boston, MA 02108
617–727–2200
(information and referral to local consumer
offices that work in conjunction with the
Department of Attorney General)
Fax: 617–727–5765

Priscilla H. Douglas, Secretary
Executive Office of Consumer Affairs
and Business Regulation
One Ashburton Place, Room 1411
Boston, MA 02108
617–727–7780
(information and referral only)
Fax: 617–227–6094

Thomas J. McCormick
Assistant Attorney General
Western Massachusetts Consumer
Protection Division
Department of Attorney General
436 Dwight Street
Springfield, MA 01103
413–784–1240
Fax: 413–784–1244

County Offices
Paul Finnegan, Case Coordinator
Consumer Fraud Prevention
North Western District Attorney's Office
238 Main Street
Greenfield, MA 01301
413–774–5102
Fax: 413–773–3278

Stephen Gary-Saindon, Director
Consumer Fraud Prevention
Hampshire County District Attorney's Office
1 Court Square
Northampton, MA 01060
413–586–9225
Fax: 413–584–3635

D'Shone Swiney, Director
Consumer Council of Worcester County
484 Main Street, 2nd Floor
Worcester, MA 01608–1690
508–754–1176
Fax: 508–754–0203

City Offices
Donna M. Mueller, Commissioner
Mayor's Office of Consumer Affairs
and Licensing
Boston City Hall, Room 817
Boston, MA 02201
617–635–4165
Fax: 617–635–4174

Jean Courtney, Director
Consumer Information Center
Springfield Action Commission
P.O. Box 1449 Main Office
Springfield, MA 01101
413–263–6513
(Hamden and Hampshire Counties)
Fax: 413–263–6514

Michigan
State Offices
Frederick H. Hoffecker
Assistant in Charge
Consumer Protection Division
Office of Attorney General
P.O. Box 30213
Lansing, MI 48909
517–373–1140
Fax: 517–335–1935

Rodger James, Director
Bureau of Automotive Regulation
Michigan Department of State
Lansing, MI 48918–1200
517–373–4777
Toll free in MI: 800–292–4204
Fax: 517–373–0964

County Offices
Juliane M. Tanner, Chief Investigator
Bay County Consumer Protection Unit
Bay County Building
Bay City, MI 48708–5994
517–895–4139

Margaret DeMuynck, Director
Consumer Protection Department
Macomb County
Office of the Prosecuting Attorney
Macomb Court Building, 6th Floor
Mt. Clemens, MI 48043
810–469–5350
TDD: 810–466–8714
Fax: 810–469–5609

City Office
Esther K. Shapiro, Director
City of Detroit
Department of Consumer Affairs
1600 Cadillac Tower
Detroit, MI 48226
313–224–3508
Fax: 313–224–2796

Minnesota
State Office
Curt Loewe, Director
Consumer Services Division
Office of Attorney General
1400 NCL Tower
445 Minnesota Street
St. Paul, MN 55101
612–296–3353

County Office
Hennepin County Citizen Information Hotline
Office of the Hennepin County Attorney
C–2000 County Government Center
Minneapolis, MN 55487
612–348–4528
Fax: 612–348–9712

City Office
James Moncur, Director
Minneapolis Department of
Licenses & Consumer Services
One C City Hall
Minneapolis, MN 55415
612–673–2080
Fax: 612–673–3399

Mississippi
State Offices
Leyser Q. Morris
Special Assistant Attorney General
Director, Office of Consumer Protection
P.O. Box 22947
Jackson, MS 39225–2947
601–359–4230
Fax: 601–359–4231
Toll free in MS: 800–281–4418

Joe B. Hardy, Director
Bureau of Regulatory Services
Department of Agriculture and Commerce
121 North Jefferson Street
P.O. Box 1609
Jackson, MS 39201
601–354–7063
Fax: 601–354–6502

Missouri
State Office
Doug Ommen, Chief Counsel
Consumer Protection Division
Office of Attorney General
P.O. Box 899
Jefferson City, MO 65102
573–751–3321
Toll free in MO: 800–392–8222
Fax: 314–751–7948

Montana
State Office
Annie Bartos, Chief Legal Counsel
Consumer Affairs Unit
Department of Commerce
1424 Ninth Avenue
Box 200501
Helena, MT 59620–0501
406–444–4312
Fax: 406–444–2903

Nebraska
State Office
Paul N. Potadle
Assistant Attorney General
Consumer Protection Division
Department of Justice
2115 State Capitol
P.O. Box 98920
Lincoln, NE 68509
402–471–2682
Fax: 402–471 3297

Nevada
State Offices
Patricia Morse Jarman
Commissioner of Consumer Affairs
Department of Business and Industry
1850 East Sahara, Suite 101
Las Vegas, NV 89158
702–486–7355
Toll free in NV: 800–326–5202
TDD: 702–486–7901
Fax: 702–486–7371

Ray Trease, Supervisory Compliance
Investigator
Consumer Affairs Division
Department of Business and Industry
4600 Kietzke Lane, B–113
Reno, NV 89502
702–688–1800
Toll free in NV: 800–326–5202
TDD: 702–486–7901
Fax: 702–688–1803

New Hampshire
State Office
Chief
Consumer Protection and Antitrust Bureau
Office of Attorney General
33 Capitol Street
Concord, NH 03301
603–271–3641
Fax: 603–271–2110

New Jersey
State Offices
Mark S. Herr, Director
Division of Consumer Affairs
P.O. Box 45027
Newark, NJ 07101
201–504–6534
Fax: 201–648–3538

Lauren F. Carlton
Deputy Attorney General
New Jersey Division of Law
P.O. Box 45029
124 Halsey Street, 5th Floor
Newark, NJ 07101
201–648–7579
Fax: 201–648–3879

County Offices
William H. Ross III, Director
Atlantic County Consumer Affairs
1333 Atlantic Avenue, 8th Floor
Atlantic City, NJ 08401
609–345–6700
Fax: 609–343–2164

John Wassberg, Director
Bergen County Office of Consumer
Protection
21 Main Street, Room 101–E
Hackensack, NJ 07601–7000
201–646–2650
Fax: 201–489–6095

Renee L. Borstad, Director
Burlington County Office
of Consumer Affairs
49 Rancocas Road
Mount Holly, NJ 08060
609–265–5098
Fax: 609–265–5065

Patricia M. Tuck, Director
Director/Superintendent, Camden County
Consumer Protection/Weights and Measures
Jefferson House
Lakeland Road
Blackwood, NJ 08012
609–374–6161
Fax: 609–232–0748

E. Robert Spiegel, Director
Cape May County Consumer Affairs
4 Moore Road
Cape May Court House, NJ 08210
609–463–6475

Louis G. Moreno, Director
Cumberland County Department of
Consumer Affairs and Weights
and Measures
788 East Commerce Street
Bridgeton, NJ 08302
609–453–2203
Fax: 609–453–2206

Esther Chernofsky, Senior Contact Person
Essex County Consumer Services
15 South Munn Avenue, 2nd Floor
East Orange, NJ 07018
201–678–8071
201–678–8928

Joseph Silvestro, Director
Gloucester County Department of Consumer
Protection/Weights & Measures
152 North Broad Street
Woodbury, NJ 08096
609–853–3349
609–853–3358
TDD: 609–848–6616

Barbara Donnelly, Director
Hudson County Division
of Consumer Affairs
595 Newark Avenue
Jersey City, NJ 07306
201–795–6295
Fax: 201–795–6462

Helen Mataka, Director
Hunterdon County Consumer Affairs
P.O. Box 283
Lebanon, NJ 08833
908–236–2249

Donna Giovannetti, Division Chief
Mercer County Consumer Affairs
640 South Broad Street, Room 229
P.O. Box 8068
Trenton, NJ 08650–0068
609–989–6671
Fax: 609–989–6670

Lawrence Cimmino, Director
Middlesex County Consumer Affairs
10 Corporate Place South
Piscataway, NJ 08854
908–463–6000
908–463–6008

Dorothy H. Avallone, Director
Monmouth County Consumer Affairs
50 East Main Street
P.O. Box 1255
Freehold, NJ 07728–1255
908–431–7900
Fax: 908–294–5965

Kenneth J. Leake, Director
Ocean County Department of
Consumer Affairs
1027 Hooper Avenue, Bldg. 2
Toms River, NJ 08754–2191
908–929–2105
908–506–5330

Mary Ann Maloney, Director
Passaic County Consumer Affairs
401 Grand, Room 532
Paterson, NJ 07505
201–881–4547
Fax: 201–881–0012

Marianne Mattei
Somerset County Consumer Affairs
County Administration Building
P.O. Box 3000
Somerville, N.J. 08876–1262
908–231–7000, ext. 7400
Fax: 908–707–4127

Ollie Boone, Director
Union County Consumer Affairs
300 North Avenue East
P.O. Box 186
Westfield, NJ 07091
908–654–9840

City Offices
John Ostrowski, Administrator
Cinnaminson Consumer Affairs
P.O. Box 2100
1621 Riverton Road
Cinnaminson, NJ 08077
609–829–6000
Fax: 609–829–3361

Clark Consumer Affairs
430 Westfield Avenue
Clark, NJ 07066
908–388–3600
Fax: 908–388–3839

Elizabeth Consumer Affairs
City Hall
50–60 Winfield Scott Plaza
Elizabeth, NJ 07201
908–820–4183
Fax: 908–820–0112

Bernadine Jacobs, Director
Livingston Consumer Affairs
357 South Livingston Avenue
Livingston, NJ 07039
201–535–7976
Fax: 201–740–9408

Mary Mosley, Director
Maywood Consumer Affairs
459 Maywood Avenue
Maywood, NJ 07607
201–845–2900
201–845–5749
Fax: 201–909–0673

Genevieve Ross, Director
Middlesex Borough Consumer Affairs
1200 Mountain Avenue
Middlesex, NJ 08846
908–356–8090

Mildred Pastore, Director
Mountainside Consumer Affairs
1455 Coles Avenue
Mountainside, NJ 07092
908–232–6600

Max Moses, Deputy Mayor
Director Consumer Affairs
Municipal Building
4233 Kennedy Blvd.
North Bergen, NJ 07047
201–392–2157
201–330–7291
201–330–7292

Annmarie Nicolette, Director
Nutley Consumer Affairs
Public Safety Building
228 Chestnut Street
Nutley, NJ 07110
201–284–4936

Beatrice Albarran, Investigator
Perth Amboy Consumer Affairs
City Hall
1 Olive Street
Perth Amboy, NJ 08861
908–826–0290, ext. 72
Fax: 908–826–8069

Priscilla Castles, Director
Plainfield Action Services
510 Watchung Avenue
Plainfield, NJ 07060
908–753–3519
Fax: 908–753–3540

Secaucus Department of Consumer Affairs
Municipal Government Center
Secaucus, NJ 07094
201–330–2019

Marion Cramer, Director
Union Township Consumer Affairs
Municipal Building
1976 Morris Avenue
Union, NJ 07083
908–688–6763
Fax: 908–686–1633

Charles A. Stern, Director
Wayne Township Consumer Affairs
475 Valley Road
Wayne, NJ 07470
201–694–1800, ext. 3290

John Weitzel, Director
Weehawken Consumer Affairs
400 Park Avenue
Weehawken, NJ 07087
201–319–6005
Fax: 201–319–0112

Herb Gilsenberg
Woodbridge Consumer Affairs
Municipal Building
One Main Street
Woodbridge, NJ 07095
908–634–4500, ext. 6058
Fax: 908–602–6016

New Mexico

State Office
Consumer Protection Division
Office of Attorney General
P.O. Drawer 1508
Santa Fe, NM 87504
505–827–6060
Toll free in NM: 800–678–1508

New York

State Offices
Susan Somers, Deputy Chief
Bureau of Consumer Frauds and Protection
Office of Attorney General
State Capitol
Albany, NY 12224
518–474–5481
Toll free: 800–771–7755 (hotline)
Fax: 518–474–3618

Timothy S. Carey
Chairman and Executive Director
New York State Consumer Protection Board
5 Empire State Plaza, Suite 2101
Albany, NY 12223–1556
518–474–8583
Fax: 518–474–2474

Shirley Sarna
Assistant Attorney General in Charge
Bureau of Consumer Frauds and Protection
Office of Attorney General
120 Broadway
New York, NY 10271
212–416–8345
TDD: 212–416–8940
Toll free: 800–771–7755

Regional Offices
Michael Hanuszczak
Assistant Attorney General in Charge
Central New York Regional Office
44 Hawley Street, 17th Floor
State Office Building
Binghamton, NY 13901
607–721–8779

John R. Drexelius, Jr.
Assistant Attorney General in Charge
Buffalo Regional Office
Office of Attorney General
65 Court Street
Buffalo, NY 14202
716–847–7184
Toll free: 800–771–7755

M. Kevin Coffey
Assistant Attorney General in Charge
Poughkeepsie Regional Office
Office of Attorney General
235 Main Street
Poughkeepsie, NY 12601
914–485–3920
Toll free: 800–771–7755

Charles Genese
Assistant Attorney General in Charge
Rochester Regional Office
Office of Attorney General
144 Exchange Boulevard
Rochester, NY 14614
716–546–7430
TDD: 716–327–3249
Toll free: 800–771–7755

Lynda Nicolino
Assistant Attorney General in Charge
Suffolk Regional Office
Office of Attorney General
300 Motor Parkway
Hauppauge, NY 11788
516–231–2400

Michael L. Hanuszczak
Assistant Attorney General in Charge
Syracuse Regional Office
Office of Attorney General
615 Erie Boulevard West, Suite 102
Syracuse, NY 13204–2465
315–448–4848
Toll free: 800–771–7755

Steven R. Fortnam
Assistant Attorney General in Charge
Utica Regional Office
Office of Attorney General
207 Genesee Street
Utica, NY 13501
315–793–2225
315–793–2228
Toll free: 800–771–7755

County Offices
Nelson Kranker, Director
Dutchess County Department
of Consumer Affairs
38–A Dutchess Turnpike
Poughkeepsie, NY 12603
914–486–2949
Fax: 914–486–2947

Candace K. Vogel
Assistant District Attorney
Consumer Fraud Bureau
Erie County District Attorney's Office
25 Delaware Avenue
Buffalo, NY 14202
716–858–2424

James E. Picken, Commissioner
Nassau County Office of Consumer Affairs
160 Old Country Road
Mineola, NY 11501
516–571–2600
Fax: 515–571–3389

John McCullough, Executive Director
New Justice Conflict
Resolution Services Inc.
1153 West Fayette Street, Suite 301
Syracuse, NY 13204
315–471–4676

Francis D. Phillips II, District Attorney
Orange County District Attorney's Office
255 Main Street
County Government Center
Goshen, NY 10924
914–294–5471

Commissioner
Rockland County Office
of Consumer Protection
County Office Building
18 New Hempstead Road
New City, NY 10956
914–638–5280

Dennis S. Abbey, Director
Steuben County Department of
Weights, Measures and Consumer Affairs
3 East Pulteney Square
Bath, NY 14810
607–776–9631
Voice/TDD: 607–776–9631, ext. 2406

Charles A. Gardner, Director
Suffolk County Executive's Office
of Consumer Affairs
North County Complex, Bldg. 340
Veterans Memorial Highway
Hauppauge, NY 11788
516–853–4600

Jon Van Vlack, Director
Ulster County Consumer Fraud Bureau
P.O. Box 1800
Kingston, NY 12402
914–339–5680

Frank D. Castaldi, Jr.
Chief, Frauds Bureau
Westchester County Courthouse
District Attorney's Office
111 Grove Street
White Plains, NY 10601
914–285–3414
Fax: 914–285–3594

Richard Linkowski, Deputy Director
Westchester County Department
of Consumer Protection
112 East Post Road, 4th Floor
White Plains, NY 10601
914–285–2155
Fax: 914–285–3115

City Offices
Ivan E. Young, Citizen Advocate
Office of Citizen Services
Babylon Town Hall
200 E. Sunrise Highway
Lindenhurst, NY 11757
516–957–7474

Town of Colonie Consumer Protection
Memorial Town Hall
Newtonville, NY 12128
518–783–2790

Stephen Pedone, Commissioner
Mt. Vernon Office of Consumer Protection
City Hall
Mt. Vernon, NY 10550
914–665–2433
Fax: 914–665–2496

José Maldonado, Commissioner
New York City Department
of Consumer Affairs
42 Broadway
New York, NY 10004
212–487–4401
TDD: 212–487–4465
Fax: 212–487–4497

Isabel Butler, Director
Queens Neighborhood Office
New York City Department
of Consumer Affairs
120–55 Queens Blvd., Room 301A
Kew Gardens, NY 11424
718–286–2990
Fax: 718–286–2997

Schenectady Bureau of
Consumer Protection
City Hall, Room 204
Jay Street
Schenectady, NY 12305
518–382–5061

Ralph A. Capozzi, Director
Yonkers Office of Consumer Protection,
Weights and Measures
201 Palisade Avenue
Yonkers, NY 10703
914–377–6807

North Carolina
State Office
Alan S. Hirsch
Special Deputy Attorney General
Consumer Protection Section
Office of Attorney General
Raney Building
P.O. Box 629
Raleigh, NC 27602
919–733–7741
Fax: 919–715–0577

North Dakota
State Offices
Heidi Heitkamp
Office of Attorney General
600 East Boulevard
Bismarck, ND 58505
701–224–2210
Toll free in ND: 800–472–2600

Darrell Grossman, Director
Consumer Protection Division
Office of Attorney General
600 East Boulevard
Bismarck, ND 58505
701–224–3404
Toll free in ND: 800–472–2600

County Office
Kent Keys, Executive Director
Community Action Agency
1013 North 5th Street
Grand Forks, ND 58201
701–746–5431

Ohio
State Offices
Helen MacMurray
Consumer Frauds and Crimes Section
Office of Attorney General
30 East Broad Street
State Office Tower, 25th Floor
Columbus, OH 43266–0410
614–466–4986 (complaints)
TDD: 614–466–1393
Toll free in OH: 800–282–0515

Robert F. Tongren
Office of Consumers' Counsel
77 South High Street, 15th Floor
Columbus, OH 43266–0550
Voice/TDD: 614–466–9605
Toll free in OH: 800–282–9448

County Offices
Tim Ryan, Director
Corrupt Activities Prosecution Unit
Franklin County Office
of Prosecuting Attorney
369 South High Street
Columbus, OH 43215
614–462–3555
Fax: 614–462–6103

George Patricoff
Assistant Prosecuting Attorney
Montgomery County Fraud
and Economic Crimes Division
301 West 3rd Street
Dayton Montgomery County Courts Building
Dayton, OH 45402
513–225–4747
Fax: 513–225–3470

Victor Vigluicci, Prosecuting Attorney
Portage County Office
of Prosecuting Attorney
466 South Chestnut Street
Ravenna, OH 44266–3000
330–296–4593
Fax: 330–297–3856

Maureen O'Connor, Prosecuting Attorney
Summit County Office
of Prosecuting Attorney
53 University Avenue
Akron, OH 44308–1680
330–643–2800
Fax: 330–643–2137 (civil)
Fax: 330–643–8277 (criminal)

City Offices
Department of Neighborhood Services
Division of Human Services
City Hall, Room 126
801 Plum Street
Cincinnati, OH 45202
513–352–3971
Fax: 513–352–5241

Levon Hays
Youngstown Office of Consumer Affairs
and Weights and Measures
26 South Phelps Street
City Hall
Youngstown, OH 44503–1318
330–742–8884
Fax: 330–743–1335

Oklahoma

State Offices
Jane Wheeler
Assistant Attorney General
Office of Attorney General
Consumer Protection Unit
4545 N. Lincoln Blvd., Suite 260
Oklahoma City, OK 73105
405–521–4274
405–521–2029 (consumer hotline)
Fax: 405–528–1867

Charles Jones, Administrator
Department of Consumer Credit
4545 N. Lincoln Blvd., Suite 104
Oklahoma City, OK 73105–3408
405–521–3653
Fax: 405–521–6740

Oregon

State Office
Peter Sheperd, Attorney in Charge
Financial Fraud Section
Department of Justice
1162 Court St. N.E.
Salem, OR 97310
503–378–4732
Fax: 503–373–7067

Pennsylvania

State Offices
Joseph Goldberg, Director
Bureau of Consumer Protection
Office of Attorney General
Strawberry Square, 14th Floor
Harrisburg, PA 17120
717–787–9707
Toll free in PA: 800–441–2555

Irwin A. Popowsky, Consumer Advocate
Office of Consumer Advocate-Utilities
Office of Attorney General
1425 Strawberry Square
Harrisburg, PA 17120
717–783–5048 (utilities only)
Fax: 717–783–7152

Michael Butler
Deputy Attorney General
Bureau of Consumer Protection
Office of Attorney General
1251 South Cedar Crest Blvd.
Suite 309
Allentown, PA 18103
610–821–6690

Mitchell Miller, Director
Bureau of Consumer Services
Pennsylvania Public Utility Commission
P.O. Box 3265
Harrisburg, PA 17105–3265
717–783–1740
Toll free in PA: 800–782–1110
Fax: 717–787–4193

Jesse Harvey
Deputy Attorney General
Bureau of Consumer Protection
Office of Attorney General
919 State Street, Room 203
Erie, PA 16501
814–871–4371
Fax: 814–871–4848

E. Barry Creany
Senior Deputy Attorney General
Bureau of Consumer Protection
Office of the Attorney General
171 Lovell Avenue, Suite 202
Ebensburg, PA 15931
814–949–7900
Toll free in PA: 800–441–2555
Fax: 814–949–7942

John E. Kelly, Deputy Attorney General
Bureau of Consumer Protection
Office of Attorney General
21 South 12th Street, 2nd Floor
Philadelphia, PA 19107
215–560–2414
Toll free in PA: 800–441–2555

Stephanie L. Royal
Deputy Attorney General
Bureau of Consumer Protection
Office of Attorney General
Manor Complex, 6th Floor
564 Forbes Avenue
Pittsburgh, PA 15219
412–565–5394
Toll free in PA: 800–441–2555

J.P. McGowan
Deputy Attorney General
Bureau of Consumer Protection
Office of Attorney General
214 Samters Building
101 Penn Avenue
Scranton, PA 18503–2025
717–963–4913
Fax: 717–963–3418

Regional Office
Office of the Attorney General
Bureau of Consumer Protection
132 Kline Village
Harrisburg, PA 17104
717–787–7109

County Offices
Sidney Elkin, Director
Beaver County Alliance for
Consumer Protection
699 Fifth Street
Beaver, PA 15009–1997
412–728–7267

A. Courtney Yelle, Director/Chief Sealer
Bucks County Consumer Protection,
Weights and Measures
50 North Main Street
Doylestown, PA 18901
215–348–7442
Fax: 215–348–4570

Robert Taylor, Director
Chester County Weights and
Measures/Consumer Affairs
Government Services Center, Suite 390
601 Westtown Road
West Chester, PA 19382–4547
610–344–6150
Toll free in PA: 800–692–1100

Consumer Mediator
Cumberland County Consumer Affairs
One Courthouse Square
Carlisle, PA 17013–3330
717–240–6180
Fax: 717–240–6490

Evelyn Yancoskie, Director
Delaware County Office of
Consumer Affairs, Weights and Measures
Government Center Building
Second and Olive Streets
Media, PA 19063
610–891–4865
Fax: 610–566–3947

Helen Dunigan, Director
Montgomery County Consumer
Affairs Department
County Courthouse
Norristown, PA 19404
610–278–3565
Fax: 610–278–3556

City Office
Bruce Sagel, Chief
Economic Crime Unit
Philadelphia District Attorney's Office
1421 Arch Street
Philadelphia, PA 19102
215–686–8750
Fax: 215–686–8765

Puerto Rico
Jóse Antonio Alicia Rivera, Secretary
Department of Consumer Affairs (DACO)
Minillas Station, P.O. Box 41059
Santurce, PR 00940–1059
787–721–0940
787–726–6570

Pedro R. Pierluisi, Secretary
Department of Justice
P.O. Box 192
San Juan, PR 00902
787–721–2900

Rhode Island
State Offices
Steve Bucci, President
Consumer Credit Counseling Services
535 Centerville Road, Suite 103
Warwick, RI 02886
401–732–1800
Toll free: 800–781–2227
Fax: 401–732–0250

Christine S. Jabour, Esq.
Consumer Protection Division
Department of Attorney General
72 Pine Street
Providence, RI 02903
401–274–4400
TDD: 401–453–0410
Toll free in RI: 800–852–7776
Fax: 401–277–1331

South Carolina
State Offices
Haviard Jones
Senior Assistant Attorney General
Office of Attorney General
P.O. Box 11549
Columbia, SC 29211
803–734–3970
Fax: 803–734–3677

Philip S. Porter
Administrator, Consumer Advocate
Department of Consumer Affairs
P.O. Box 5757
Columbia, SC 29250–5757
803–734–9452
TDD: 803–734–9455
Toll free in SC: 800–922–1594

W. Jefferson Bryson, Jr.
State Ombudsman
Office of Executive Policy and Program
1205 Pendleton Street, Room 308
Columbia, SC 29201
803–734–0457
TDD: 803–734–1147
Fax: 803–734–0546

South Dakota
State Office
Division of Consumer Protection
Office of Attorney General
500 East Capitol
State Capitol Building
Pierre, SD 57501–5070
605–773–4400
TDD: 605–773–6585
Toll free in SD: 800–300–1986
Fax: 605–773–4106

Tennessee
State Offices
Mark Williams, Director
Division of Consumer Affairs
Fifth Floor
500 James Robertson Parkway
Nashville, TN 37243–0600
615–741–4737
Toll free in TN: 800–342–8385
(All complaints must be sent to
the above address at Consumer
Affairs for processing)

Cynthia Carter
Deputy Attorney General
Division of Consumer Protection
Office of Attorney General
500 Charlotte Avenue
Nashville, TN 37243–0491
615–741–3491
Fax: 615–532–2910

Texas
State Offices
Tom Perkins
Assistant Attorney General and Chief
Consumer Protection Division
Office of Attorney General
P.O. Box 12548
Austin, TX 78711
512–463–2070

Robert E. Reyna
Assistant Attorney General
Consumer Protection Division
Office of Attorney General
714 Jackson Street, Suite 800
Dallas, TX 75202–4506
214–742–8944
Fax: 214–939–3930

Valli Jo Acosta
Assistant Attorney General
Consumer Protection Division
Office of Attorney General
6090 Surety Drive, Room 113
El Paso, TX 79905
915–772–9476
Fax: 915–772–9046

Richard Tomlinson
Assistant Attorney General
Consumer Protection Division
Office of Attorney General
1019 Congress Street, Suite 1550
Houston, TX 77002–1702
713–223–5886

Assistant Attorney General
Consumer Protection Division
Office of Attorney General
916 Main Street, Suite 806
Lubbock, TX 79401–3997
806–747–5238
Fax: 806–747 6307

Ric Madrigal
Assistant Attorney General
Consumer Protection Division
Office of Attorney General
3201 North McColl Rd., Suite B
McAllen, TX 78501
210–682–4547
Fax: 210–682–1957

Aaron Valenzuela
Assistant Attorney General
Consumer Protection Division
Office of Attorney General
115 East Travis Street, Suite 925
San Antonio, TX 78205–1615
210–224–1007

Office of Public Insurance Counsel
333 Guadalupe, Suite 3–120
Austin, TX 78701
512–322–4143
Fax: 512–322–4148

County Offices
Richard Reed
Assistant District Attorney and Chief
Dallas County District Attorney's Office
Specialized Crime Division
133 North Industrial Blvd., LB 19
Dallas, TX 75207–4399
214–653–3820
Fax: 214–653–3845

Russel Turbeville
Assistant District Attorney and Chief
Harris County Consumer Fraud Division
Office of District Attorney
201 Fannin, Suite 200
Houston, TX 77002–1901
713–755–5836

City Offices
Beverly Weaver, Director
Department of Environmental and
Health Services
City Hall
1500 Marilla, Room 7A–North
Dallas, TX 75201
214–670–5216

Michael Marcotte, Director
Economic Development
City Hall
500 Marilla, Room 5C–South
Dallas, TX 75201
214–670–1686

Utah

State Office
Francine A. Giani, Director
Division of Consumer Protection
Department of Commerce
160 East 300 South
Box 146704
Salt Lake City, UT 84114–6704
801–530–6601
Toll free in UT: 800–721–7233
Fax: 801–530–6001

Vermont

State Offices
John Hasen
Assistant Attorney General and Chief
Public Protection Division
Office of Attorney General
109 State Street
Montpelier, VT 05609–1001
802–828–3171
Fax: 802–828–2154

Bruce Martell, Supervisor
Consumer Assurance Section
Department of Agriculture, Food and Market
120 State Street
Montpelier, VT 05620–2901
802–828–2436

Virgin Islands

Vera Falu, Commissioner
Department of Licensing and
Consumer Affairs
Property and Procurement Building
Subbase #1, Room 205
St. Thomas, VI 00802
809–774–3130
Fax: 809–776–0605

Virginia

State Offices
Frank Seales, Jr., Chief
Antitrust and Consumer Litigation Section
Office of Attorney General
900 East Main Street
Richmond, VA 23219
804–786–2116
Fax: 804–371–2086/2087

Robert E. Colvin
Project Manager, Office of Consumer Affairs
Department of Agriculture and
Consumer Services
Washington Building, Suite 100
P.O. Box 1163
Richmond, VA 23219
804–786–2042
TDD: 804–371–6344
Toll free in VA: 800–552–9963
Fax: 804–371–7479

County Offices
Office of Citizen and Consumer Affairs
#1 Court House Plaza, Suite 310
2100 Clarendon Boulevard
Arlington, VA 22201
703–358–3260
Fax: 703–358–3295

Ronald B. Mallard, Director
Fairfax County Department of
Consumer Affairs
12000 Government Center Parkway
Suite 433
Fairfax, VA 22035
Fax: 703–222–5921 (mail complaints only)

City Offices
Prescott Barbash, Administrator
Alexandria Office of Consumer Affairs
City Hall
P.O. Box 178
Alexandria, VA 22313
703–838–4350
TDD: 703–838–5056

Robert L. Gill, Coordinator
Division of Consumer Affairs
City Hall
Norfolk, VA 23510
757–664–4888
TDD: 757–624–8410

Dolores Daniels
Assistant to the City Manager
for Community Relations
364 Municipal Building
215 Church Avenue, S.W.
Roanoke, VA 24011
540–981–2583
Fax: 540–224–3138

Cathy Townsend Parks, Director
Consumer Affairs Division
Office of the Commonwealth's Attorney
Judicial Center, Bldg. 10B
2305 Judicial Blvd.
Virginia Beach, VA 23456–9050
757–426–5836
Fax: 757–427–8779

Washington

State Offices
Mala Nagarajan, Supervisor
Consumer Protection Division
Office of the Attorney General
103 E. Holly Street, Suite 308
Bellingham, WA 98225
360–738–6185
TDD: 206–464–7293
Toll free in WA: 800–551–4636
TDD toll free: 800–276–9883

Christy Martinez, Supervisor
Consumer Protection Division
Office of the Attorney General
500 N. Morain Street, Suite 1250
Kennewick, WA 99336–2607
509–734–7140
TDD: 206–464–7293
Toll free in WA: 800–551–4636
TDD toll free in WA: 800–276–9883

Larry D. Keyes, Supervisor
Consumer Protection Division
Office of the Attorney General
P.O. Box 40118
Olympia, WA 98504–0118
360–753–6210
TDD: 206–464–7293
Toll free in WA: 800–551–4636
TDD toll free in WA: 800–276–9883

Sally Sterling
Director of Consumer Services
Consumer and Business
Fair Practices Division
Office of the Attorney General
900 Fourth Avenue, Suite 2000
Seattle, WA 98164
206–464–6684
TDD: 206–464–7293
Toll free in WA: 800–551–4636
TDD toll free: 800–276–9883

Owen Clarke, Chief
Consumer and Business
Fair Practices Division
Office of the Attorney General
West 1116 Riverside Avenue
Spokane, WA 99201
509–456–3123
TDD: 206–464–7293
Toll free in WA: 800–551–4636
TDD toll free: 800–276–9883
Fax: 509–458–3548

Cynthia Lanphear, Contact Person
Consumer and Business
Office of the Attorney General
1019 Pacific Avenue, 3rd Floor
Tacoma, WA 98402–4411
206–593–2904
TDD: 206–464–7293
Toll free in WA: 800–551–4636
TDD toll free: 800–276–9883
Fax: 206–593–2449

June Bachman, Supervisor
Consumer Protection Division
Office of the Attorney General
500 West 8th Street, Suite 55
Vancouver, WA 98660
360–690–4751
TDD: 206–464–7293
Toll free in WA: 800–551–4636
TDD toll free in WA: 800–276–9883
Fax: 360–690–4762

City Offices
Kristie Anderson, Director
Department of Weights and Measures
3200 Cedar Street
Everett, WA 98201
206–259–8810
Fax: 206–259–8856

C. Patrick Sainsbury
Chief Deputy Prosecuting Attorney
Fraud Division
900 4th Avenue, #1002
Seattle, WA 98164
206–296–9010

Dwight Dively, Director
Seattle Department of Finance,
Revenue and Consumer Affairs
600 4th Avenue, #103
Seattle, WA 98104–1891
206–684–8484
Fax: 206–684–8625

Craig Leisy
Consumer Affairs Supervisor
Seattle Department of Finance,
Revenue and Consumer Affairs
600 4th Avenue, #103
Seattle, WA 98104–1891
206–386–1298
Fax: 206–386–1129

Ed Gonzaga
Consumer Affairs Inspector
Seattle Department of Finance,
Revenue and Consumer Affairs
600 4th Avenue, #103
Seattle, WA 98104–1891
206–233–7837
Fax: 206–684–5170

West Virginia
State Offices
Jill Miles
Deputy Attorney General
Consumer Protection Division
Office of Attorney General
812 Quarrier Street, 6th Floor
Charleston, WV 25301
304–558–8986
Toll free in WV: 800–368–8808
Fax: 304–558–0184

Karl H. Angell, Jr. Director
Division of Labor
Weights and Measures Section
570 MacCorkle Avenue
St. Albans, WV 25177
304–348–7890
Fax: 304–722–0605

City Office
Nemo Nearman, Director
City of Charleston
Department of Consumer Protection
P.O. Box 2749
Charleston, WV 25330
304–348–6439
Fax: 304–348–8157

Wisconsin
State Offices
William Oemichen, Administrator
Division of Trade and Consumer Protection
Department of Agriculture, Trade
and Consumer Protection
2811 Agriculture Drive
P.O. Box 8911
Madison, WI 53708
608–224–4950
Toll free in WI: 800–422–7128
Fax: 608–224–4939

Margaret Quaid, Regional Supervisor
Division of Trade and Consumer Protection
Department of Agriculture, Trade
and Consumer Protection
927 Loring Street
Altoona, WI 54720
715–839–3848
Toll free in WI: 800–422–7128
Fax: 715–839–1645

Judy Cardin
Regional Supervisor
Division of Trade and Consumer Protection
Department of Agriculture, Trade
and Consumer Protection
200 North Jefferson Street, Suite 146A
Green Bay, WI 54301
414–448–5111
Toll free in WI: 800–422–7128
TDD: 608–224 5058

Elmer Prenzlow
Regional Supervisor
Consumer Protection Regional Office
Department of Agriculture, Trade
and Consumer Protection
10930 W. Potter Road, Suite C
Milwaukee, WI 53226–3450
414–266–1231

County Offices
Fredric Matestic
Assistant District Attorney
Milwaukee County District Attorney's Office
Consumer Fraud Unit
821 West State Street, Room 412
Milwaukee, WI 53233–1485
414–278–4585
Fax: 414–223–1955

James A. Dehne
Consumer Fraud Investigator
Racine County Sheriffs Department
717 Wisconsin Avenue
Racine, WI 53403
414–636–3125
Fax: 414–636–3346

Wyoming
State Office
Mark Moran,
Assistant Attorney General
Office of Attorney General
123 State Capitol Building
Cheyenne, WY 82002
307–777–7874
Fax: 307–777–6869

State Agencies on Aging

The offices listed in this section coordinate services for older Americans. They provide information on services, programs and opportunities for these consumers. (This list is printed in larger type for the benefit of older consumers.)

Alabama

Martha Murph Beck
Executive Director
Alabama Commission on Aging
RSA Plaza, Suite 470
770 Washington Avenue
Montgomery, AL 36130
334–242–5743
Fax: 334–242–5594
TDD: 334–242–0995

Alaska

Jane Demmert, Director
Alaska Commission on Aging
Division of Senior Services
P.O. Box 110211
Juneau, AK 99811–0211
907–465–3250
Fax: 907–465–4716

Arizona

Art Olin, Administrator
Aging and Adult Administration
Site Code 950A
Department of Economic Security
1789 West Jefferson Street
Phoenix, AZ 85007
602–542–4446
Fax: 602–542–6575

Arkansas

Herb Sanderson, Director
Division of Aging and
Adult Services
Department of Human Services
P.O. Box 1437, Slot 1412
Little Rock, AR 72203–1437
501–682–2441
Fax: 501–682–8155

California

Dixon Arnett, Director
Department of Aging
1600 K Street
Sacramento, CA 95814
916–322–3887
Fax: 916–324–1903
**TDD toll free nationwide:
800–735–2929**

Colorado

Rita Barreras, Director
Aging and Adult Service
Department of Social Services
110 16th Street, Suite 200
Denver, CO 80202–4147
Voice/TDD: 303–620–4147
Fax: 303–620–4191

Connecticut

Christine M. Lewis
Director, Community Services
Department of Social Services
Elderly Services Division
25 Sigourney Street, 10th Floor
Hartford, CT 06106–5033
860–424–5277
Fax: 860–424–4966
Toll Free in CT: 800–842–1508

Delaware

Eleanor L. Cain, Director
Div. Services for Aging and Adults
with Physical Disabilities, DDHSS
1901 North DuPont Highway
New Castle, DE 19720
302–577–4791
Toll free nationwide:
800–223–9074
Fax: 301–577–4793

District of Columbia

Jearline F. Williams
Executive Director
D.C. Office on Aging
441 Fourth Street, N.W.
Suite 900 South
Washington, DC 20001
202–724–5622
Fax: 202–724–4979
TDD: 202–724–8925

Florida

Bentley Lipscomb, Secretary
Florida Department of Elder Affairs
4040 Esplanade Way
Tallahassee, FL 32399–7000
904–414–2000
Fax: 904–414–2004
TDD: 904–414–2001

Georgia

Judy Hagebak, Director
Division of Aging Services
Department of Human Resources
2 Peachtree Street, N.E.
18th Floor
Atlanta, GA 30303
404–657–5258
Fax: 404–657–5285

Guam

Donna Renee Anderson,
Administrator
Division of Senior Citizens
Department of Public Health and
Social Services
P.O. Box 2816
Agana, GU 96910
671–475–0263
Fax: 671–477–2930

Hawaii

Marilyn Seely, Director
Executive Office on Aging
250 South Hotel Street, Suite 107
Honolulu, HI 96813–2831
808–586–0100
Toll free in HI: 800–468–4644
Ext. 60100
Fax: 808–586– 0185

Idaho

Arlene D. Davidson, Director
Idaho Commission on Aging
700 West Jefferson, Room 108
P.O. Box 83720
Boise, ID 83720-0007
208-334-3833
Fax: 208-334-3033

Illinois

Maralee Lindley, Director
Department on Aging
421 East Capitol Avenue, Suite 100
Springfield, IL 62701–1789
217–785–2870
**Voice/TDD toll free in IL:
800–252–8966**
Fax: 217–785–4477
Chicago Office: 312–814–2630

Indiana

Bobby Conner, Director
Division of Disability, Aging
and Rehabilitative Service
Bureau of Aging and In-Home
Services
402 W. Washington Street
Indianapolis, IN 46207–7083
317–232–1147
Toll free nationwide:
800–545–7763
**Voice/TDD toll free in IN:
800–962–8408**
Fax: 317–232–7867

Iowa

Betty Grandquist,
Executive Director
Department of Elder Affairs
Clemens Building, 3rd Floor
200 Tenth Street
Des Moines, IA 50309–3609
515–281–5187
Fax: 515–281–4036
TDD: 515–281–5188

Kansas

Thelma Hunter Gordon, Secretary
Department on Aging
Docking State Office Building,
Room 150
915 S.W. Harrison
Topeka, KS 66612–1505
913–296–4986
Toll free in KS: 800–432–3535
TDD: 913–291–3167

Kentucky

Department of Social Services
CHR Bldg. - 5th West
275 East Main Street
Frankfort, KY 40621
502–564–6930
Fax: 502–564–4595

Louisiana

Richard W. Collins
Governor's Office of Elderly Affairs
P.O. Box 80374
Baton Rouge, LA 70898-0374
504–925–1700
Toll Free in LA: 800–259–4990
(elderly protection/ombudsman
Hotline)
Fax: 504–925–1749

Maine

Christine Gianopoulos, Director
Bureau of Elder and Adult Services
Department of Human Services
35 Anthony Avenue
State House, Station 11
Augusta, ME 04333–0011
207–624–5335
Fax: 207–624–5361

Maryland

Sue Fryer Ward, Director
Office on Aging
State Office Bldg., Room 1004
301 West Preston Street
Baltimore, MD 21201
410–767–1102
Toll free in MD: 800–243–3425
Fax: 410–333–7943
TDD: 410–767–1083

Massachusetts

Franklin P. Ollivierre, Secretary
Executive Office of Elder Affairs
One Ashburton Place, 5th Floor
Boston, MA 02108
617–727–7750
Toll free in MA: 800–882–2003
Fax: 617–727–9368
TDD Toll free: 800–872–0166

Michigan

Carol Parr, Acting Director
Office of Services to the Aging
P.O. Box 30026
Lansing, MI 48909
517–373–8230
Fax: 517–373–4092
TDD: 517–373–4096

Minnesota

James G. Varpness, Executive
Secretary
Minnesota Board on Aging
444 Lafayette Road
St. Paul, MN 55155–3843
612–296–2770
Toll free nationwide:
800–882–6262
Fax: 612–297–7855

Mississippi

Eddie Anderson, Director
Division of Aging and
Adult Services
750 North State Street
Jackson, MS 39202
601–359–4925
Toll free in MS: 800–948–3090
Fax: 601–359–4370

Missouri

Greg Vadner, Director
Division on Aging
Department of Social Services
P.O. Box 1337
615 Howerton Court
Jefferson City, MO 65102–1337
573–751–3082
Fax: 573–751–8687
**TDD toll free nationwide:
800–735–2966**

Montana

Charles Rehbein,
Bureau Chief
Office on Aging
111 North Sanders, Room 210
Helena, MT 59620
406–444–4077
Toll free nationwide:
800–332–2272
**Voice/TDD toll free
nationwide: 800–833–8503**
Fax: 406–444–7433

Nebraska

Dennis H. Loose, Director
Department on Aging
P.O. Box 95044
301 Centennial Mall–South
Lincoln, NE 68509–5044
402–471–2306
**Voice/TDD toll free in NE:
800–942–7830**
Fax: 402–471–4619

Nevada

Mary Liveratti,
Acting Administrator
Division for Aging Services
Department of Human Resources
340 North 11th Street, Suite 203
Las Vegas, NV 89101
702–486–3545
Fax: 702–486–3572
TDD: 702–486–3420

New Hampshire

Thomas E. Pryor, Director
Division of Elderly and
Adult Services
State Office Park South
115 Pleasant St., Annex Bldg. #1
Concord, NH 03301–6501
603–271–4680
Toll free in NH: 800–351–1888
Fax: 603–271–4643
**TDD Toll free in NH:
800–735–2964**

New Jersey

Ruth Reader, Assistant
Commissioner
Department of Health and
Senior Services
Division of Senior Affairs
101 South Broad Street-CN 807
Trenton, NJ 08625–0807
609–292–3766
Toll free in NJ: 800–792–8820
Fax: 609–633–6609

New Mexico

Michelle Lujan Grishan, Director
State Agency on Aging
La Villa Rivera Building
228 East Palace Avenue,
Ground Floor
Santa Fe, NM 87501
505–827–7640
Toll free in NM: 800–432–2080
Fax: 505–827–7649

New York

Walter G. Hoefer, Director
New York State Office
for the Aging
2 Empire State Plaza
Albany, NY 12223–1251
518–474–5731
**Voice/TDD toll free in NY:
800–342–9871**
Fax: 518–474–0608

North Carolina

Bonnie Cramer, Director
Division of Aging
CB 29531
693 Palmer Drive
Raleigh, NC 27626–0531
919–733–3983
Fax: 919–733–0443

North Dakota

Linda Wright, Director
Department of Human Services
600 South Second Street, Suite 1C
Bismarck, ND 58507–5729
701–328–8910
Toll free in ND: 800–755–8521
Fax: 701–328–8989

Ohio

Judith V. Brachman, Director
Ohio Department of Aging
50 West Broad Street, 9th Floor
Columbus, OH 43215–5928
614–466–5500
Fax: 614–466–5741

Oklahoma

Roy R. Keen, Division Administrator
Services for the Aging
Department of Human Services
P.O. Box 25352
Oklahoma City, OK 73125
405–521–2281; 521–2327
Toll free in OK: 800–211–2116
Fax: 405–521–2086

Oregon

Roger Averback, Administrator
Senior and Disabled
Services Division
500 Summer St. NE, 2nd Floor
Salem, OR 97310–1015
Voice/TDD: 503–945–5811
Toll free in OR: 800–282–8096
Fax: 503–373–7823

Pennsylvania

Richard Browdie, Secretary
Department of Aging
400 Market Street, 6th Floor
Harrisburg, PA 17101–2301
717–783–1550
Fax: 717–772–3382

Puerto Rico

Ruby Rodriguez Ramirez
M.H.S.A Executive Director
Governor's Office of Elderly Affairs
Call Box 50063
Old San Juan Station, PR 00902
787–721–5710; 721–4560;
721–6121
Fax: 787–721–6510

Rhode Island

Barbara Casey Ruffino, Director
Department of Elderly Affairs
160 Pine Street
Providence, RI 02903–3708
401–277–2858
**Voice/TDD toll free in RI:
800–322–2880**
Fax: 401–277–1490
TDD: 401–277–2880

South Carolina

Constance C. Rinehart, Executive
Director
South Carolina Division on Aging
202 Arbor Lake Drive, Suite 301
Columbia, SC 29223–4535
803–737–7500
Toll free in SC: 800–868–9095
Fax: 803–737–7501

South Dakota

Gail Ferris, Administrator
Office of Adult Services and Aging
Richard Kneip Building
700 Governors Drive
Pierre, SD 57501–2291
605–773–3656
Fax: 605–773–6834

Tennessee

Emily Wiseman, Director
Commission on Aging
500 Deaderick Street
Andrew Jackson Building,
9th Floor
Nashville, TN 37243–0860
615–741–2056
Fax: 615–741–3309
**TDD toll free nationwide:
800–848–0298
Voice relay service:
800–848–0299**

Texas

Mary Sapp, Executive Director
Department on Aging
4900 North Lamar
Austin, TX 78751–2399
512–424–6840
Toll free nationwide:
800–252–9240
Fax: 512–424–6890

Utah

Helen Goddard, Director
Division of Aging and
Adult Services
P.O. Box 45500
120 North 200 West, Suite 401
Salt Lake City, UT 84145–0500
801–538–3910
Fax: 801–538–4395

Vermont

David Yacozone, Commissioner
Department of Aging and Disabilities
Waterbury Complex
103 South Main Street
Waterbury, VT 05676
Voice/TDD: 802–241–2400
Fax: 802-241-2325

Virgin Islands

Catherine L. Mills, Commissioner
Department of Human Services
Knud Hansen Complex, Bldg. A
1303 Hospital Ground
Charlotte Amalie, VI 00802
809–774–0930
Fax: 809–774–3466

Virginia

Thelma Bland, Commissioner
Department for the Aging
700 East Franklin Street,
10th Floor
Richmond, VA 23219–2327
Voice/TDD: 804–225–2271
Toll free in VA: 800–552–3402
Fax: 804–371–8381

Washington

Ralph Smith, Assistant Secretary
Aging and Adult Services
Administration
Dept. of Social and Health Services
P.O. Box 45600
Olympia, WA 98504–5600
360–493–2500
Toll free nationwide:
800–422–3263
Fax: 360–493–9484
TDD: 360–493–2637

West Virginia

William E. Lytton, Jr.
Interim Executive Director
Commission on Aging
1900 Kanawha Blvd, East
Holly Grove-Building 10
Charleston, WV 25305–0160
304–558–3317
Fax: 304–558–0004

Wisconsin

Donna McDowell, Director
Bureau on Aging
Department of Health and
Family Services
217 South Hampton Street,
Suite 300
Madison, WI 53703
608–266–2536
Fax: 608–267–3203

Wyoming

Deborah Fleming, Administrator
Department of Health
Division on Aging
139 Hathaway Building, Room 139
Cheyenne, WY 82002–0480
307–777–7986
Toll free nationwide:
800–442–2766
Fax: 307–777–5340

State Banking Authorities

The officials listed below regulate and supervise state-chartered banks. Many of them handle or refer problems and complaints about other types of financial institutions as well. Some also answer general questions about banking and consumer credit. If you are dealing with a federally chartered bank, check the listing of "Selected Federal Agencies," beginning on page 107. Also see the information in "Selecting a Financial Institution" on page 18.

Alabama
Kenneth R. McCartha
Superintendent of Banks
101 South Union Street
Montgomery, AL 36130
334–242–3452

Alaska
Willis F. Kirkpatrick
Director of Banking, Securities
and Corporations
P.O. Box 110807
Juneau, AK 99811–0807
907–465–2521
TDD: 907–465–5437
Fax: 907–465–2549

Arizona
Richard C. Houseworth
Superintendent of Banks
Arizona State Banking Dept.
2910 North 44th Street
Suite 310
Phoenix, AZ 85018
602–255–4421
Toll free in AZ: 800–544–0708

Arkansas
Bill J. Ford
Bank Commissioner
Tower Building
323 Center Street, Suite 500
Little Rock, AR 72201–2613
501–324–9019
Fax: 501–324–9028

California
Conrad W. Hewitt
Superintendent of Banks
111 Pine Street, Suite 1100
San Francisco, CA
94111–5613
415–263–8501
Toll free in CA: 800–622–0620
For consumer complaints against
CA state–licensed banks, the
"800" number reaches the
Consumer Services Office,
located in Sacramento, CA.

Colorado
Barbara M.A. Walker
State Bank Commissioner
Division of Banking
1560 Broadway St., Suite 1175
Denver, CO 80202
303–894–7575

Connecticut
John Burke
Banking Commissioner
260 Constitution Plaza
Hartford, CT 06103
860–240–8299
Toll free in CT: 800–831–7225

Delaware
Timothy R. McTaggart
State Bank Commissioner
555 E. Lockerman Street
Suite 210
Dover, DE 19901
302–739–4235
Toll free: 800–638–3376
(complaints DE only)
Fax: 302–739–2356

District of Columbia
Anthony Romero
Superintendent of Banking and
Financial Institutions
717 14th Street, N.W.
11th Floor
Washington, DC 20005
202–727–1563

Florida
Robert F. Milligan
State Comptroller
State Capitol
Tallahassee, FL 32399–0350
904–488–6311
Toll free in FL: 800–848–3792

Georgia
Edward D. Dunn
Commissioner
Banking and Finance
2990 Brandywine Road
Suite 200
Atlanta, GA 30341–5565
404–986–1633

Guam
Joaquin Blaz
Director
Department of Revenue
and Taxation
855 West Marine Drive
Agana, GU 96910
011–671–477–5107

Hawaii
Lynn Y. Wakatsuki, Commissioner
Financial Institutions
P.O. Box 2054
Honolulu, HI 96805
808–586–2820
Fax: 808–586–2818

Idaho
Gavin M. Gee, Acting Director
Department of Finance
700 West State Street, 2nd Floor
Boise, ID 83720–0031
208–334–3313
Fax: 208–334–2216

Illinois
Richard Luft
Commissioner of Banks
and Trust Companies
500 E. Monroe Street
Springfield, IL 62701
217–785–2837
TDD: 217–524–6644

Indiana
Charles W. Phillips, Director
Department of Financial
Institutions
402 W. Washington Street
Room W066
Indianapolis, IN 46204–2759
317–232–3955
Toll free in IN: 800–382–4880

Iowa
Michael Guttau
Superintendent of Banking
200 East Grand, Suite 300
Des Moines, IA 50309
515–281–4014

Kansas
W. Newton Male
State Bank Commissioner
700 Jackson Street, Suite 300
Topeka, KS 66603–3714
913–296–2266
Fax: 913–296–0168

Kentucky
Larry D. Lander
Commissioner
Department of Financial
Institutions
477 Versailles Road
Frankfort, KY 40601
502–573–3390

Louisiana
Larry L. Murray, Commissioner
Financial Institutions
P.O. Box 94095
Baton Rouge, LA 70804–9095
504–925–4660

Maine
H. Donald DeMatteis
Superintendent of Banking
36 State House Station
Augusta, ME 04333–0036
207–624–8570
TDD: 207–624–8563
Fax: 207–624–8590

Maryland
H. Robert Hergenroeder, Jr.
Commissioner of Financial
Regulation
501 St. Paul Place, 13th Floor
Baltimore, MD 21202
410–333–6812

Massachusetts
Thomas J. Curry
Commissioner of Banks
100 Cambridge Street
Boston, MA 02202
617–727–3145
TDD: 617–727–7625
Toll free: 800–495–2265

Michigan
Patrick McQueen, Commissioner
Financial Institutions Bureau
P.O. Box 30224
Lansing, MI 48909
517–373–3460
Fax: 517–335–1109
Fax: 517–335–0908

Minnesota
David B. Gruenes
Commissioner of Commerce
133 East 7th Street
St. Paul, MN 55101
612–296–2135
Fax: 612–296–8591

Mississippi
John S. Allison
Acting Commissioner
Department of Banking and
Consumer Finance
P.O. Box 23729
Jackson, MS 39225–3729
601–359–1031
Toll free in MS: 800–844–2499

Missouri
Earl L. Manning
Commissioner of Finance
P.O. Box 716
Jefferson City, MO 65102
573–751–3242
Toll free in MO: 800–722–3321
**TDD toll free:
800–735–2966**
Fax: 573–751–9192

Montana
Donald W. Hutchinson
Commissioner
Financial Institutions
846 Front Street
P.O. Box 200546
Helena, MT 59620–0546
406–444–2091
Fax: 406–444–4186

Nebraska
James A. Hansen
Director of Banking and Finance
1200 N Street, Suite 311
Lincoln, NE 68508
402–471–2171

Nevada
L. Scott Walshaw
Commissioner
Financial Institutions
406 East Second Street
Carson City, NV 89710
702–687–4260
Fax: 702–687–6909

New Hampshire
A. Roland Roberge
Bank Commissioner
169 Manchester Street
Concord, NH 03301
603–271–3561
Fax: 603–271–1090

New Jersey
Elizabeth Randall
Commissioner
Departments of Banking and
Insurance
20 West State Street CN–325
Trenton, NJ 08625
609–292–3420

New Mexico
William J. Verant
Director
Financial Institutions Division
P.O. Box 25101
Santa Fe, NM 87504
505–827–7100
Fax: 505–827–7107

New York
Neil D. Levin
Superintendent of Banks
Two Rector Street
New York, NY 10006–1894
212–618–6553
Toll free in NY: 800–522–3330
(general consumer information)
Toll free in NY: 800–832–1838
(small business information)

North Carolina
Hal D. Lingerfelt
Commisioner of Banks
P.O. Box 29512
Raleigh, NC 27626–0512
919–733–3016

North Dakota
Gary D. Preszler
Commissioner of Banking and
Financial Institutions
2900 North 19th Street, #3
Bismarck, ND 58501–5305
701–328–9933
TDD toll free: 800–366–6888
Fax: 701–328–9955

Ohio
W. Curtis Stitt
Superintendent
Division of Financial Institutions
77 South High Street, 21st Floor
Columbus, OH 43266–0121
614–466–2932
Fax: 614–644–1631

Oklahoma
Mick Thompson
Bank Commissioner
4545 North Lincoln Boulevard
Suite 164
Oklahoma City, OK 73105
405–521–2783
Fax: 405–525–9701

Oregon
Cecil R. Monroe
Administrator
Division of Finance and
Corporate Securities
350 Winter Street, N.E.
Room 21
Salem, OR 97310
503–378–4140
TDD: 503–378–4387
Fax: 503–378–4178

Pennsylvania
Richard C. Rishel
Secretary of Banking
333 Market Street, 16th Floor
Harrisburg, PA 17101–2290
717–787–6991
Toll free in PA: 800–PA–BANKS
TDD toll free: 800–679–5070
Fax: 717–787–8773

Puerto Rico
Joseph P. O'nell
Commissioner of Financial
Institutions
1492 Ponce de Leon Avenue
Suite 600
San Juan, PR 00907–4192
787–723–3131

Rhode Island
Edward D. Pare, Jr.
Associate Director and
Superintendent of Banking
233 Richmond Street
Suite 231
Providence, RI 02903–4231
401–277–2405
TDD: 401–277–2223
Fax: 401–331–9123

South Carolina
Louie A. Jacobs
Commissioner of Banking
1015 Sumter Street, Room 309
Columbia, SC 29201
803–734–2001
Fax: 803–734–2013

South Dakota
Richard A. Duncan
Director of Banking
State Capitol Building
500 East Capitol Avenue
Pierre, SD 57501–5070
605–773–3421
Fax: 605–773–5367

Tennessee
Bill Houston
Commissioner
Financial Institutions
John Sevier Building
500 Charlotte Avenue, 4th Floor
Nashville, TN 37243–0705
615–741–2236
Fax: 615–741–2883

Texas
Catherine A. Ghiglieri
Banking Commissioner
2601 North Lamar
Austin, TX 78705
512–475–1300

Utah
G. Edward Leary
Commissioner
Financial Institutions
P.O. Box 89
Salt Lake City, UT 84110–0089
801–538–8830

Vermont
Elizabeth Costle
Commissioner
Banking, Insurance and Securities
89 Main Street, 2nd Floor
Montpelier, VT 05620–3101
802–828–3307

Virgin Islands
Kenneth L. Mapp
Lieutenant Governor
Commissioner of Banking and
Insurance
18 Kongens Gade
Charlotte Amalie
St. Thomas, VI 00801
809–774–2991

Virginia
Sidney A. Bailey
Commissioner
Financial Institutions
1300 E. Main Street
Suite 800
P.O. Box 640
Richmond, VA 23218–0640
804–371–9657
TDD: 804–371–9206
Toll free in VA: 800–552–7945

Washington
John L. Bley
Supervisor of Banking
P.O. Box 41023
Olympia, WA 98504–1203
360–753–6520
Toll free: 800–372–8303

West Virginia
Sharon G. Bias
Commissioner of Banking
State Capitol Complex
Building 3, Room 311
1900 Kanawha Blvd., East
Charleston, WV 25305–0240
304–558–2294
Toll free in WV: 800–642–9056

Wisconsin
Richard L. Dean, Secretary
Department of Financial
Institutions
101 E. Wilson, 5th Floor
P.O. Box 7876
Madison, WI 53707–7876
608–261–9555
Toll free in WI: 800–452–3328
(consumer inquiries)

Wyoming
L. Bruce Hendrickson
Commissioner
Division of Banking
Herschler Building
3rd Floor, East
Cheyenne, WY 82002
307–777–7797

State Insurance Regulators

Each state has its own laws and regulations for all types of insurance, including car, homeowner and health insurance. The officials listed below enforce these laws. Many of these offices can provide you with information to help you make informed insurance buying decisions.

Your local library also has information that can help you compare insurance companies before making a purchase.

If you have a question or complaint about your insurance company's policies, contact the company before you contact the state insurance regulator.

Alabama
Michael DeBellis
Acting Commissioner
Department of Insurance
135 South Union Street, #200
Montgomery, AL 36130
334–269–3550
Fax: 334–241–4192

Alaska
Marianne K. Burke
Director
Department of Commerce and Economic Development
Division of Insurance
P.O. Box 110805
Juneau, AK 99811–0805
907–465–2515

Thelma Walker
Drputy Director
Division of Insurance
3601 C Street
Suite 1324
Anchorage, AK 99503–5948
907–269–7900

American Samoa
Albert Atuatsi
Insurance Commissioner
Office of the Governor
Pago Page, AS 96799
011–684–633–4116

Arizona
John King, Director
Department of Insurance
2910 North 44th Street
Suite 210
Phoenix, AZ 85018–7256
602–912–8444

Arkansas
Lee Douglas
Commissioner
Department of Insurance
1200 West 3rd Street
Little Rock, AR 72201–1904
501–371–2600
Toll free: 800–852–5494

California
Charles Quackenbush
Commissioner
Department of Insurance
300 Capitol Mall
Suite 1500
Sacramento, CA 95814
916–445–5544
Toll free in CA: 800–927–4357

Colorado
Jack Ehnes
Commissioner
1560 Broadway
Suite 850
Denver, CO 80202
303–894–7499, ext. 400

Connecticut
George M. Reider, Jr.
Commissioner
Department of Insurance
P. O. Box 816
Hartford, CT 06142–0816
860–297–3800

Delaware
Donna Lee H. Williams
Commissioner
Department of Insurance
841 Silver Lake Blvd.
P.O. Box 7007
Dover, DE 19903–1507
302–739–4251
Toll free in DE: 800–282–8611

District of Columbia
Patrick Kelly
Acting Commissioner
Insurance Administration
441 4th Street, N.W.
8th Floor North
Washington, DC 20001
202–727–8000, ext. 3007

Florida
Bill Nelson
Commissioner
Department of Insurance
State Capitol
Plaza Level Eleven
Tallahassee, FL 32399–0300
904–922–3130
Toll free in FL: 800–342–2762

Georgia
John Oxendine
Commissioner
Department of Insurance
2 Martin L. King, Jr. Drive
Atlanta, GA 30334
404–656–2070

Guam
Joseph T. Duenas
Commissioner
Department of Revenue and Taxation
Government of Guam
378 Chalan San Antonio
Tamuning, Guam 96911
011–671–445–5000

Hawaii
Wayne C. Metcalf
Commissioner
Insurance division
Department of Commerce and Consumer Affairs
250 S. King Street
5th Floor
Honolulu, HI 46813–3614
808–586–2790
Toll free: 800–586–2790

Idaho
James Alcorn
Director
Department of Insurance
700 W. State Street
Boise, ID 83720
208–334–4320
Toll free in ID: 800–721–3272

Illinois
Mark Boozell
Director
Department of Insurance
320 West Washington Street
Springfield, IL 62767
217–782–4515

100 West Randolph Street
Suite 15–100
Chicago, IL 60601
312–814–2420

Indiana
Marjorie Maginn
Commissioner
Department of Insurance
311 West Washington Street
Suite 300
Indianapolis, IN 46204–2787
317–232–2395
Toll free in IN: 800–622–4461

Iowa
Theresa Vaughan
Commissioner
Division of Insurance
Lucas State Office Building
6th Floor
Des Moines, IA 50319
515–281–5705

Kansas
Kathleen Sebelius
Commissioner
Department of Insurance
420 S.W. 9th Street
Topeka, KS 66612
913–296–7829
Toll free in KS: 800–432–2484

Kentucky
George Nicoles
Commisioner
Department of Insurance
215 West Main Street
Frankfort, KY 40601
502–564–6088

Louisiana
James H. "Jim" Brown, Jr.
Commissioner
Department of Insurance
P.O. Box 94214
Baton Route, LA 70801–9214
504–342–1259

Maine
Brian Atchinson
Superintendent
Bureau of Insurance
State House Station 34
Augusta, ME 04333–0034
207–624–8475
Toll free in ME: 800–300–5000

Maryland
Dwight K. Bartlett, III
Commissioner
Insurance Administration
501 St. Paul Place
7th Floor
Baltimore, MD 21202
410–333–1782
Toll free in MD: 800–492–6116

Massachusetts
Linda Ruthardt
Commissioner
Division of Insurance
470 Atlantic Avenue
6th Floor
Boston, MA 02210–2223
617–521–7777

Michigan
D. Joseph Olson
Commissioner
Insurance Bureau
611 West Ottawa Street
2nd Floor North
Lansing, MI 48933
517–373–0240

Minnesota
David B. Gruenes
Commissioner
Department of Commerce
133 East 7th Street
St. Paul, MN 55101
612–296–2488

Mississippi
George Dale
Commissioner
Department of Insurance
1804 Walter Sillers Building
Jackson, MS 39205
601–359–3569
Toll free in MS: 800–562–2957

Missouri
Jay Angoff
Director
Department of Insurance
301 West High Street
6 North
Jefferson City, MO
65102–0690
573–751–2640
Toll free in MO: 800–726–7390

Montana
Mark O'Keefe
Commissioner
Department of Insurance
126 North Sanders
Mitchell Building
Room 270
Helena, MT 59601
406–444–2040
Toll free in MT: 800–332–6148

Nebraska
Robert Lange
Director
Department of Insurance
941 O Street
Suite 400
Lincoln, NE 68508
402–471–2201

Nevada
Alice Molasky
Commissioner
Division of Insurance
1665 Hot Springs Road, #152
Carson City, NV 89710
702–687–4270
Toll free in NV: 800–992–0900

New Hampshire
Charles Blossom
Commissioner
Department of Insurance
169 Manchester Street
Concord, NH 03301–5151
603–271–2261

New Jersey
Elizabeth E. Randall
Commissioner
Department of Insurance
20 West State Street
CN329
Trenton, NJ 08625
609–984–2444

New Mexico
Christopher P. Krahling
Superintendent
Department of Insurance
P.O. Drawer 1269
Santa Fe, NM 87504–1269
505–827–4698
Toll free in NM: 800–947–4722

New York
Edward Muhl
Superintendent
Department of Insurance
160 West Broadway
New York, NY 10013–3393
212–602–2488
Toll free in NY: 800–342–3736

Agency Building One
Empire State Plaza
Albany, NY 12257
518–474–6600

North Carolina
James E. Long
Commissioner
Department of Insurance
Dobbs Building
430 North Salisbury Street
P.O. Box 26387
Raleigh, NC 27611
919–733–2004
Toll free in NC: 800–662–7777

North Dakota
Glenn R. Pomeroy
Commissioner
Department of Insurance
600 East Boulevard Avenue
Bismarck, ND 58505–0320
701–328–2440
Toll free in ND: 800–247–0560

Ohio
Harold T. Duryee
Director
Department of Insurance
2100 Stella Court
Columbus, OH 43215–1067
614–644–2658
Toll free: 800–522–0071

Oklahoma
John Crawford
Commissioner
Department of Insurance
3814 Santa Fe
Oklahoma City, OK 73118
405–521–2991
Toll free in OK: 800–522–0071

Oregon
Kerry Barnett
Director
Department of Consumer and
Business Services
350 Winter Street, N.E.
Room 200
Salem, OR 97310–0700
503–378–4636

Pennsylvania
Linda S. Kaiser
Commissioner
Insurance Department
1326 Strawberry Square, 13th
Floor
Harrisburg, PA 17120
717–787–2317

Puerto Rico
Juan Antonio Garcia
Commissioner
Office of the Commissioner of
Insurance
Fernandez Juncos Station
1607 Ponce de Leon Avenue
Santurce, PR 00910
809–722–8686

Rhode Island
Alfonso E. Mastrostefano
Commissioner
Insurance Division
233 Richmond Street
Providence, RI 02903–4233
401–277–2223

South Carolina
Lee P. Jedziniak
Director
Department of Insurance
1612 Marion Street
P.O. Box 100105
Columbia, SC 24201
803–737–6150
Toll free in SC: 800–768–3467

South Dakota
Darla L. Lyon
Director
Division of Insurance
Department of Commerce
and Regulation
500 E. Capitol
Pierre, SD 57501–3940
605–773–3563

Tennessee
Doug Sizemore
Commissioner
Department of Commerce
and Insurance
500 James Robertson Parkway
Nashville, TN 37243–0565
615–741–2218
Toll free in TN: 800–342–4029

Texas
Elton Bomer
Commissioner
Department of Insurance
333 Guadalupe Street
P.O. Box 149104
Austin, TX 78714–9104
512–463–6464
Toll free: 800–252–3439

Utah
Robert E. Wilcox
Commissioner
Department of Insurance
3110 State Office Building
Salt Lake City, UT 84114
801–538–3805
Toll free in UT: 800–439–3805

Vermont
Elizabeth R. Costle
Commissioner
Department of Banking,
Insurance
and Securities
Health Care Administration
89 Main Street, Drawer 20
Montpelier, VT 05620–3101
802–828–4884

Virgin Islands
Gwendolyn Brady
Director
Division of Banking and
Insurance
Lt. Governor's Office
Kongens Gade 18
St. Thomas, VI 00802
809–774–7166

Virginia
Alfred W. Gross
Commissioner
State Corporation Commission
Bureau of Insurance
1300 East Main Street
Richmond, VA 23219
804–371–9694
Toll free in VA: 800–552–7945

Washington
Deborah Senn
Commissioner
Insurance Building-Capitol
Campus
14th Avenue and Water Street
P.O. Box 40255
Olympia, WA 98504–0255
360–753–3613

West Virginia
Henry C. Clark
Commissioner
Department of Insurance
2019 Washington Street, East
P.O. Box 50540
Charleston, WV 25305–0540
304–558–3856
Toll free in WV: 800–642–9004

Wisconsin
Josephine W. Musser
Commissioner
Office of the Commissioner of
Insurance
121 E. Wilson
Madison, WI 53702
608–266–0103
Toll free in WI: 800–236–8517

Wyoming
John McBride
Commissioner
Department of Insurance
Herschler Building
122 West 25th Street
Cheyenne, WY 82002–0440
307–777–7402
Toll free in WY: 800–438–5768

State Securities Administrators

Each state has its own laws and regulations for securities brokers and for all types of securities, including stocks, mutual funds, commodities, real estate offerings, uninsured investment products sold by banks and others. The officials and agencies listed below enforce these laws and regulations. Many of these offices can provide you with information to help you make informed investment decisions.

State securities agencies are responsible also for preventing fraud and abuse in the sale of all but the largest securities offerings.

If you have a question or complaint about an investment you have made or are about to make, call the company or bank involved. If your complaint or question is not resolved, call the appropriate state securities agency below.

Alabama
Joseph P. Borg
Director
Securities Commission
770 Washington Street,
Suite 570
Montgomery, AL 36130–4700
334–242–2984
Fax:334–242–0240
Toll free in AL: 800–222–1253

Alaska
L.P. Carroll
Senior Examiner, State of
Alaska
Department of Commerce
and Economic Development
Banking and Securities
P.O. Box 110807
Juneau, AK 99811–0807
907–465–2521
Fax: 907–465–2549

Arizona
Duty Investigator
Corporation Commission
Securities Division
1300 West Washington, 3rd Floor
Phoenix, AZ 85007
602–542–4242
Fax: 602–594–7470

Arkansas
Mac Dodson
Commissioner
Securities Department
Heritage West Building
201 East Markham, 3rd Floor
Little Rock, AR 72201–1692
501–324–9260
Fax: 501–324–9268

California
Commissioner
Department of Corporations
3700 Wilshire Boulevard
Suite 600
Los Angeles, CA 90010–3001
213–736–2741
Fax: 213–736–2117

Colorado
Philip A. Feigin
Securities Commissioner
Division of securities
1580 Lincoln, Suite 420
Denver, CO 80203–1506
303–894–2320
Fax: 303–861–2126
TDD: 303–894–7880

Connecticut
John Burke
Banking Commissioner
Department of Banking
260 Constitution Plaza
Hartford, CT 06103
860–240–8299
Fax: 860–240–8178

Delaware
Richard W. Hubbard
Securities Commissioner
Department of Justice
Division of Securities
State Office Building
820 N. French Street, 8th Floor
Wilmington, DE 19801
302–577–2515
Fax: 302–655–0576

District of Columbia
Veda M. Shamsid-Deen
Acting Director
D.C. Public Service Commission
Office of Securities
450 5th Street, N.W., Suite 821
Washington, DC 20001
202–626–5105
Fax: 202–737–2080

Florida

Robert F. Milligan
Comptroller
Division of Securities
The Capitol LL–22
Tallahassee, FL 32399–0350
904–488–9805
Fax: 904–681–2428
Toll free in FL: 800–372–8792

Georgia

Lewis A. Massey
Secretary of State
Office of the Secretary of State
Division of Securities and
Business Regulation
Two Martin Luther King, Jr.
Drive
Suite 802, West Tower
Atlanta, GA 30334
404–656–2894
Fax: 404–657–8410

Hawaii

Russell H. Yamashita
Commissioner of Securities
Department of Commerce
and Consumer Affairs
P.O. Box 40
Honolulu, HI 96810
808–586–2744
808–586–2740 (Securities
Enforcement Unit)
Fax: 808–586–2733
Toll free in HI: 800–468–4644,
ext. 62727

Idaho

Gavin M. Gee, Director
Department of Finance
Marilyn Scanlan, Bureau Chief
Securities Bureau
P.O. Box 83720
Boise, ID 83720–0031
208–334–3684
Fax: 208–332–8098

Ilinois

Director
Illinois Securities Department
Office of Secretary of State
Robert Newtson
Lincoln Tower, Suite 200
520 S. Second Street
Springfield, IL 62701
217–782–2256
Toll free in IL: 800–628–7937

Indiana

Bradley W. Skolnik
Securities Commissioner
Office of the Secretary of State
Securities Division
302 West Washington
Room E–111
Indianapolis, IN 46204
317–232–6681
Toll free in IN: 800–223–8791
Fax: 317–233–3675

Iowa

Enforcement Section
Securities Bureau
Lucas State Office Building
2nd Floor
Des Moines, IA 50319
515–281–4441
Fax: 515–281–6467

Kansas

David Brant
Securities Commissioner
Office of the Securities
Commissioner
618 South Kansas Avenue
2nd Floor
Topeka, KA 66603–3804
913–296–3307
Fax: 913–296–6872
Toll free in KA: 800–232–9580

Kentucky

Larry D. Lander
Commissioner of Financial Institutions
477 Versailles Road
Frankfort, KY 40601–3868
502–573–3390
Fax: 502–573–8787

Louisiana

Harry C. Stansbury
Deputy Commissioner of
Securities
Securities Commission
Energy Centre
1100 Poydras Street, Suite
2250
New Orleans, LA 70163
504–568–5515

Maine

Stephen L. Diamond
Securities Administrator
Securities Division
21 State House Station
Augusta, ME 04333
207–624–8551
Fax: 207–624–8590

Maryland

Robert N. McDonald
Securities Commissioner
Office of the Attorney General
Division of Securities
200 Saint Paul Place, 20th Floor
Baltimore, MD 21202–2020
410–576–6360
Fax: 410–576–6532
TDD: 410–576–6372

Massachusetts

William Francis Galvin
Secretary of the Commonwealth
Securities Division
One Ashburton Place,
Room 1701
Boston, MA 02108
617–727–3548
Fax: 617–248–0177
Toll free in MA: 800–269–5428

Michigan

Carl L. Tyson, Director
Department of Consumer
and Industry Services
Corporation, Securities and
Land Development Bureau
P.O. Box 30054
Lansing, MI 48909–7554
517–334–6212
Fax: 517–334–6155

Minnesota

David Gruenes
Commissioner of Commerce
Department of Commerce
133 East Seventh Street
St. Paul, MN 55101
612–296–4026
Fax: 612–296–4328
Toll free in MN: 800–657–3602

Mississippi

Leslie Scott
Assistant Secretary of State for
Business Services
P.O. Box 136
Jackson, MS 39205 or
202 North Congress Street
Suite 601
Jackson, MS 39201
601–359–6371
Fax: 601–359–2894

Missouri

Douglas F. Wilburn
Commissioner of Securities
P.O. Box 1276
Jefferson City, MO 65102
573–751–4136
Toll free in MO: 800–721–7996
Fax: 573–526–3124

Montana

Mark O'Keefe
State Auditor & Securities
Commissioner
Office of the State Auditor
Securities Department
P.O. Box 4009
Helena, MT 59604
406–444–2040
Fax: 406–444–3497
Toll free in MT: 800–332–6148
TDD: 404–444–3246

Nebraska

Jack Herstein
Assistant Director
Department of Banking & Finance
Bureau of Securities
P.O. Box 95006
Lincoln, NE 68509–5006
402–471–3445

Nevada

Donald J. Reis
Deputy Secretary of State
Office of the Secretary of State
Securities Division
555 E. Washington Avenue
Suite 5200
Las Vegas, NV 89101
702–486–2440
Fax: 702–486–2452

New Hampshire

Peter C. Hildreth
Director of Securities
Bureau of Securities Regulation
Department of State
State House, Room 204
Concord, NH 03301–4989
603–271–1463
Fax: 603–271–7933

New Jersey

Thomas J. Gaynor
Bureau Chief
Department of Law and
Public Safety
Division of Consumer Affairs
Bureau of Securities
P.O. Box 47029
Newark, NJ 07101
201–504–3600
Fax: 201–504–3601

New Mexico

Michael J. Vargon
Deputy Director
Regulation & Licensing
Department
Securities Division
725 St. Michaels Drive
Santa Fe, NM 87501
505–827–7140 (general
information)
Fax: 505–984–0617

New York

Dennis Vacol
Attorney General
Department of Law
Bureau of Investor Protection
and Securities
120 Broadway, 23rd Floor
New York, NY 10271
212–416–8200
Fax: 212–416–8816

North Carolina

Rufus L. Edmisten
Secretary of State
Department of the Secretary
of State
Securities Division
300 North Salisbury Street
Suite 100
Raleigh, NC 27603–5909
919–733–3924
Fax: 919–821–0818
Toll free: 800–688–4507

North Dakota

Nancy Lewis
Office of the Securities
Commissioner
600 East Boulevard
Bismarck, ND 58505–0510
701–224–2910
Toll free in ND: 800–297–5124
Fax: 701–255–3113

Ohio

Tom Geyer
Acting Commissioner
Division of Securities
77 South High Street
22nd Floor
Columbus, OH 43215
614–644–7381
Fax: 614–466–3316

Oklahoma

Irving L. Faught
Administrator
Department of Securities
1st National Center
120 N. Robinson, Suite 860
Oklahoma City, OK 73102
405–235–0230
Fax: 405–280–7742

Oregon

Kerry E. Barnett, Director
Cecil Monroe, Administrator
Department of Consumer and
Business Services
Division of Finance & Corporate
Securities
350 Winter Street, N.E., Room 21
Salem, OR 97310
503–378–4387 (Corporate
Securities Section)
503–378–4140 (Finance Section)
Fax: 503–378–4178

Pennsylvania

Robert M. Lam, Chairman
Securities Commission
Eastgate Office Building
1010 North 7th Street, 2nd Floor
Harrisburg, PA 17102–1410
717–787–8061
Toll free in PA: 800–600–0007
Fax: 717–783–5122
**TDD/AT&T Relay Center toll
free: 800–654–5984**

Puerto Rico

Joseph P. O'Neil
Commissioner
Office of the Commissioner of
Financial Institutions
Securities Division
Centro Europa Building
Suite 600
1492 Ponce de Leon Avenue
San Juan, PR 00907–4127
787–723–3131
Fax: 787–723–4042

Juan Rivera
Assistant Securities
Commissioner
787–723–8359
787–723–8403

Felipe B. Cruz
Associate Director Securities
Hotline: 787–723–8445

Rhode Island

Maria D'Alessandro Piccirilli
Associate Director and
Superintendent of Securities
Department of Business
Regulation
233 Richmond Street, Suite 232
Providence, RI 02903–4232
401–277–3048
Fax: 401–273–5202
TDD: 401–277–2223

South Carolina

Tracey Myers
Deputy of Security Commission
Department of State
Securities Division
1205 Pendleton Street, Suite 525
Columbia, SC 29201
800–734–1087
Fax: 803–734–2164

South Dakota

Gail Sheppick
Enforcement Director
Division of Securities
118 West Capitol Avenue
Pierre, SD 57501–2017
605–773–4823
Fax: 605–773–5953

Tennessee

Kenneth T. McClellan
Assistant Commissioner
Department of Commerce
and Insurance
Securities Division
Davy Crockett Tower, Suite 680
500 James Robertson Parkway
Nashville, TN 37243–0485
615–741–2947
Toll free in TN: 800–863–9117
Fax: 615–532–8375

Texas

Denise Voigt Crawford
Securities Commissioner
State Securities Board
P.O. Box 13167
Austin, TX 78711–3167
512–305–8300
Fax: 512–305–8310

Utah

Mark J. Griffin
Director, Securities Division
Department of Commerce
P.O. Box 146760
Salt Lake City, UT
84114–6760
801–530–6600
Fax: 801–530–6980
Toll free in UT: 800–721–SAFE

Vermont

Richard S. Cortese
Deputy Commissioner
Department of Banking,
Insurance & Securities
Securities Division
89 Main Street, Drawer 20
Montpelier, VT 05620–3101
802–828–3420
802–828–2896

Virginia

Ron Thomas
Director
State Corporation Commission
Division of Securities & Retail
Franchising
P.O. Box 1197
Richmond, VA 23218
804–371–9051
Toll free in VA: 800–552–7945
Fax: 804–371–9911
TDD: 804–371–9203

Washington

Deborah Bortner
Administrator
Department of Financial
Institutions
Securities Division
P.O. Box 9033
Olympia, WA 98507–9033
360–902–8760
Fax: 360–586–5068
Toll free in WA: 800–372–8303
TDD: 360–664–8126

West Virginia

William E. Schneider
Deputy Commissioner of
Securities
State Auditor's Office
Securities Division
State Capitol Building
1900 Kanawha Boulevard East
Room 118–West
Charleston, WV 25305
304–558–2257
Fax: 304–344–2229

Wisconsin

Patricia Struck
Administrator
Department of Financial
Institutions
Division of Securities
P.O. Box 1768
Madison, WI 53702–1768
608–266–3431
Fax: 608–256–1259
Toll free in WI: 800–47–CHECK

Wyoming

Diana J. Ohman
Secretary of State & Securities
State Capitol Building
Cheyenne, WY 82002–0020
307–777–7370
Fax: 307–777–5339
TDD: 307–777–5351

State Utility Commissions

State utility commissions regulate consumer service and rates for gas, electricity and a variety of other services within your state. These services include rates for telephone calls and moving household goods. In some states, the utility commissions regulate water and transportation rates. Rates for utilities and services provided between states are regulated by the Federal government.

Many utility commissions handle consumer complaints. Sometimes, if a number of complaints are received about the same utility matter, they will conduct investigations.

Alabama
James Sullivan
President, Public Service
Commission
P.O. Box 991
Montgomery, AL 36101–0991
334–242–5207
Toll free in AL: 800–392–8050
Fax: 334–242–0509

Alaska
Robert A. Lohr
Executive Director
Alaska Public Utilities
Commission
1016 West 6th Avenue
Suite 400
Anchorage, AK 99501
907–276–6222
Toll free in AK: 800–390–2782
Fax: 907–276–0160
TDD: 907–276–4533

Arizona
Renz Jennings
Chairman, Corporation
Commission
1200 West Washington Street
Phoenix, AZ 85007
602–542–3935
Toll free in AZ: 800–222–7000
Fax: 602–542–5560
TDD: 602–542–2105

Arkansas
Sam I. Bratton, Jr.
Chairman, Public Service
Commission
P.O. Box 400
Little Rock, AR 72203–0400
501–682–1453
Toll free in AR: 800–482–1164
(complaints)
Fax: 501–682–5731

California
P. Gregory Conlon
President, Public Utilities
Commission
505 Van Ness Avenue
Room 5218
San Francisco, CA 94102
415–703–3703
Toll free in CA: 800–649–7570
(complaints)
Fax: 415–703–1758
TDD: 415–703–2032

Colorado
Robert Hix
Chairman, Public Utilities
Commission
1580 Logan Street
Logan Tower—Office Level 2
Denver, CO 80203
303–894–2000
Toll free in CO: 800–888–0170
Fax: 303–894–2065
TDD: 303–894–2512

Connecticut
Reginald J. Smith
Chairperson, Department of
Public Utility Control
10 Franklin Square
New Britain, CT 06051
860–827–1553
Toll free in CT: 800–382–4586
Fax: 860–827–2613
TDD: 860–827–2837

Delaware
Arnetta McRae
Commissioner, Public Service
Commission
1560 South DuPont Highway
Dover, DE 19901
302–739–4247
Toll free in DE: 800–282–8574
Fax: 302–739–4849
TDD: 302–739–4333

District of Columbia
Marlene L. Johnson
Chairperson, Public Service
Commission
450 Fifth Street, N.W.
Suite 800
Washington, DC 20001
202–626–5120
Fax: 202–393–1389
TDD: 202–638–2428

Florida
Susan F. Clark
Chairman, Public Service
Commission
2540 Shumard Oak Boulevard
Tallahassee, FL 32399–0850
904–413–6140
Toll free in FL: 800–342–3552;
800–955–8771
Fax: 800–511–0809
TDD toll free in FL:
800–955–8770

Georgia
Dave Baker
Commissioner, Public Service
Commission
244 Washington Street, S.W.
Atlanta, GA 30334
404–656–4512
Toll free in GA: 800–282–5813
Fax: 404–656–2341

Hawaii
Yukio Naito, Chairman
Dennis Yamada, Commissioner
Gregory Pai, Commissioner
Public Utilities Commission
465 South King Street
Room 103
Honolulu, HI 96813
808–586–2020
Toll free for other Islands:
800–468–4644
Fax: 808–586–2066

Idaho
Ralph Nelson, President
Marsha H. Smith, President
Public Utilities Commission
P.O. Box 83720
Boise, ID 83720–0074
208–334–3912
Toll free in ID: 800–377–3529
Fax: 208–334–3762
TDD: 208–334–3151

Illinois
Dan Miller
Chairman, Illinois Commerce
Commission
527 East Capitol Avenue
P.O. Box 19280
Springfield, IL 62794–9280
217–782–7907
Fax: 217–524–6859
TDD: 217–782–7434

Indiana
John R. Mortell
Chairman, Utility Regulatory
Commission
302 West Washington Street
Suite E–306
Indianapolis, IN 46204
317–232–2701
Toll free: 851–4268
Fax: 317–232–6758
TDD: 317–232–8556

Iowa
Allan T. Thoms
Chairperson, Iowa Utilities Board
Lucas State Office Building
5th Floor
Des Moines, IA 50319
515–281–5979
Fax: 515–281–8821

Kansas
Tim McKee
Chairman, State Corporation
Commission
1500 SW Arrowhead Road
Topeka, KS 66604–4027
913–271–3166
Toll free in KS: 800–662–0027
Fax: 913–271–3354

Kentucky
Linda Breathitt
Chair, Public Service Commission
730 Schenkel Lane
P.O. Box 615
Frankfort, KY 40602
502–564–3940
Toll free in KY: 800–772–4636
(complaints only)
Fax: 502–564–1582

Louisiana
Irma Muse Dixon
Chair, Public Service Commission
P.O. Box 91154
Baton Rouge, LA 70821–9154
504–342–6687
Toll free in LA: 800–256–2413
Fax: 504–342–2008

Maine
Thomas C. Welch
Chairman, Public Utilities
Commission
242 State Street
Augusta, ME 04333
207–287–3831
Toll free in ME: 800–452–4699
Fax: 207–287–1039

Maryland

H. Russell Frisby
Chairman, Public Service
Commission
6 St. Paul Street, 16th Floor
Baltimore, MD 21202
410–767–8000
Toll free in MD: 800–492–0474
Fax: 410–333–6495
**TDD toll free in MD:
800–735–2258**

Massachusetts

John Howe
Chairman, Department of
Public Utilities
100 Cambridge Street
12th Floor
Boston, MA 02202
617–727–3500
Fax: 617–723–8812
**TDD toll free:
800–323–3298**

Michigan

John Strand
Chairperson, Public Service
Commission
6545 Mercantile Way
P.O. Box 30221
Lansing, MI 48909
517–334–6445
Toll free in MI: 800–292–9555
Fax: 517–882–5170
**TDD toll free in MI:
800–649–3777**

Minnesota

Joel Jacobs
Chairman, Public Utilities
Commission
121 Seventh Place East
Suite 350
St. Paul, MN 55101–2147
612–296–7124
Toll Free in MN: 800–657–3782
Fax: 612–297–7073
TDD: 612–297–1200

Mississippi

Neilsen Cochran
Chairman, Public Service
Commission
P.O. Box 1174
Jackson, MS 39215
601–961–5400
Toll free in MS: 800–356–6430
Fax: 601–961–5469

Northern District
Toll free in MS: 800–356–6428

Central District
Toll free in MS: 800–356–6430

Southern District
Toll free in MS: 800–356–6429

Missouri

Karl Zobrist
Chairman, Public Service
Commission
P.O. Box 360
Jefferson City, MO 65102
573– 751–3243
Toll free in MO: 800–392–4211
Fax: 573–526–1500
**TDD toll free in MO:
800–735–2966**

Montana

Nancy McCaffee
Chair, Public Service
Commission
1701 Prospect Avenue
P.O. Box 202601
Helena, MT 59620–2601
Voice/TDD: 406–444–6199
Toll free in MT: 800–646–6150
Fax: 406–444–7618

Nebraska

Rod Johnson
Chairman, Public Service
Commission
300 The Atrium
1200 "N" Street
Lincoln, NE 68509
or
P.O. Box 94927
Lincoln, NE 68509–4927
402–471–3101
Toll free in NE: 800–526–0017
Fax: 402–471–0254
TDD: 402–471–0213

Nevada

John F. Mendoza
Chairman, Public Service
Commission
555 East Washington Avenue
Room 4600
Las Vegas, NV 89101
702–486–2600
Toll free in NV: 800–992–0900
Fax: 702–486–2595
TDD: 702–687–6000

New Hampshire

Douglas L. Patch
Chairman, Public Utilities
Commission
8 Old Suncook Road
Building No. 1
Concord, NH 03301
603–271–2431
Toll free in NH: 800–852–3793
Fax: 603–271–3878
TDD toll free : 800–735–2964

New Jersey

Herbert H. Tate
President, Board of Public
Utilities
Two Gateway Center
Newark, NJ 07102
201–648–2027
Toll free in NJ: 800–621–0241
Fax: 201–648–2836
TDD: 201–648–7983

New Mexico

Wayne Shirley
Chairman, New Mexico Public
Utility Commission
Marian Hall
224 East Palace Avenue
Sante Fe, NM 87501–2013
505–827–6940
Toll free in NM: 800–663–9782
Fax: 505–827–6973
TDD: 505–827–6911

New York

John F. O'Mara
Chairman, Public Service
Commission
3 Empire State Plaza
Albany, NY 12223
518–474–2530
Toll free in NY: 800–342–3377
(complaints);
800–342–3355 (emergency
service cutoff)
Fax: 518–474–7146
**TDD toll free in NY:
800–662–1220**

North Carolina

Hugh A. Wells
Chairman, Utilities Commission
P.O. Box 29510
Raleigh, NC 27626–0510
919–733–4249
919–733–9277 (consumer
services; complaints)
Fax: 919–733–7300

North Dakota

Susan Wefald, President
Leo Reinbold, Commissioner
Bruce Hagen, Commissioner
Public Service Commission
State Capitol, 12th Floor
Bismarck, ND 58505–0480
701–328–2400
Fax: 701–328–2410
TDD: 800–366–6888

Ohio

Craig A. Glazer
Chairman, Public Utilities
Commission
180 East Broad Street
Columbus, OH 43215–3793
614–466–3292
Toll free in OH: 800–686–7826
(consumer services)
Fax: 614–752–8351
TDD: 614–466–8180
**TDD toll free in OH:
800–686–1570**

Oklahoma

Cody Graves
Chairman, Corporation
Commission
Jim Thorpe Office Building
2101 North Lincoln Boulevard
Oklahoma City, OK 73105
405–521–2267
Toll free in OK: 800–522–8154
Fax: 405–521–6045

Oregon

Roger Hamilton
Chairman, Public Utility
Commission
550 Capitol St. NE
Salem, OR 97310–1380
503–378–6611
Toll free in OR: 800–522–2404
Fax: 503–378–5743
**TDD toll free in OR:
800–735–2900**

Pennsylvania

John M. Quain
Chairman, Public Utility
Commission
P.O. Box 3265
Harrisburg, PA 17105
717–783–7349
Toll free in PA: 800–782–1110
Fax: 717–787–4193

Puerto Rico

Nydia E. Rodriguez Martinez
Chairman, Public Service
Commission
P.O. Box 190870
San Juan, PR 00919–0810
787–756–1943

Rhode Island

James J. Malachowski
Chairman, Public Utilities
Commission
100 Orange Street
Providence, RI 02903
Voice/TDD: 401–277–3500
Toll free in RI: 800–341–1000
Fax: 401–277–6805

South Carolina
Rudolph Mitchell
Chairman, Public Service
Commission
P.O. Drawer 11649
Columbia, SC 29211
803–737–5100
Toll free in SC: 800–922–1531
Fax: 803–737–5246
TDD toll free in SC:
800–735–2905

South Dakota
Ken Stofferahn, Chairman
Jim Burg, Vice Chairman
Laska Schoenfelder,
Commissioner
Public Utilities Commission
500 East Capitol Avenue
Pierre, SD 57501–5070
605–773–3201
Toll free in SD: 800–332–1782
Fax: 605–773–3809

Tennessee
Lynn Greer, Chairman
Tennessee Regulatory Authority
460 James Robertson Parkway
Nashville, TN 37243–0505
615–741–3668
Voice/TDD toll free in TN:
800–342–8359
Fax: 615–741–5015

Texas
Pat Wood, III, Chairman
Judy Walsh, Commissioner
Robert W. Gee, Commissioner
Public Utility Commission
7800 Shoal Creek Boulevard
Suite 400N
Austin, TX 78757
512–458–0100
Fax: 512–458–8340
TDD: 512–458–0221

Utah
Stephen F. Mecham
Chairman, Public Service
Commission
160 East 300 South
Salt Lake City, UT 84111
801–530–6716
Fax: 801–530–6796
TDD: 801–530–6706

Vermont
Richard H. Cowart
Chairman, Vermont Public
Service Board
112 State Street
Montpelier, VT 05620–2701
802–828–2358
Fax: 828–3351
TDD: 800–253–0191

Virgin Islands
Walter Challenger
Acting Chairman
Public Services Commission
P.O. Box 40
Charlotte Amalie
St. Thomas, VI 00804
809–776–1291
Fax: 809–774–4971

Virginia
Theodore V. Morrison, Jr.
Chairman, State Corporation
Commission
P.O. Box 1197
Richmond, VA 23209
804–371–9608
Toll free in VA: 800–552–7945
Fax: 371–9376
TDD: 804–371–9206

Washington
Sharon Nelson
Chairman, Utilities and
Transportation Commission
P.O. Box 47250
Olympia, WA 98504–7250
360–753–6423
Toll free in WA: 800–562–6150
Fax: 360–586–1150
TTY: 360–586–8206

West Virginia
Boyce Griffith
Chairman, Public Service
Commission
P.O. Box 812
Charleston, WV 25323
Voice/TDD: 304–340–0300
Toll free in WV: 800–344–5113
Fax: 304–340–0325

Wisconsin
Cheryl L. Parrino
Chairman, Public Service
Commission
610 North Whitneyway
Madison, WI 53705–2729
608–266–5481
Toll free in WI: 800–225–7729
Fax: 608–266–3957
TDD: 608–267–1479

Wyoming
Steven Ellenbecker, Chairman
Bill Tucker, Chairman
Public Service Commission
700 West 21st Street
Cheyenne, WY 82002
307–777–7427
Toll free in WY: 800–877–9965
Fax: 307–777–5700

State Vocational and Rehabilitation Agencies

State vocational and rehabilitation agencies coordinate and provide a number of services for disabled persons. These services can include counseling, evaluation, training and job placement. There are also services for the sight and hearing impaired. For more information, call or write the office nearest you.

Alabama
Lamona H. Lucas,
Commissioner
Department of Rehabilitation
Services
P.O. Box 11586
Montgomery, AL 36111–0586
334–281–8780
Toll free in AL: 800–441–7607

Alaska
Duane French, Director
Division of Vocational
Rehabilitation
801 W. 10th St., Suite 200
Juneau, AK 99801–1894
Voice/TDD: 907–465–2814
Toll free in AK: 800–478–2815

American Samoa
Peter Galeai, Director
Vocational Rehabilitation
Department of Manpower
Resources
Pago Pago, AS 96799
011–684–633–2336

Arizona
Roger J. Hodges, Administrator
Rehabilitation Services
Administration (930A)
1789 West Jefferson
2nd Floor N.W.
Phoenix, AZ 85007
602–542–3332
Voice/TDD: 602–542–6049

Arkansas
Bobby C. Simpson,
Commissioner
Arkansas Rehabilitation Services
Division of Vocational &
Technical Education Department of Education
P.O. Box 3781
Little Rock, AR 72203
501–296–1616
Toll free in AR: 800–330–0632
Fax: 501–296–1675
TDD: 501–296–6669

James C. Hudson , Director
Division of Services
for the Blind
Department of Human Services
P.O. Box 3237
Little Rock, AR 72203
Toll free in AR: 800–960–9270
TDD: 501–324–9271

California
Brenda Premo, Director
Department of Rehabilitation
830 K Street Mall
Sacramento, CA 95814
Voice/TDD: 916–445–3971

Colorado
Dina Huerta, Director
Division of Vocational
Rehabilitation
110 16th Street, 2nd Floor
Denver, CO 80202
Voice/TDD: 303–620–4153
Fax: 303–620–4189

Connecticut

Richard Carlson, Chief
Division of Client Services
State Department of Social
Services
Bureau of Rehabilitation
Services
10 Griffin Road North
Windsor, CT 06095
860–298–2000
Toll free in CT: 800–537–2549
TDD: 860–298–2231

George Precourt,
Executive Director
Board of Education and S
ervices for the Blind
170 Ridge Road
Wethersfield, CT 06109
860–249–8525
Toll free in CT: 800–842–4510
Fax: 860–278–6920

Delaware

Michelle Pointer, Director
Division of Vocational
Rehabilitation
Department of Labor
4425 North Market Street
P.O. Box 9969
Wilmington, DE 19809–0969
302–761–8300
Voice/TDD: 302–761–8349

Debra Wallace, Director (Acting)
Division for the Visually Impaired
Department of Health and
Social Services
1901 N. DuPont Highway
New Castle, DE 19720
302–577–4731

District of Columbia

Ruth Royall Hill, Administrator
D.C. Rehabilitation Services
Administration
Department of Human Services
800 9th Street, S.W.,
Fourth Floor
Washington, DC 20024
202–645–5703

Florida

Tamara Bibb Allen, Director
Division of Vocational
Rehabilitation
Department of Labor and
Employment Security
20002 Old St. Augustine Road
Building A
Tallahassee, FL 32399–0696
904–488–6210
Voice/TDD: 904–488–2867

Whit Springfield, Director
Division of Blind Services
Department of Labor and
Employment Security
2540 Executive Center
Circle West
Douglas Building, Room 203
Tallahassee, FL 32399
Voice/TDD: 904–488–1330
Toll free in FL: 800–342–1828

Georgia

Peggy Rosser, Director
Division of Rehabilitation
Services
Department of Human
Resources
2 Peachtree Street, N.W., 23rd
Floor
Atlanta, GA 30330–3166
Voice/TDD: 404–657–3000

Guam

Norbert F. Ungacta,
Acting Director
Department of Vocational
Rehabilitation
122 Harmon Plaza, Room
B–201
Harmon Industrial Park,
GU 96911
011–671–475–4645
001–671–475–4635
(consumer information)

Hawaii

Neil Shim, Administrator
Division of Vocational
Rehabilitation
and Services for the Blind
Department of Human Services
P.O. Box 339
Honolulu, HI 96809
808–586–5355
808–586–5366

Idaho

George Pelletier, Jr.,
Administrator
Division of Vocational
Rehabilitation
Len B. Jordan Building
Room 150
650 West State
Boise, ID 83720–0096
Voice/TDD: 208–334–3390
Toll free in ID: 800–856–2720

James E. Monroe, Administrator
Idaho Commission for the Blind
341 West Washington
Boise, ID 83702
208–334–3220
Toll free in ID: 800–542–8688

Illinois

Audrey McCrimon, Director
Department of Rehabilitation
Services
623 East Adams Street
Springfield, IL 62794
217–785–0218
Toll free in IL: 800–ASK–DORIS
TDD: 217–782–5734

Indiana

Bobby Conner, Director
Division of Disability, Aging and
Rehabilitative Services
402 West Washington Street,
Room W–451
P.O. Box 7083
Indianapolis, IN 46207–7083
317–232–1147
Toll free: 800–545–7763
**TDD toll free in IN:
800–962–8408**

Iowa

Marge Knudsen, Administrator
Division of Vocational
Rehabilitation Services
Department of Education
510 East 12th Street
Des Moines, IA 50319
Voice/TDD: 515–281–4311
Toll free in IA: 800–532–1486

Creig Slayton, Director
Department for the Blind
524 4th Street
Des Moines, IA 50309
Voice/TDD: 515–281–1333
Toll free in IA: 800–362–2587

Kansas

Joyce Cussimanio
Commissioner
Rehabilitation Services
Department of Social and
Rehabilitation Services
300 S.W. Oakley
Biddle Building, 1st Floor
Topeka, KS 66606
913–296–3911
TDD: 913–296–7029

Kentucky

Sam Serraglio, Commissioner
Department of Vocational
Rehabilitation
209 St. Clair
Frankfort, KY 40601
Voice/TDD: 502–564–4440
Toll free in KY: 800–372–7172
TDD: 502–564–6742

Denise Placido,
Commissioner (Acting)
Department for the Blind
Workforce Development Cabinet
209 St. Clair
Frankfort, KY 40601
502–564–4754
Toll free: 800–321–6668

Louisiana

May Nelson, Director
Louisiana Rehabilitation
Services
Department of Social Services
8225 Florida Boulevard
Baton Rouge, LA 70806–4834
504–925–4168
Toll free in LA: 800–737–2958
Voice/TDD: 504–925–4179

Maine

Harold Lewls, Director
Division of the Blind & Visually
Impaired
Margaret Brewster, Director
Division of Vocational
Rehabilitation
Department of Labor
35 Anthony Avenue
Augusta, ME 04333–0150
207–624–5300
Toll free in ME: 800–332–1003
Voice/TDD: 207–624–5322

Mariana Islands

Manny Villagomez, Chief
Vocational Rehabilitation Division
Commonwealth of Northern
Mariana Islands
P.O. Box 1521
SaiPan, Mariana Islands 96950
011–670–234–6538

Maryland

Robert Burns, Assistant State
Superintendent
Division of Rehabilitation
Services
State Department of Education
2301 Argonne Drive
Baltimore, MD 21218
410–554–9385
Fax: 410–554–9412
TDD: 410–554–9411

Massachusetts

Charles Crawford, Commissioner
Commission for the Blind
88 Kingston Street
Boston, MA 02111–2227
617–727–5550
Toll free in MA: 800–392–6450
**TDD toll free in MA:
800–392–6556**

Elmer C. Bartels, Commissioner
Massachusetts Rehabilitation
Commission
4 Point Place
27–43 Wormwood Street
Boston, MA 02210
617–727–2172
TDD: 617–727–9063

Michigan
Joseph Skiba
State Director
Michigan Rehabilitation
Services
Michigan Jobs Commission
P.O. Box 30010
Lansing, MI 48909
517–373–3390
Toll free in MI: 800–605–6722
TDD: 517–373–4035

Philip E. Peterson,
Executive Director
Michigan Commission for
the Blind
Family Independence Agency
201 North Washington Square
P.O. Box 30652
Lansing, MI 48909
517–373–2062
Toll free in MI: 800–292–4200
Voice/TDD: 517–373–4025

Linda Dorn, State Director
Disability Determination Service
Family Independence Agency
P.O. Box 30011
Lansing, MI 48909
517–373–7830
517–373–4533
Toll Free in MI: 800–366–3404

Minnesota
Norena A. Hale, Assistant
Commissioner
Department of Economics
and Security
Rehabilitation Services Branch
390 North Robert Street
5th Floor
St. Paul, MN 55101
612–296–1822
TDD: 612–296–3900

Richard C. Davis, Assistant
Commissioner
Services for the Blind
2200 University Avenue
West #240
St. Paul, MN 55114–1840
612–642–0500
Toll free in MN: 800–652–9000
Voice/TDD: 612–642–0506

Mississippi
Mike Gandy, Office Director
Office of Vocational
Rehabilitation for the Blind
P.O. Box 1698
Jackson, MS 39215
601–853–5100
Voice/TDD: 800–443–1000

Noll C. Carnoy, Executive Director
Vocational Rehabilitation Division
Department of Rehabilitation
Services
1281 Highway 51
P.O. Box 22806
Madison, MS 39110
601–853–5100
Toll free in MS: 800–443–1000

Missouri
Don Gann, Assistant
Commissioner
Division of Vocational
Rehabilitation
State Department of Education
3024 W. Truman Blvd.
Jefferson City, MO 65109
Voice/TDD: 573–751–3251

Sally Howard, Deputy Director
Rehabilitation Services
for the Blind
Division of Family Services
619 East Capitol
Jefferson City, MO 65101
573–751–4249

Montana
Joe A. Mathews, Administrator
Department of Public Health
and Human Services
Disability Services Division
P.O. Box 4210
Helena, MT 59604–4210
Voice/TDD: 406–444–2590

Nebraska
Frank Lloyd, Assistant Com-
missioner/Director
Division of Vocational
Rehabilitation Services
State Department of Education
P.O. Box 94987
Lincoln, NE 68509
402–471–3649
Voice/TDD: 402–471–3659

James S. Nyman, Director
Services for the Visually
Impaired
Department of Public Institutions
4600 Valley Road
Lincoln, NE 68510
Voice/TDD: 402–471–2891

Nevada
Elizabeth Breshears,
Administrator
Nevada Rehabilitation Division
505 East King Street
505 East King Street
Room 502
Carson City, NV 89710
Voice/TDD: 702–687–4440

New Hampshire
Paul K. Leather, Director
Division of Adult Learning and
Rehabilitation
State Department of Education
78 Regional Drive, Building 2
Concord, NH 03301
Voice/TDD: 603–271–3471

New Jersey
Jamie C. Hilton, Executive
Director
New Jersey Commission for
the Blind
and Visually Impaired
153 Halsey Street, 6th Floor
P.O. Box 47017
Newark, NJ 07101
201–648–2324
Voice/TDD: 201–648–6276
TDD: 201–648–4559

Thomas G. Jennings, Director
Division of Vocational
Rehabilitation Services
135 East State Street, CN 398
Trenton, NJ 08625–0398
609–292–5987
Voice/TDD: 609–292–2919

New Mexico
Terry Brigance, Director
Department of Education
Division of Vocational
Rehabilitation
435 St. Michaels Drive
Building D
Santa Fe, NM 87505
Toll Free: 800–235–5387
(complaints)
Voice/TDD: 505–827–3500

New York
Lawrence C. Gloeckler, Deputy
Commissioner
Office of Vocational and
Educational Services for
Individuals with Disabilities
New York State Education
Department
One Commerce Plaza
Room 1606
Albany, NY 12234
518–474–2714
Toll free in NY: 800–222–JOBS
(employment hotline)
TDD: 518–486–3773

Eugene Luini, Director
State Department
of Social Services
Commission for the Blind and
Visually Handicapped
40 N. Pearl Street
Albany, NY 12243
518–473–1801
Toll free in NY: 800–342–3715
TDD: 518–474–7501

North Carolina
Bob Philbeck, Director
Division of Vocational
Rehabilitation Services
Department of Human
Resources
State Office
P.O. Box 26053
Raleigh, NC 27611
919–733–3364
Fax: 919–733–7968
Voice/TDD: 919–733–5924

John DeLuca, Director
Division of Services
for the Blind
Department of Human
Resources
309 Ashe Avenue
Raleigh, NC 27606
919–733–9822
Voice/TDD: 919–733–9700

North Dakota
Gene Hysjulien, Director
Division of Vocational
Rehabilitation
Department of Human Services
Dacotah Foundation Bldg.
600 S. Second Street, Suite 1B
Bismarck, ND 58504–5729
701–328–8950
Toll free in ND: 800–755–2745
TDD: 701–328–8968

Ohio
Robert L. Rabe, Administrator
Rehabilitation Services
Commission
400 East Campus View Boule-
vard
Columbus, OH 43235–4604
Voice/TDD: 614–438–1210
Toll free in OH: 800–282–4536,
ext. 1210

Oklahoma
Linda Parker, Director
Department of Rehabilitation
Services
3535 N.W. 58, Suite 500
Oklahoma City, OK 73112
405–951–3400

Oregon

Charles Young, Administrator
Commission for the Blind
535 S.E. 12th Avenue
Portland, OR 97214
503–731–3221
Fax: 503–731–3230
TDD: 503–731–3224

Joil Southwell, Administrator
Division of Vocational
Rehabilitation
Department of Human
Resources
Human Resources Building
500 Summer St. NE
Salem, OR 97310–1018
503–945–5880
TDD: 503–378–3933

Pennsylvania

Gil Selders, Executive Director
Office of Vocational Rehabilitation
Labor and Industry Building
7th and Forster Streets
Harrisburg, PA 17120
717–787–5244
Voice/TDD: 717–783–8917
Toll free in PA: 800–442–6351

Robert Eschbach, Director
Bureau of Blindness
and Visual Services
Department of Public Welfare
P.O. Box 2675
Harrisburg, PA 17105–2675
717–787–6176
Toll free in PA: 800–622–2842

Puerto Rico

Jose R. Santana, Administrator
Administration for Vocational
Rehabilitation
Department of Family
P.O. Box 191118
San Juan, PR 00919–1118
809–725–1792

Rhode Island

Raymond Carroll,
Administrator (Acting)
Department of Human Services
Division of Community Services
Office of Rehabilitation Services
40 Fountain Street
Providence, RI 02903–1898
401–421–7005
TDD: 401–421–7016

Jack Thompson, Deputy
Administrator
Office of Rehabilitation Services
Services for the Blind and
Visually Impaired
Department of Human Services
40 Fountain Street
Providence, RI 02903
401–277–2300
Voice/TDD: 401–277–3010
Toll free in RI: 800–752–0888

South Carolina

Donald Gist, Commissioner
Commission for the Blind
1430 Confederate Avenue
Columbia, SC 29201
803–734–7522
Toll free in SC: 800–922–2222

P. Charles LaRosa, Jr.,
Commissioner
Vocational Rehabilitation
Department
1410 Boston Avenue
P.O. Box 15
West Columbia, SC 29171
803–896–6504
Voice/TDD: 803–896–6635

South Dakota

David L. Miller, Division Director
Division of Rehabilitation Services
Department of Human Services
East Highway 34, Hillsview Plaza
c/o 500 E. Capitol
Pierre, SD 57501–5070
Voice/TDD: 605–773–3195
Toll free in SD: 800–265–9684

Grady Kickul, Division Director
Division of Service to the Blind
and Visually Impaired
East Highway 34, Hillsview Plaza
c/o 500 E. Capitol
Pierre, SD 57501–5070
605–773–4644
TDD: 605–773–5990

Tennessee

Jack Van Hooser, Assistant
Commissioner
Rehabilitation Services
Department of Human Services
Citizens Plaza State Office
Bldg., 15th Floor
400 Deaderick Street
Nashville, TN 37248–0060
Voice/TDD: 615–313–4714

Texas

Vernon M. Arrell, Commissioner
Texas Rehabilitation Commission
4900 North Lamar
Austin, TX 78751
512–483–4001
Toll free: 800–628–5115

Pat D. Westbrook,
Executive Director
Texas Commission for the Blind
4800 N. Lamar Blvd.
Austin, TX 78756
512–459–2500
Voice/TDD: 512–459–2608
**Voice/TDD toll free in TX:
800–252–5204**

Utah

Blaine Petersen,
Executive Director
Utah State Office of
Rehabilitation
250 East Fifth South
Salt Lake City, UT 84111
Voice/TDD: 801–538–7530
Toll free in UT: 800–473–7530

William G. Gibson, Director
Services for the Visually
Handicapped
State Office of Rehabilitation
309 East First South
Salt Lake City, UT 84111
801–323–4343
Toll free: 800–284–1823

Vermont

Diane Dalmasse, Director
Vocational Rehabilitation Division
103 South Main Street
Waterbury, VT 05671–2303
Voice/TDD: 802–241–2186

Steve Stone, Director
Division for the Blind
and Visually Impaired
103 South Main Street
Waterbury, VT 05676
802–241–2210

Virgin Islands

Sedonie Halbert, Administrator
Division for Disabilities and
Rehabilitation Services
Virgin Islands Department of
Human Services
1303 Hospital Ground
Knud Hansen Complex
St. Thomas, VI 00802
809–774–0930

Virginia

John R. Vaughn, Commissioner
Department of Rehabilitative
Services
4901 Fitzhugh Avenue
P.O. Box 11045
Richmond, VA 23230
804–367–0316
Voice/TDD: 804–367–0315
Toll free in VA: 800–552–5019

W. Roy Grizzard, Jr.,
Commissioner
Department for the
Visually Handicapped
397 Azalea Avenue
Richmond, VA 23227
Voice/TDD: 804–371–3140
Toll free in VA: 800–622–2155

Washington

Jeanne Munro, Director
Division of Vocational
Rehabilitation
Department of Social and
Health Services
P.O. Box 45340
Olympia, WA 98504–5340
Voice/TDD: 360–427–2135
Toll free in WA: 800–637–5627

Shirley Smith, Director
Department of Services for
the Blind
1400 South Evergreen Park Drive
P.O. Box 40933
Olympia, WA 98504–0933
360–586–1224
Toll free in WA: 800–552–7103
TDD: 360–586–6437

West Virginia

William L. Tanzey, Director
Division of Rehabilitation
Services
P.O. Box 50890
State Capitol Complex
Charleston, WV 25305–0890
304–766–4600
Voice/TDD: 304–766–4970
Toll free in WV: 800–642–3021

Wisconsin

Judy R. Norman–Nunnery,
Administrator
Division of Vocational
Rehabilitation
Department of Workforce
Development
2917 International Lane, 3rd Floor
P.O. Box 7852
Madison, WI 53707–7852
608–243–5600
TDD: 608–243–5601

Wyoming

Gary W. Child, Administrator
Division of Vocational
Rehabilitation
Department of Employment
1 East Herschler Building
Cheyenne, WY 82002
307–777–7385
Voice/TDD: 307–777–7389

State Weights and Measures Offices

State Weights and Measures offices enforce laws and regulations about the labeling, weight, measure or count of such packaged items as food and household products. These offices also check the accuracy of weighing and measuring devices, for example, supermarket scales, gasoline pumps, taxicab meters and rental car odometers.

Some city and county offices have weights and measures functions in addition to the state offices listed below. Contact the state office for the appropriate weights and measures office or check your local telephone directory under the government listings for your local weights and measures office. The office might be listed under either the city or county bureau of standards, agriculture or consumer protection.

Alabama

Steadman Hollis, Director
Weights and Measures Division
Department of Agriculture
P.O. Box 3336
Montgomery, AL 36109–0336
334–240–7133
Toll free in AL: 800–321–0018
Fax: 334–240–7193

Alaska

Edward Moses, Director
Aves D. Thompson, Chief
Inspector
Weights and Measures
Department of Commerce and
Economic Development
Division of Measurement
Standards
12050 Industry Way
Huffman Business Park
Building O
Anchorage, AK 99515
907–345–7750
Toll free in AK: 800–478–7636

Arizona

John Hays, Director
Department of Weights and
Measures
9535 E. Doubletree Ranch Road
Scottsdale, AZ 85258–5539
602–255–5211
Toll free in AZ: 800–277–6675
Fax: 602–255–1950

Arkansas

James M. Hile, Director
Bureau of Standards
4608 West 61st Street
Little Rock, AR 72209
501–324–9681
Fax: 501–562–7605

California

Darrell A. Guensler, Director
Division of Measurement
Standards
Department of Food and
Agriculture
8500 Fruitridge Road
Sacramento, CA 95826
916–229–3000
Fax: 916–229–3026

Colorado

David Wallace, Chief
Measurements Standards
Section
Department of Agriculture
3125 Wyandot Street
Denver, CO 80211
303–866–2845
Fax: 303–866–2836

Connecticut

Allan M. Nelson, Director
Weights and Measures Division
Department of Consumer
Protection
State Office Building,
Room 110
165 Capitol Avenue
Hartford, CT 06106
860–566–5230
Fax: 860–566–7630

Delaware

Steven Connors, Administrator
Office of Weights and Measures
Department of Agriculture
2320 South DuPont Highway
Dover, DE 19901–5515
302–739–4811
Fax: 302–697–6287

District of Columbia

Jeffrey Mason, Chief
Weights and Measures
Market Branch
Department of Consumer and
Regulatory Affairs
1110 U Street, S.E.
Washington, DC 20020
202–645–6706
Fax: 202–645–6705

Florida

Max Gray, Chief
Bureau of Weights and
Measures
Department of Agriculture and
Consumer Services
3125 Conner Blvd.,
Mail Stop L–29
Building #2
Tallahassee, FL 32399–1650
904–488–9140
Fax: 904–922–6655

Georgia

Bill Truby, Assistant
Commissioner
Division of Weights and
Measures
Department of Agriculture
Agriculture Building
Atlanta, GA 30334
404–656–3605
Toll free in GA: 800–282–5852
Fax: 404–656–9380

Hawaii

Masao Hanaoka, Administrator
Measurement Standards
Department of Agriculture
725 Ilalo Street
Honolulu, HI 96813–5524
808–586–0886
Fax: 808–586–0889

Idaho

James R. Boatman, Chief
Bureau of Weights and
Measures
Department of Agriculture
2216 Kellogg Lane
Boise, ID 83712
208–332–8690
Fax: 208–334–2170

Illinois

Sidney A. Colbrook, Manager
Bureau of Weights and
Measures
Department of Agriculture
801 East Sangamon Avenue
P.O. Box 19281
Springfield, IL 62794–9281
217–782–3817
Toll Free in IL: 800–582–0468
Fax: 217–524–7801

Indiana

Larry Stump, Division Director
Weights and Measures Division
State Department of Health
1330 West Michigan Street
P.O. Box 1964
Indianapolis, IN 46206–1964
317–383–6350
Fax: 317–383–6776

Iowa

Jerry L. Bane, Bureau Chief
Weights and Measures
Department of Agriculture and
Land Stewardship
H.A. Wallace Building
Des Moines, IA 50319
515–281–5716
Fax: 515–281–6800

Kansas

Constantine Cotsoradis, Director
Weights and Measures Division
Department of Agriculture
2016 South West 37th Street
Topeka, KS 66611–2570
913–267–4641
Fax: 913–267–2518

Kentucky

Vicki Van Hoose, Director
Division of Weights and
Measures
Department of Agriculture
106 West Second Street
Frankfort, KY 40601–2882
502–564–4870
Fax: 502–564–5669

Louisiana

Ronald Harrell, Director
Weights and Measures
Department of Agriculture
P.O. Box 3098
Baton Rouge, LA 70821–3098
504–925–3780
Fax: 504–922–0477

Maine

David E. Gagnon, Director
Quality Assurance and
Regulations
State House Station 28
Augusta, ME 04333–0028
207–287–3841
Fax: 207–287–5576

Maryland

Louis E. Straub, Chief
Weights and Measures Section
Maryland Department of
Agriculture
50 Harry S. Truman Parkway
Annapolis, MD 21401
410–841–5790
Fax: 410–841–2765

Massachusetts

Charles H. Carroll
Assistant Director of Standards
Division of Standards
One Ashburton Place
McCormick Building,
Room 1115
Boston, MA 02108
617–727–3480
Fax: 617–727–5705

Michigan

Edward Heffron, Division
Director
Department of Agriculture,
Food Division
Ottawa Building, 4th Floor
P.O. Box 30017
Lansing, MI 48909
517–373–1060
Fax: 517–373–3333

Minnesota

Michael F. Blacik, Director
Division of Weights and
Measures
Department of Public Service
2277 Highway 36
St. Paul, MN 55113–3800
612–639–4010
Fax: 612–639–4014

Mississippi

William P. Eldridge, Director
Weights and Measures Division
Department of Agriculture
21 N. Jefferson Street
P.O. Box 1609
Jackson, MS 39201
601–354–7077
Fax: 601–354–6502

Missouri

Roy Humphreys, Division
Director
Weights and Measures Division
Department of Agriculture
P.O. Box 630
Jefferson City, MO
65102–0630
573–751–4316
Fax: 573–751–1784; 573–0281

Montana

Jack Kane, Bureau Chief
Bureau of Weights and
Measures
Department of Commerce
Capitol Station
Helena, MT 59620
406–444–3164
Fax: 406–444–4305

Nebraska

Steven A. Malone, Director
Division of Weights and
Measures
Department of Agriculture
301 Centennial Mall South,
4th Floor
P.O. Box 94757
Lincoln, NE 68509
402–471–4292
Fax: 402–471–3252

Nevada

Edward M. Hoganson,
Supervisor
Department of Business
and Industry
Division of Agriculture
Weights and Measures
2150 Frazier Avenue
Sparks, NV 89431
702–688–1166
Fax: 702–688–2533

New Hampshire

Stephen Taylor, Commissioner
Department of Agriculture,
Markets and Food
Bureau of Weights and
Measures
P.O. Box 2042
Concord, NH 03302–2042
603–271–3700
Fax: 603–271–1109

New Jersey

William J. Wolfe, State
Superintendent
Office of Weights and Measures
1261 Routes 1 and 9 South
Avenel, NJ 07001–1647
908–815–4840
Fax: 908–382–5298

New Mexico

Gary West, Director
Consumer Services, Dept. 3170
Department of Agriculture
P.O. Box 30005
Las Cruces, NM 88003–8005
505–646–1616
Fax: 505–646–3303

New York

Ross Andersen,
Assistant Director
Bureau of Weights and
Measures
Department of Agriculture
and Markets
1 Winners Circle
Albany, NY 12235
518–457–3452
Fax: 518–457–5693

North Carolina

N. David Smith, Director
Standards Division
Department of Agriculture
P.O. Box 27647–Dept. SD
Raleigh, NC 27611
919–733–3313
Fax: 919–715–0524

North Dakota

Alan Moch, Director
Division of Testing and Safety
State Capitol
Bismarck, ND 58505–0480
701–328–2413
Fax: 701–328–2410

Ohio

James C. Truex,
Inspection Manager
Division of Weights
and Measures
Department of Agriculture
8995 East Main Street, Bldg. 5
Reynoldsburg, OH 43068
614–728–6290
Fax: 614–728–6424

Oklahoma

Ernest Hellwege, Director
Plant Industry and Consumer
Services
Department of Agriculture
2800 North Lincoln Boulevard
Oklahoma City, OK 73105
405–521–3864, ext. 261
Fax: 405–522–4584

Oregon

Kendrick J. Simila,
Administrator
Measurement Standards
Department of Agriculture
635 Capitol Street, N.E.
Salem, OR 97310–0110
503–986–4670
Fax: 503–986–4784

Pennsylvania

Charles Bruckner, Director
Bureau of Ride and
Measurement Standards
Department of Agriculture
2301 North Cameron Street
Harrisburg, PA 17110
717–787–9089
Fax: 717–772–2780

Puerto Rico

Francisco F. Aponte Ortiz
Auxiliary Secretary for
Complaints
Department of Consumer Affairs
P.O. Box 41059
Minillas Station
Santurce, PR 00940
787–721–3190
Fax: 787–726–5707

Rhode Island

Lynda L. Maurer, Supervising
Metrologist
Mercantile Division
Department of Labor
610 Manton Avenue
Providence, RI 02909
401–457–1867
Fax: 401–457–1873

South Carolina

Carol P. Fulmer, Assistant
Commissioner
Consumer Services Division
Department of Agriculture
P.O. Box 11280
Columbia, SC 29211–1280
803–737–9690
Fax: 803–737–9703

South Dakota

Michael Mehlhaff, Director
Division of Commercial
Inspection and Regulation
118 West Capitol
Pierre, SD 57501–2036
605–773–3697
Fax: 605–773–6631

Tennessee

Robert Williams, Standards
Administrator
Weights and Measures
Department of Agriculture
P.O. Box 40627
Melrose Station
Nashville, TN 37204
615–360–0109
Fax: 615–360–0608

Texas

Ed Price, Director
Weights and Measures Program
Department of Agriculture
P.O. Box 12847
Austin, TX 78711
512–463–7602
Fax: 512–463–7643

Utah

Kyle R. Stephens, Director
Division of Regulatory Services
State Department of Agriculture
P.O. Box 146500
Salt Lake City, UT
84114–6500
801–538–7150
Fax: 801–538–7126

Vermont

Bruce A. Martell, Supervisor
Consumer Assurance Section
Department of Agriculture
Food & Markets
116 State Street
Drawer 20
Montpelier, VT 05620–2901
802–828–2436
Fax: 802–828–2361

Virgin Islands

Maurice Illidge, Director
Weights and Measures Division
Dept. of Licensing and
Consumer Affairs
Golden Rock Shopping Center
Christiansted
St. Croix, VI 00820
809–773–2226
Fax. 809–778–8250
Toll free: 888–800–3522

Virginia

J. Alan Rogers, Program
Manager
Office of Product and Industry
Standards, Room 402
Richmond, VA 23218–1163
804–786–2476
Fax: 804–786–1571

Washington

Bob Arrington, Program
Manager
Weights and Measures
Department of Agriculture
P.O. Box 42560
Olympia, WA 98504–2560
360–902–1857
Fax: 360–902–2086

West Virginia

Karl Angell, Jr., Director
Division of Labor
Weights and Measures Section
570 W. MacCorkle Avenue
St. Alban, WV 25177
304–722–0602
Fax: 304–722–0605

Wisconsin

Alan Porter, Manager
Bureau of Consumer Protection
Department of Agriculture
Trade and Consumer Protection
2811 Agriculture Drive
P.O. Box 8911
Madison, WI 53708
608–224–4945
Toll free In WI: 800–422–7128
Fax: 608–224–4939

Wyoming

Jim Bigelow, Technical Services
Manager
Consumer/Compliance Division
Department of Agriculture
2219 Carey Avenue
Cheyenne, WY 82002–0100
307–777–6590
Fax: 307–777–6593

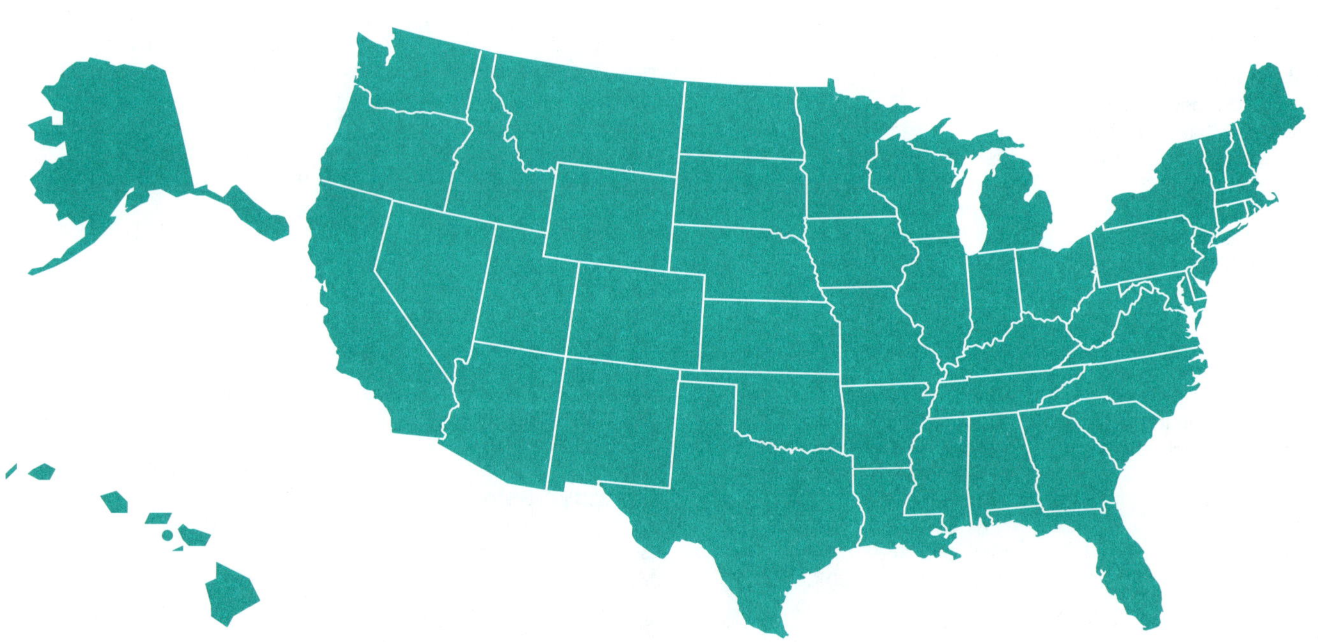

Military Commissary and Exchange Offices

Consumers who shop at military commissaries and exchanges and who have a question or problem should contact the local manager before contacting the regional offices in this section. If your problem is not resolved at the local level, then write or call the regional office nearest you. Be sure to discuss the problem with the local and regional offices before contacting the national headquarters of a commissary or exchange.

Defense Commissary Agency

Northeast Region

Defense Commissary Agency
Northeast Region
Huber Road, Building 2257
Fort George G. Meade, MD
20755–5220
301–677–9782/9823
Fax: 301–677–9222/9230

Northwest/Pacific Region

Defense Commissary Agency
Northwest/Pacific Region
Box 339542
Fort Lewis, WA 95433–9542
206–967–3364/3663
Fax: 206–967–3663

Southwest Region

Defense Commissary Agency
Southwest Region
Marine Corps Air Station El Toro
Building 694, P.O. Box 96017
Santa Ana, CA 92709–6017
714–726–3079
Fax: 714–726–4330

Midwest Region

Defense Commissary Agency
Midwest Region
300 AFCOMS Way, Bldg. 3030
Kelly Air Force Base, TX
78241–6132
210–925–6655, ext. 328
Fax: 210–925–2619

Central Region

Defense Commissary Agency
Central Region
5151 Bonney Road, Suite 201
Virginia Beach, VA
23462–4314
804–363–3500
Fax: 804–363–3565

Southern Region

Defense Commissary Agency
Southern Region
60 West Maxwell Boulevard
Maxwell Air Force Base, AL
36112–6307
334–953–6318/6319
Fax: 334–953–2346/3725

European Region

Defense Commissary Agency
Europe Region
DeCA–EU
Unit 3060
Kapaun Air Station, Germany
APO AE 09094–3060
011–49–631–3523–150
Fax: 011–49–631–3523–104

DeCA Headquarters

Defense Commissary Agency
1300 E Avenue
Fort Lee, VA 23801–1800
804–734–8717
Fax: 804–734–8244

Army and Air Force Exchange Service

Northeast Region

P.O. Box 660320
Dallas, TX 75266–0320
214–277–7103

Southeast Region

P.O. Box 650447
Dallas, TX 75265–0447
214–277–7303

Central Region

P.O. Box 660320
Dallas, TX 75266–0320
214–277–7203

Western Region

P.O. Box 650429
Dallas, TX 75265–0429
214–277–7403

U.S. Headquarters

Army and Air Force Exchange
Service Headquarters
P.O. Box 660202
Dallas, TX 75266–0202
214–312–3993

Europe Region

Unit 24580
APO AE 09245
or
Europe Region
In der Witz 14–18
Building 4001
55252 **Mainz–Kastel,** Germany
011–49–911–06134–715–2863

Pacific Region

Unit 35163
APO AP 96378–5163
Okinawa, Japan
011–81–611–745–7703

Marine Corps Exchange Service

Regional Headquarters

Marine Corps Exchange
Marine Corps Logistics Base,
Bldg. 7500
Albany, GA 31704–5003
912–888–6801
Fax: 912–439–0324

Marine Corps Exchange
Headquarters Battalion
Henderson Hall
P.O. Box 4009, Bldg. 26
Arlington, VA 22204–4009
703–979–8420
Fax: 703–979–0972

Marine Corps Exchange
Marine Corps Logistics Base,
Bldg. 319
Barstow, CA 92311–5003
619–256–0212
Fax: 619–256–7027

Marine Corps Exchange
Marine Corps Air Station
P.O. Box 50018
Beaufort, SC 29904–5018
803–522–7578
Fax: 803–522–7077

Marine Corps Exchange
Marine Corps Base, Bldg. 895
Camp Lejeune, NC
28542–5003
910–451–2481
Fax: 910–353–4105

Marine Corps Exchange
Marine Corps Base, Bldg. 1108
Camp Pendleton, CA
92055–5003
619–725–6233
Fax: 619–385–0446

Marine Corps Exchange
Marine Corps Air Station
Bldg. 3918
Cherry Point, NC 28533–5003
919–447–7041
Fax: 919–447–2922

Marine Corps Exchange
P.O. Box 63073, Bldg. 1404
Kanehoe Bay, HI 96863–5003
808–254–7522
Fax: 808–254–7508

Marine Corps Exchange
Camp Elmore
1251 Yalu Street
Norfolk, VA 23515–5003
804–423–1187
Fax: 804–423–5819

Marine Corps Exchange
Marine Corps Recruit
Depot/ERR
Bldg. 202
Parris Island, SC 29905–5003
803–525–3301
Fax: 803–525–2872

Marine Corps Exchange
Marine Corps Combat
Development Command
P.O. Box 229, Bldg. 3500
Quantico, VA 22134–0229
703–640–8800
Fax: 703–640–6708

Marine Corps Exchange
Marine Corps Recruit
Depot/WRR
3800 Chosin Avenue
San Diego, CA 92140–5196
619–297–2500
Fax: 619–543–9025

Marine Corps Exchange
Marine Corps Air Bases West
P.O. Box 5010
El Toro, CA 92630
714–551–6532
Fax: 714–857–4031

Marine Corps Exchange
Marine Corps Air/Ground
Combat Center, Bldg. 1533
Twentynine Palms, CA
92278–8150
619–830–6163
Fax: 619–368–3298

Marine Corps Exchange
Marine Corps Air Station
Bldg. 693
Yuma, AZ 85369–5003
520–341–2363
Fax: 520–344–1902

Retail Services Exchange
PSC 561, P.O. Box 1866
FPO AP 96310–1866
Iwakuni, Japan
011–81–6117–53–5641
Fax: 011–81–827–21–7363

Marine Corps Exchange Service
Headquarters U.S. Marine Corps
Quantico, VA 22134
703–784–3821
Fax: 703–784–5354

Navy Exchange Service Centers

Navy Exchange Officer
Navy Exchange Service Center
Box 2
Jacksonville, FL 33212–0104
904–777–7200
Fax: 904–777–7221
General Manager

Navy Exchange Service Center
1560 Arleigh Burke Crescent
Norfolk, VA 23511–3898
804–440–2200
Fax: 804–444–2131

General Manager
Navy Exchange Service Center
P.O. Box 133
Pearl Harbor, HI 96860
808–423–3201
Fax: 808–422–7897

Navy Exchange Officer
Navy Exchange Service Center
Naval Station
Box 368036
San Diego, CA 92136–8036
619–544–2100
Fax: 619–231–7826

Commanding Officer
U.S. Navy Exchange Service
Center **Europe**
PSC 810, Box 33
FPO AE 09619–0033
011–39–81–724–42
Fax: 011–39–81–724–43

Selected Federal Agencies

Many Federal agencies have enforcement and/or complaint-handling duties for products and services used by the general public. Others act for the benefit of the public, but do not resolve individual consumer problems.

Agencies also have fact sheets, booklets and other information which might be helpful in making purchase decisions and dealing with consumer problems. If you wish to access Federal agencies electronically, the websites and/or e-mail addresses are listed for a number of them. The numbers for text telephones (TDD/TTY) are in **bold type**.

If you need help in deciding whom to contact with your consumer problem, check the index at the end of this book or call the Federal Information Center (FIC) toll free on 800–688–9889.

The Federal agencies listed below respond to consumer complaints and inquiries.

Architectural and Transportation Barriers Compliance Board (ACCESS Board)

1331 F Street, N.W., Suite 1000
Washington, DC 20004–1111
202–272–5434
Fax: 202 272 5447
Toll free: 800–872–2253

Commission on Civil Rights

Look in your telephone directory under "U.S. Government, Civil Rights Commission." If it does not appear, call the FIC toll free on 800–688–9889 or contact:
Commission on Civil Rights
624 9th Street, N.W.
Washington, DC 20425
202–376–8513 (complaint referral in DC)
Toll free: 800–552–6843 (complaint referral outside DC)
TDD nationwide:
202–376–8116
(complaint referral)
202–376–8128 (publications)
202–376–8312 (public affairs)

Commodity Futures Trading Commission (CFTC)

Lafayette Centre
1155 21st Street, N.W.
Washington, DC 20581
202–418–5506 (complaints)
202–418–5080 (information)
TDD: 202–418–5514
(complaints)
TDD: 202–418–5515
(information)
Website: www.cftc.gov

Consumer Product Safety Commission (CPSC)

Call the CPSC hotline to report a hazardous product or product-related injury weekdays from 8:30 a.m. to 5 p.m. Recorded messages on safety recommendations and product recalls are available 24 hours a day, 7 days a week. Call or write:
Product Safety Hotline
U.S. Consumer Product Safety Commission
Washington, DC 20207
Toll free: 800–638–CPSC (2772)
TDD toll free: 800–638–8270
E-mail: info@cpsc.gov
Website: www.cpsc.gov
Fax-on-demand:
301–504–0051

Department of Agriculture (USDA)

Animal and Plant Health Inspection Service
Public Affairs
Department of Agriculture
4700 River Road, Unit 51
Riverdale, MD 20737
301–734–7799
Website: www.aphis.usda.gov

Center for Nutrition Policy and Promotion
Department of Agriculture
1120 20th Street, N.W.,
Room 200
Washington, DC 20036
202–418–2312
E-mail: cnpp-web@www.usda.gov
Website:
www.usda.gov/fcs/cnpp.html

Cooperative State Research, Education and Extension Service
Department of Agriculture
1400 Independence Avenue,
S.W., Room 3328–S
Washington, DC 20250
202–720–2332
E-mail:
webmaster@reeusda.gov
Website: www.reeusda.gov
Or consult county or city government listings in your local telephone directory for the number of your local Cooperative Extension Service office.

Food and Consumer Service
Office of Consumer Affairs
Department of Agriculture
3101 Park Center Drive,
Room 813–B
Alexandria, VA 22302
703–305–1626
E-mail: fcs-web@www.usda.gov
Website: www.usda.gov/fcs

Inspector General's Hotline
Office of the Inspector General
Department of Agriculture
P.O. Box 23399
Washington, DC 20026
202–690–1622
Toll free: 800–424–9121

Meat and Poultry Hotline Food Safety and Inspection Service
Department of Agriculture
1400 Independence Avenue,
S.W., Room 2925–S
Washington, DC 20250
Voice/TDD: 202–720–3333
Voice/TDD toll free outside DC: 800–535–4555
Website: www.usda.gov/fsis

Office of Communications
Department of Agriculture
1400 Independence Avenue,
S.W., Room 507–A
Washington, DC 20250
202–720–2791

Rural Economic and Community Development

Department of Agriculture
1400 Independence Avenue,
S.E., Room 5037–S
Washington, DC 20250
202–720–4323
E-mail:
webmaster@rurdev.usda.gov
Website: www.rurdev.usda.gov

Department of Commerce

Bureau of the Census
Customer Services
Washington, DC 20233
301–457–4100
Fax: 301–457–4714
Fax-on-demand:
900–555–2FAX

Office of Consumer Affairs
Department of Commerce
Room 5718
Washington, DC 20230
202–482–5001
Fax: 202–482–6007
Fax-on-demand:
202–501–1191
E-mail: CAffairs@doc.gov

National Institute of Standards and Technology
Office of Weights and Measures
Gaithersburg, MD 20899
301–975–4004
Fax: 301–926–0647
Fax-on-demand:
800–925–2453
E-mail: owm@nist.gov
Website: www.nist.gov/owm

Metric Program
Gaithersburg, MD 20899
301–975–3690
Fax: 301–948–1416
E-mail: metric_prg@nist.gov
Website: www.nist.gov/metric

National Marine Fisheries Service
Inspection Services Division
Department of Commerce
National Oceanic and Atmospheric Administration
1315 East–West Highway
Silver Spring, MD 20910
301–713–2355
Fax: 301–713–1081
Toll free: 800–HACCP50
(voluntary fishery products inspection program)

National Weather Service
Constituent Affairs
Washington, DC 20230
202–482–6090
Fax: 202–482–3154
Website: www.noaa.gov

Patent and Trademark Office
2121 Crystal Drive, Suite 0100
Arlington, VA 22202
703–305–8341
Fax: 703–308–5258
Website: www.uspto.gov/

Department of Defense

Office of National Ombudsman
National Committee for Employer Support of the Guard and Reserve
1555 Wilson Boulevard, Suite 200
Arlington, VA 22209–2405
703–696–1391
Toll free outside DC:
800–336–4590
Provides assistance with employer/employee problems for members of the Guard and Reserve and their employers.

Department of Education

Clearinghouse on Disability Information
Department of Education
330 C Street, S.W., Room 3132
Washington, DC 20202–2524
Voice/TDD: 202–205–8241

National Clearinghouse on Bilingual Education Hotline
Department of Education
1118 22nd Street, N.W.
Washington, DC 20037
202–467–0867
Toll free outside DC:
800–321–NCBE

Office of Governmental and Interagency Affairs
Department of Education
600 Independence Avenue, S.W.
Room 3061
Washington, DC 20202
202–401–3679

Office of Public Affairs
Department of Education
600 Independence Avenue, S.W.
Room 2200
Washington, DC 20202
202–401–1576

Student Financial Aid Information
Department of Education
P.O. Box 84
Washington, DC 20044
Toll free: 800–4FED–AID
(433–3243) (For general information on student loans, grants and scholarships available from the Department of Education.)
For questions on a defaulted account, call the Default Line:
Toll free 800–621–3115.

Department of Energy

For information about conservation and renewable energy:
Energy Efficiency and Renewable Energy Clearinghouse
Department of Energy
P.O. Box 3048
Merrifield, VA 22116
Toll free: 800–363–3732
**TDD toll free:
800–273–2957**
BBS: 800–273–2955
E-mail: doe.erec@nciinc.com

For inquiries about weatherization assistance:
Office of Energy Efficiency and Renewable Energy
Department of Energy
Washington, DC 20585
202–586–4074

Office of Intergovernmental and External Affairs
Department of Energy
Washington, DC 20585
202–586–5373

Office of Scientific and Technical Information
Department of Energy
P.O. Box 62
Oak Ridge, TN 37831
(written inquiries only)

Department of Health and Human Services (HHS)
Website: www.os.dhhs.gov

**AIDS Hotline
Acquired Immune Deficiency Syndrome**
Toll Free: 800–342–AIDS
(342–2437) (24 hrs.)
Toll free: 800–344–SIDA
(344–7432) (for Spanish speaking, 8 a.m.-2 a.m.)
**TDD toll free:
800–243–7889** (Mon.-Fri., 10 a.m.-10 p.m.)

Cancer Hotline
Toll free: 800–4–CANCER

Child Abuse and Neglect Hotline
703–385–7565
Toll free outside DC:
800–394–3366

Food and Drug Administration (FDA)
Look in your telephone directory under "U.S. Government, Health and Human Services Department, Food and Drug Administration." If it does not appear, call the Federal Information Center toll free on 800–688–9889 or contact:

Consumer Affairs and Information Staff
Food and Drug Administration (HFE–88)
Department of Health and Human Services
5600 Fishers Lane, Room 16–75
Rockville, MD 20857
301–443–3170 or
Toll free: 800–532–4440

Food Safety and Applied Nutrition
202–205–4314 or
Toll free: 800–332–4010

Health Care Financing Administration (HCFA)
Division of Beneficiary Services
Department of Health and Human Services
6325 Security Boulevard
Baltimore, MD 21207
Toll free: 800–638–6833
(This is a taped answering service; a specialist will return your call.)

Hill–Burton Free Hospital Care Hotline
Toll free in MD: 800–492–0359
Toll free outside MD:
800–638–0742

Inspector General's Hotline
HHS/OIG/Hotline
P.O. Box 23489
Washington, DC 20026
Toll free: 800–HHS–TIPS

National Health Information Center
Department of Health and Human Services
P.O. Box 1133
Washington, DC 20013–1133
301–565–4167 (DC Metro Area)
Toll free: 800–336–4797

National Runaway Switchboard
Toll free: 800–621–4000

Office of Child Support Enforcement
Department of Health and Human Services
Washington, DC 20447
202–401–9373

Office for Civil Rights
Department of Health and Human Services
Washington, DC 20201
202–619–0403
215–546–1570 (Spanish)
Toll free outside DC:
800–368–1019
TDD toll free: 800–537–7697

Office of Managed Care
HCFA
Department of Health and Human Services
7500 Security Boulevard
Baltimore, MD 21244
410–786–4287
Medicare Hotline toll free:
800–638–6833

President's Council on Physical Fitness and Sports
Department of Health and Human Services
701 Pennsylvania Ave., N.W.
Suite 250
Washington, DC 20004
202–272–3421

Department of Housing and Urban Development (HUD)

Home Improvement Insurance Branch
Department of Housing and Urban Development
L'Enfant Plaza
Room 3214
Washington, DC 20410
202–755–7400

Home Mortgage Insurance Division Single Family Housing
Department of Housing and Urban Development
451 Seventh Street, S.W.
Room 9272
Washington, DC 20410
202–700–2700

Inspector General's Fraud Hotline
202-708-4200
Toll free outside DC:
800-347-3735

Interstate Land Sales/RESPA Division
Department of Housing and Urban Development
451 Seventh Street, S.W.
Room 9146
Washington, DC 20410
202–708–4560

Manufactured Housing and Construction Standards Division
Department of Housing and Urban Development
L'Enfant Plaza
Room 3214
Washington, DC 20410
202–755–7430

Office of Affordable Housing Programs
Department of Housing and Urban Development
451 Seventh Street, S.W.
Room 7164
Washington, DC 20410
202–708–2685

Office of Fair Housing and Equal Opportunity
Department of Housing and Urban Development
451 Seventh Street, S.W.
Room 5100
Washington, DC 20410
202–708–4252
Toll free: 800–669–9777
(hotline complaints)

Department of the Interior

Bureau of Indian Affairs
Department of the Interior
Washington, DC 20240
202–208–3711

Bureau of Land Management
Department of the Interior
Washington, DC 20240
202–452–5125

Fish and Wildlife Service
Department of the Interior
Washington, DC 20240
202–208–4131

Geological Survey
Department of the Interior
12201 Sunrise Valley Drive
Reston, VA 22092
703–648–4427

National Park Service
Department of the Interior
Washington, DC 20240
202–208–6843

Department of Justice

Antitrust Division
Department of Justice
Washington, DC 20530
202–514–2401

Civil Rights Division
Look in your telephone directory under "U.S. Government, Justice Department, Civil Rights Division." If it does not appear, call the Federal Information Center toll free on 800–688–9889 or contact:
Civil Rights Division
Department of Justice
Washington, DC 20530
202–514–2151

Drug Enforcement Administration (DEA)
Look in your telephone directory under "U.S. Government, Justice Department, Drug Enforcement Administration." If it does not appear, call the Federal Information Center toll free on 800–688–9889 or contact: Drug Enforcement Administration
Department of Justice
Washington, DC 20537
202–307–8000

Federal Bureau of Investigation (FBI)
Look inside the front cover of your telephone directory for the number of the nearest FBI office. If it does not appear, look under "U.S. Government, Justice Department, Federal Bureau of Investigation." You also may contact:
Federal Bureau of Investigation
Department of Justice
Washington, DC 20535
202–324–3000

Immigration and Naturalization Service (INS)
Look in your telephone directory under "U.S. Government, Justice Department, Immigration and Naturalization Service." If it does not appear, call the Federal Information Center toll free on 800–688–9889 or contact:
Immigration and Naturalization Service
Department of Justice
425 I Street, N.W.
Washington, DC 20536
202–514–2648
TDD: 202–514–0139

Department of Labor

Office of Public Affairs
Department of Labor
Washington, DC 20210
202–219–7316 (general inquiries)

Employment and Training Administration
Look in your telephone directory under "U.S. Government, Labor Department, Employment and Training Administration." If it does not appear, call the Federal Information Center toll free on 800–688–9889 or contact:
Employment and Training Administration
Office of Public Affairs
Department of Labor
Washington, DC 20210
202–219–6871

Employment Standards Administration
Office of Public Affairs
Department of Labor
Washington, DC 20210
202–219–8743

Mine Safety and Health Administration
Office of Information and Public Affairs
Department of Labor
Ballston Towers #3
Arlington, VA 22203
703–235–1452

Occupational Safety and Health Administration (OSHA)
Look in your telephone directory under "U.S. Government, Labor Department, Occupational Safety and Health Administration." If it does not appear, call the Federal Information Center toll free on 800–688–9889 or contact:
Occupational Safety and Health Administration
Office of Information and Consumer Affairs
Department of Labor
Washington, DC 20210
202–219–8148

Office of the Assistant Secretary for Veterans' Employment and Training
Department of Labor
Washington, DC 20210
202–219–5573
Toll free: 800–442–2VET
(Veterans' Job Rights Hotline)

Office of Labor Management Standards
Department of Labor
Washington, DC 20210
202–219–7320

Pension and Welfare Benefits Administration
Office of Program Services
Department of Labor
Washington, DC 20210
202–219–8776

Women's Bureau
The Women's Bureau Clearinghouse has available a "Know Your Rights" series of information covering women's work issues such as sexual harassment, pregnancy discrimination, and family and medical leave. The Clearinghouse also provides information to employers and employees about the work and family issues of dependent care (child and/or elder care) policies.
Contact: Women's Bureau
Department of Labor
Washington, DC 20210
202–219–4486
Toll free: 800–827–5335
(24 hours)
Website: www.dol.gov/dol/wb/

Department of State

Bureau of Consular Affairs Overseas Citizens Services
Department of State
Washington, DC 20520
202–647–5225 (emergencies and non-emergencies, Mon.-Fri., 8:15a.m.-10 p.m.)
After hours emergencies, Sundays, holidays, call 202–647–4000 and ask for duty officer.)
Website: www.travel.state.gov

Passport Services
Washington Passport Agency
1111 19th Street, N.W.
Washington, DC 20524
202–647–0518

Visa Services
Department of State
Washington, DC 20520
202–663–1225

Department of Transportation (DOT)

Federal Aviation Administration (AOA–20)
Washington, DC 20591
Toll free: 800–FAA–SURE
(consumer hotline)

Air Safety:
Federal Aviation Administration (ASY–300)
Washington, DC 20591
Toll free: 800–255–1111
(safety hotline)

Airline Service Complaints:
Federal Aviation Administration (C 75)
Aviation Consumer Protection Division
Washington, DC 20590
202–366–2220

Auto Safety Hotline and Fax-on-Demand Service
National Highway Traffic Safety Administration (NHTSA)
Washington, DC 20590
202–366–0123
Toll free outside DC:
800–424–9393
TDD: 202–366–7899
TDD toll free outside DC:
800–424–9153
Website: www.nhtsa.dot.gov

Boating Safety Classes:
Boat U.S. Foundation
880 S. Pickett Street
Alexandria, VA 22304
703–823–9550
Toll free: 800–336–2628

Boating Safety Hotline:
United States Coast Guard
(G–NAB–5)
2100 Second Street, S.W.
Washington, DC 20593
202–267–1587
Toll free: 800–368–5647

Oil and Chemical Spills:
United States Coast Guard
National Response Center
2100 Second Street, S.W.
Room 2611
Washington, DC 20593–0001
202–267–2100
Toll free: 800–424–8802

Railway Safety:
Federal Railroad Administration
Office of Safety (RRS)
400 Seventh Street, S.W.
Washington, DC 20590
202–632–3310

Department of the Treasury

Bureau of Alcohol, Tobacco and Firearms
Look in your telephone directory under "U.S. Government, Treasury Department, Bureau of Alcohol, Tobacco and Firearms." If it does not appear, call the Federal Information Center toll free on 800–688–9889 or contact:
Bureau of Alcohol, Tobacco and Firearms
Department of the Treasury
650 Massachusetts Avenue, N.W.
Washington, DC 20226
202–927–8500

To report lost or stolen explosives, or to report explosive incidents or bombings, call:
202–927–7777
Toll outside DC: 800–283–4867
Website: www.ustreas.gov/treasury/bureaus/atf/atf.html

Bureau of Engraving and Printing
Office of Communications
Department of the Treasury
14th and C Streets, S.W.,
Room 109M
Washington, DC 20228
202–874–2517
Website: www.ustreas.gov/treasury/bureaus/bep/bep.html

Bureau of the Public Debt
Public Affairs Officer
Office of the Commissioner
Department of the Treasury
999 E Street, N.W., Room 553
Washington, DC 20239–0001
202–219–3302
Website: www.ustreas.gov/treasury/bureaus/pubdebt/pubdebt.html

Comptroller of the Currency
The Comptroller of the Currency handles complaints about national banks, i.e., banks that have the word "National" in their names or the initials "N.A" after their names. For assistance, look in your telephone directory under "U.S. Government, Treasury Department, Comptroller of the Currency." If it does not appear, call the Federal Information Center toll free on 800–688–9889 or contact:
Comptroller of the Currency
Compliance Management, Customer Assistance Unit
250 E Street, S.W.
Mail Stop 3–9
Washington, DC 20219–0001
Toll free: 800–613–6743
Website: www.occ.treas.gov

Financial Management Service
Office of Legislative and Public Affairs
Department of the Treasury
401 14th Street, S.W.,
Room 555
Washington, DC 20227
202–874–6740
Website: www.ustreas.gov/treasury/bureaus/finman/finman.html

Internal Revenue Service (IRS)
Look in your telephone directory under "U.S. Government, Treasury Department, Internal Revenue Service." If it does not appear, call the Federal Information Center toll free on 800–688–9889 or call:
Toll free: 800–829–1040 (information and problem resolution)
Website: www.irs.ustreas.gov

Office of Thrift Supervision
The Office of Thrift Supervision handles complaints about Federal savings and loans and Federal savings banks. For assistance, contact:
Office of Thrift Supervision
Division of Consumer and Civil Rights
1700 G Street, N.W.
Washington, DC 20552
202–906–5900
202–906–6000
Toll free: 800–842–6929
Website: www.ustreas.gov/treasury/bureaus/ots/ots/html

United States Customs Service

Look in your telephone directory under "U.S. Government, Treasury Department, U.S. Customs Service." If it does not appear, call the Federal Information Center toll free on 800–688–9889.

To report fraudulent import practices, drug smuggling activity, or other illegal food or hazardous substances, call U.S. Customs Service's Hotline: Toll free: 800–BE–ALERT. Website: www.ustreas.gov/treasury/bureaus/customs/customs.html

United States Mint

Customer Relations Division Department of the Treasury 633 Third Street, N.W. Washington, DC 20220 202–344–5027

United States Savings Bonds Division

Department of the Treasury Office of Public Affairs 800 K Street, N.W., Suite 800 Washington, DC 20226 202–622–2000 Toll free: 800–4US–BOND (toll free recording)

Department of Veterans Affairs (VA)

For information about VA medical care or benefits, write, call or visit your nearest VA facility. Your telephone directory will list a VA medical center or regional office under "U.S. Government, Department of Veterans Affairs," or under "U.S.Government, Veterans Administration." You also may contact the offices listed below.

For information about benefits:
Veterans Benefits Administration (27)
Department of Veterans Affairs 810 Vermont Avenue, N.W. Washington, DC 20420 Toll free: 800–827–1000

For information about medical care:
Veterans Health Administration (167)
810 Vermont Avenue, N.W. Washington, DC 20420 202–273–8952

For information about burials, headstones or markers, and presidential memorial certificates:
National Cemetery System (402B2)
Department of Veterans Affairs 810 Vermont Avenue, N.W. Washington, DC 20420 202–273–5221

For consumer information or general assistance:
Consumer Affairs Service (075B)
Department of Veterans Affairs 810 Vermont Avenue, N.W. Washington, DC 20420 202–273–5760

Environmental Protection Agency (EPA)

Asbestos Information
Hotline: 202–554–1404
Fax: 202–554–5603

Emergency Planning and Community Right–to–Know Information
Environmental Protection Agency Washington, DC 20460 Toll free Hotline: 800–535–0202 Fax: 703–412–3333

General Information on Environmental Issues
303–312–6312 Toll free: 800–227–8917 (CO, MO, ND, SD, UT, WY residents only) Fax: 303–312–7061

Indoor Air Quality Information Clearinghouse
202–233–9048 Toll free: 800–438–4318 Fax: 202–233–9555

Inspector General's Whistle Blower Hotline
202–260–4977 Toll free outside DC: 800–424–4000 Fax: 202–260–6976

National Pesticides Telecommunications Network (NPTN)
Toll free: 800–858–7378 Toll free outside TX: 800–858–PEST Fax: 541–737–0761

Office of Public Liaison
Environmental Protection Agency Washington, DC 20460 202–260–4454 Fax: 202–260–0130

Public Information Center PIC (3406)
Environmental Protection Agency Washington, DC 20460 202–260–2080 (general information) Fax: 202–260–6257

Resource Conservation and Recovery Act
RCRA/Superfund/UST Hotline Environmental Protection Agency Washington, DC 20460 703–412–9810 Toll free outside DC: 800–424–9346 Fax: 703–412–3333

Safe Drinking Water Hotline
Toll free: 800–426–4791 Fax: 703–285–1101

Toxic Substances Control Act Assistance Information Service
Environmental Protection Agency Washington, DC 20024 202–554–1404 Fax: 202–554–5603

Equal Employment Opportunity Commission

Look in your telephone directory under "U.S. Government, Equal Employment Opportunity Commission." If it does not appear, call the Federal Information Center toll free on 800–688–9889 or contact: Office of Communications and Legislative Affairs Equal Employment Opportunity Commission 1801 L Street, N.W. Washington, DC 20507 202–663–4900 Toll free outside DC area: 800–669–4000 (file–a–charge information) Toll free: 800–669–3362 (publications)
TDD Toll free outside DC area: 800–669–6820 (file–a–charge information) TDD toll free: 800–669–3302 (publications)

Federal Communications Commission (FCC)

General information:
Public Services Division Federal Communications Commission 1919 M Street, N.W., Room 254 Washington, DC 20554 202–418–0200 Toll free: 888–322–8255 **TTY: 202–418–2555** E-mail: fccinfo@fcc.gov Website: www.fcc.gov

Complaints about telephone systems:
Common Carrier Bureau Consumer Protection Division Federal Communications Commission 2025 M Street, N.W., Room 6202 Washington, DC 20554 202–632–7553

Complaints about radio or television:
Mass Media Bureau Enforcement Division Federal Communications Commission 2025 M Street, N.W., Room 8210 Washington, DC 20554 202–418–1430

Cable service:
Federal Communications Commission 2033 M Street, N.W. Washington, D.C. 20036 202–418–7096

Federal Deposit Insurance Corporation (FDIC)

FDIC handles questions about deposit insurance coverage and complaints about FDIC–insured state banks which are not members of the Federal Reserve System. For assistance, look in your telephone directory under "U.S. Government, Federal Deposit Insurance Corporation." If it does not appear, call the Federal Information Center toll free on 800–688–9889 or contact:

Division of Compliance and Consumer Affairs
Federal Deposit Insurance Corporation
550 17th Street, N.W.
Washington, DC 20429–9990
202–942–3100
Toll free: 800–934–3342

Federal Emergency Management Agency

Look in your telephone directory under U.S. Government, Federal Emergency Management Agency. If it does not appear, call the Federal Information Center toll free on 800–688–9889 or contact:

Federal Insurance Administration
Federal Emergency Management Agency
500 C Street, S.W.
Washington, DC 20472
202–646–2780
Toll free: 800–638–6620
Website: www.fema.gov

Office of Emergency Information and Media Affairs
E-mail: eipa@fema.gov
(general inquiries)
Fax-on-demand:
202–646–FEMA (24-hour service)

Office of Inspector General
Waste, Fraud and Abuse Hotline
Toll free: 800–323–8603

Response and Recovery Directorate
Federal Emergency Management Agency
500 C Street, S.W., Room 705
Washington, DC 20472
202–646–3454

Disaster victims living in presidentially-declared major disaster areas can find out if they are eligible to apply for disaster assistance by calling:
Toll free: 800–462–4029
TDD toll free: 800–462–7585

U.S. Fire Administration
Federal Emergency Management Agency, NETC
16825 South Seton Avenue
Emmitsburg, MD 21727
301–447–1080
202–646–2449
Website: www.usfa.fema.gov

Federal Maritime Commission

Office of Informal Inquiries and Complaints
800 North Capitol Street, N.W.
Washington, DC 20573
202–523–5807

Federal Reserve System

The Board of Governors handles consumer complaints about state–chartered banks and trust companies which are members of the Federal Reserve System. For assistance, look in your telephone directory under U.S. Government, Federal Reserve System, Board of Governors," or "Federal Reserve Bank." If neither appears, call the Federal Information Center toll free on 800–688–9889 or contact:

Board of Governors of the Federal Reserve System
Division of Consumer and Community Affairs
Washington, DC 20551
202–452–3693
TDD: 202–452–3544

Federal Trade Commission (FTC)

Look in your telephone directory under "U.S. Government, Federal Trade Commission." If it does not appear, call the Federal Information Center toll free on 800–688–9889 or contact:
Correspondence Branch
Federal Trade Commission
Washington, DC 20580
(written complaints only)

Public Reference Section
Federal Trade Commission
6th & Pennsylvania Ave., N.W., Room 130
Washington, DC 20580
202–326–2222 (publications)

General Services Administration (GSA)

Business Service Centers
Look in your telephone directory under "U.S. Government, General Services Administration." If this does not appear, call the Federal Information Center or access the GSA website: www.gsa.gov.

Consumer Information Center (CIC)
CIC publishes the free *Consumer Information Catalog* which lists more than 200 free and low–cost Federal booklets on a wide variety of consumer topics. For a free copy of the *Catalog,* write to:
Consumer Information Catalog
Pueblo, CO 81009
719–948–4000.
Website: www.pueblo.gsa.gov
(access to the *Catalog* and full text of all publications)
CIC bulletin board:
202–208–7679.

Federal Information Center
(see page 3)

Federal Information Relay Service
(see page 114)

Surplus Federal Property Sales
GSA disposes of both personal property and real estate. Look in your telephone directory under "U.S. Government, General Services Administration." If it does not appear, call the Federal Information Center toll free on 800–688–9889.

Government Printing Office (GPO)

Government Publications
Government Printing Office
P.O. Box 371954
Pittsburgh, PA 15250–7954
202–512–1800

Subscriptions to Periodicals
Government Printing Office
P.O. Box 371954
Pittsburgh, PA 15250–7954
202–512–2267

National Archives and Records Administration

8th and Pennsylvania Avenue, N.W.
Washington, DC 20408
202–501–5400
TDD: 202–501–5404
Fax: 202–501–7154

National Archives and Records Administration at College Park (Archives II)
8601 Adelphi Road
College Park, MD 20740–6001
301–713–6800
Fax: 301–713–6920
E-Mail: inquire@nara.gov
Website: www.nara.gov

Federal Register
National Archives and Records Administration
800 N. Capitol Street, N.W.
Washington, DC 20408
202–523–4534
TDD: 202–523–5229
Fax: 202–523–6866

National Council on Disability (NCD)

1331 F Street, N.W.
Suite 1050
Washington, DC 20004–1107
202–272–2004
TDD: (202) 272–2074

National Credit Union Administration

The National Credit Union Share Insurance Fund provides Federal insurance for nearly 13,000 credit unions. Look in your telephone directory under "U.S. Government, National Credit Union Administration." If it does not appear, call the Federal Information Center toll free on 800–688–9889 or contact:

National Credit Union Administration
1775 Duke Street
Alexandria, VA 22314–3428
703–518–6300

National Labor Relations Board

Office of the Executive Secretary
1099 14th Street, N.W., Room 11600
Washington, DC 20570
202–273–1940

Nuclear Regulatory Commission (NRC)

Office of Public Affairs
Washington, DC 20555
301–504–2240

Pension Benefit Guaranty Corporation

Customer Service Center
1200 K Street, N.W.
Washington, DC 20005
202–326–4000
TDD: 202–326–4179

Postal Rate Commission

Office of the Consumer Advocate
Postal Rate Commission
1333 H Street, N.W.
Suite 300
Washington, DC 20268
202–789–6830

Postal Service

If you experience difficulty when ordering merchandise or conducting business transactions through the mail, or suspect that you have been the victim of a mail fraud or misrepresentation scheme, contact your postmaster or local Postal Inspector. Look in your telephone directory under "U.S. Government, Postal Service U.S." for these local listings. If they do not appear, contact:

Chief Postal Inspector
U.S. Postal Service
Washington, DC 20260–2100
202–268–2284

For consumer convenience, all post offices and letter carriers have postage–free Consumer Service Cards available for reporting mail problems and submitting comments and suggestions. If the problem cannot be resolved using the Consumer Service Card or through direct contact with the local post office, write or call:
Consumer Advocate
United States Postal Service
Washington, DC 20260–2200
202–268–2284
TDD: 202–268–2310

President's Committee on Employment of People with Disabilities

1331 F Street, N.W., Suite 300
Washington, DC 20004–1107
202–376–6200
TDD: 202–376–6205

Railroad Retirement Board

844 North Rush Street
Chicago, IL 60611–2092
312–751–4500

Securities and Exchange Commission (SEC)

450 Fifth Street, N.W.
Mail Stop 11–2
Washington, DC 20549

For information and complaints:
Office of Investor Education and Assistance
202–942–7040
Fax: 202–942–9634
E-mail: help@sec.gov
For information and to order publications:
Toll free: 800–SEC–0330
Website: www.sec.gov

Small Business Administration (SBA)

Consumer Affairs
409 Third Street, S.W.
Washington, DC 20416
Toll free: 800–U–ASK–SBA
(information)

Social Security Administration

Office of Public Inquiries
6401 Security Boulevard
Baltimore, MD 21235
Toll free: 800–772–1213

Surface Transportation Board (STB)

1925 K Street, N.W.
Washington, DC 20006

Complaints about railroad rates and services:
Office of Compliance and Enforcement
202–927–5500

General information:
Office of Public Services
202–927–6184
Fax: 202–927–5158

Press releases:
Office of Press Service
202–927–5350
Fax: 202–927–6107

Tennessee Valley Authority (TVA)

Public Relations
400 West Summit Hill Drive
Knoxville, TN 37902
423–632–7196

United States Information Agency

301 4th Street, S.W.
Washington, DC 20547
202–619–5151
202–619–4355

TDD Services for Hearing and Speech Impaired Individuals

Hearing or speech impaired individuals who use a Telecommunications Device for the Deaf (TDD or TTY) can get assistance for calls to a TDD number by calling:

Toll free 800–855–1155

If you need assistance and you have TDD equipment, this number will put you in touch with a TDD operator who can help you with the following:

- calling card calls (with an accepted telephone calling card);
- collect calls (paid for by the person you are calling);
- person-to-person calls (a call to a specific person);
- third-party calls (calls billed to a number other than the one you are calling to or from);
- calls from a public phone (only calling card, collect, person-to-person or third-party); and
- directory assistance (provide the person's name, street address, city and state).

Telecommunications Relay Services

Telecommunications relay services are a way to link telephone conversations between hearing individuals, using a standard (voice) telephone, and hearing and speech impaired individuals, using a TDD. Relay services allow hearing individuals to call TDD numbers and allow hearing and speech impaired individuals to call standard (voice) telephone numbers. Calls can be made from a standard (voice) telephone number to a TDD number or from a TDD number to a standard (voice) telephone number.

Local Telecommunications Relay Services

To comply with the "Telecommunications" portion of the Americans with Disabilities Act (ADA), a number of states operate local relay services to link hearing and hearing- and speech-impaired individuals in their local areas. Consult your local telephone directory for information on the use, services provided and dialing instructions for your local relay.

Federal Information Relay Service

The Federal Information Relay Service (FIRS) provides telecommunications service accessibility for individuals who are deaf, hard of hearing and speech impaired to conduct official business nationwide with and in the Federal Government. FIRS serves as an intermediary for conversations between hearing individuals, deaf, hard of hearing and speech impaired individuals using Telecommunications Devices for the Deaf (TDD/TTY). FIRS toll free TDD/TTY/voice number is 800–877–8339.

For more information on relay communications or to obtain a FIRS brochure on how to use the FIRS service, call toll free: 800–877–0996 (TDD/TTY/voice).

If you would like copies of the U.S. Government TDD/TTY Directory, write:

Consumer Information Center
Department 582C
Pueblo, CO 81009

Website: www.gsa.gov/et/fic-firs/firs.htm

Books for Blind and Physically Disabled Persons

The **Library of Congress** has a free reading program for anyone who is unable to read standard printed materials as a result of temporary or permanent visual or physical limitations. More than 106,900 books, magazines and other publications in 15 million copies are available in braille and/or audio recordings. Information and catalogs for selecting reading material are issued in large print, braille, recorded, computer-diskette and CD-ROM editions, and on the Internet.

Special playback equipment is distributed on free loan from the Library of Congress. Cassettes and records can be ordered from approximately 143 cooperating libraries. Anyone who is medically certified as unable to hold a book or who is unable to read ordinary print because of a visual handicap may borrow and return these materials, postage-free. For more information, call or write:

National Library Service for the
Blind and Physically Handicapped
The Library of Congress
Washington, DC 20542
202–707–5100
Toll free: 800–424–9100

Recording for the Blind and Dyslexic (RFB&D) is a national, non-profit organization that provides recorded textbooks, library services and other educational resources for people who cannot read standard print because of a visual, perceptual or physical disability. RFB&D has a 75,000-volume lending library of audio books. Special 4-track tape players and recorders are available for purchase through RFB&D for use with the audio books. RFB&D's line of tape players and recorders includes four portable models and two desktop models—all of which are affordable, lightweight and readily available.

RFB&D also offers the non-profit sale of books on computer disk (E-Text). The E-Text collection contains more than 500 titles, ranging from computer manuals and works of literature to an assortment of reference books.

RFB&D offers two forms of membership—Individual and Institutional. There is a registration fee of $50 and an annual fee of $25 for individual members. Schools and agencies may purchase a level of institutional membership that meets the needs of the students they serve.

For more information or to request an application, call, write or visit the website:

Recording for the Blind and Dyslexic
20 Roszel Road
Princeton, NJ 08540
609–452–0606
Toll free: 800–221–4792

Website: www.rfbd.org

Index

This alphabetical index will help you find the right organization to contact for information or for assistance with your complaint. First, look for the specific topic, for example, Cars. Under this topic heading, there will be one or more contacts followed by the *Handbook* page number(s). Sometimes you will be directed to **"See"** another entry for information or a list of contacts. **"See also"** references direct you to other topics that might be related to your problem and help you locate the right contact. For company names, see the alphabetical listings under "Corporate Consumer Contacts" and "Car Manufacturers."

W